Lecture Notes in Computer Science 1549

Edited by G. Goos, J. Hartmanis and J. van Leeuwen

Springer

Berlin
Heidelberg
New York
Barcelona
Hong Kong
London
Milan
Paris
Singapore
Tokyo

Mikael Pettersson

Compiling
Natural Semantics

 Springer

Series Editors

Gerhard Goos, Karlsruhe University, Germany
Juris Hartmanis, Cornell University, NY, USA
Jan van Leeuwen, Utrecht University, The Netherlands

Author

Mikael Pettersson
Computing Science Department
Uppsala University
P.O. Box 311, S-751 05 Uppsala, Sweden
E-mail: Mikael.Pettersson@csd.uu.se

Cataloging-in-Publication data applied for

Die Deutsche Bibliothek - CIP-Einheitsaufnahme

Pettersson, Mikael:
Compiling natural semantics / Mikael Pettersson. - Berlin ;
Heidelberg ; New York ; Barcelona ; Hong Kong ; London ; Milan ;
Paris ; Singapore ; Tokyo : Springer, 1999
  (Lecture notes in computer science ; 1549)
  ISBN 3-540-65968-4

CR Subject Classification (1998): D.3, F.3

ISSN 0302-9743
ISBN 3-540-65968-4 Springer-Verlag Berlin Heidelberg New York

Typesetting: Camera-ready by author
SPIN 10693148   06/3142 – 5 4 3 2 1 0   Printed on acid-free paper

Foreword

When Mikael asked me to write this foreword, I happily agreed. Since the time I wrote my own Ph.D. thesis 1984 on incremental programming environments, compilers, and generator tools for such systems, I have been interested in the problem of automatically generating practical tools from formal semantics language specifications. This problem was unsolved in my own work at that time, which focused on incremental environment architecture, debugging, and code generation aspects, and could generate parts of incremental programming environments from specifications. However, I always wished for a good opportunity to attack the semantics problem in a practical context.

This opportunity came in the fall of 1989, when Mikael Pettersson started as a graduate student in the PELAB research group (Programming Environments Laboratory) at Linköping University, of which I recently had become leader. Mikael shared my interest in efficient programming language implementations and generator tools, and was very research minded from the start. Already during his undergraduate studies he read many research papers on language implementation techniques and formal semantics, at that time primarily Denotational Semantics, and did several experimental designs. This also became the topic of his first 3 years of research, on the problem of generating fast compilers that emit efficient code from denotational specifications. Mikael developed the DML system (Denotational Meta-Language), which included a subset of Standard ML, concrete syntax notation for pattern matching, and implementation techniques that made generated compilers both execute quickly and emit efficient code.

Around 1990–92, we became increasingly aware of the Natural Semantics specification formalism, which was gaining in popularity and seemed to be rather easy to use, yet provided high abstraction power and good modularity properties. During 1992 my group had just started to cooperate in an Esprit project with Gilles Kahn's group at the Sophia-Antipolis branch of INRIA in France. Kahn proposed the Natural Semantics formalism 1985, and his group had since then developed the Centaur system which includes Typol as the meta-language and tool for Natural Semantics specifications. This system provides a nice interactive environment for prototyping language specifications; however, generated compilers and interpreters execute quite slowly.

Therefore, Mikael, with my support, decided to slightly change his Ph.D. thesis topic. The new goal was to develop techniques and tools for generating very efficient language implementations from Natural Semantics specifications. Generated implementations should be comparable with or better than handwritten ones in performance. This was an ambitious goal that nobody had realized before.

After studying the new area, analyzing possible approaches, and implementation techniques used by logic programming and functional programming languages, Mikael completed the first RML prototype in February 1994. At that time RML was both relational and nondeterministic, similar to most logic programming languages, so the name *Relational Meta-Language* was appropriate. Even the first prototype was rather efficient compared to Typol, but better was to come. Mikael observed that the great majority of language specifications in Natural Semantics are deterministic. Only seldom is nondeterminism really needed, and in those cases specifications can usually be reformulated in a deterministic way. Mikael decided to make RML deterministic to enable further improvements in efficiency. A year later, with the addition of more sophisticated optimizations in the RML compiler, the generated code had improved another factor of five in performance. You can read about all the details in this book.

I am very proud of Mikael's work. His RML system is the first generator tool for Natural Semantics that can produce really efficient implementations. The measured efficiency of generated example implementations seems to be roughly the same as (or sometimes better than) comparable hand implementations in Pascal or C. Another important property is compatibility and modularity. Generated modules are produced in C, and can be readily integrated with existing frontends and backends.

I feel quite enthusiastic about the future prospects of automatically generating practically useful implementations from formal specifications of programming languages, using tools such as RML. Perhaps we will soon reach the point where ease of use and efficiency of the generated result will make it as attractive and common to generate semantic processing parts of translators from Natural Semantics specifications, as is currently the case for generating scanners and parsers using tools such as Lex and Yacc. Only the future will tell.

Linköping, October 1998
Peter Fritzson

Preface

Abstract

Natural Semantics has become a popular tool among programming language researchers. It is used for specifying many aspects of programming languages, including type systems, dynamic semantics, translations between representations, and static analyses. The formalism has so far largely been limited to theoretical applications, due to the absence of practical tools for its implementation. Those who try to use it in applications have had to translate their specifications by hand into existing programming languages, which can be tedious and prone to error. Hence, Natural Semantics is rarely used in applications.

Compiling high-level languages to correct and efficient code is nontrivial, hence implementing compilers is difficult and time-consuming. It has become customary to specify *parts* of compilers using special-purpose specification languages, and to compile these specifications to executable code. While this has simplified the construction of compiler front-ends, and to some extent their back-ends, little is available to help construct those parts that deal with *semantics* and translations between higher-level and lower-level representations. This is especially true for the Natural Semantics formalism.

In this thesis, we introduce the Relational Meta-Language, RML, which is intended as a practical language for natural semantics specifications. Runtime efficiency is a prerequisite if natural semantics is to be generally accepted as a *practical* tool. Hence, the main parts of this thesis deal with the problem of compiling natural semantics, actually RML, to highly efficient code.

We have designed and implemented a compiler, rml2c, that translates RML to efficient low-level C code. The compilation phases are described in detail. High-level transformations are applied to reduce the usually enormous amount of nondeterminism present in specifications. The resulting forms are often completely deterministic. Pattern-matching constructs are expanded using a pattern-match compiler, and a translation is made into a continuation-passing style intermediate representation. Intermediate-level CPS optimizations are applied before low-level C code is emitted. A new and efficient technique for mapping *tailcalls* to C has been developed.

We have compared our code with other alternative implementations. Our benchmarking results show that our code is much faster, sometimes by orders of magnitude. This supports our thesis that the given compilation strategy is suitable for a significant class of specifications.

A natural semantics specification for RML itself is given in the appendix.

Acknowledgements

I thank my thesis supervisor Peter Fritzson for giving me free rein to explore my interests in formal semantics and language implementation technology. I also thank the members of my thesis committee, Reinhard Wilhelm, Isabelle Attali, Tore Risch, and Björn Lisper, for their interest in my work, and my friends and colleagues at the Department of Computer Science at Linköping University. And finally, I thank my family for being there.

Addendum

This book is a revised version of the Ph.D. dissertation I defended in December 1995 at the University of Linköping. The RML system has evolved in several directions since then, and I summarize the main developments here.

In the RML type system, implicit logical variables have been replaced by a polymorphic type 'a lvar with explicit binding and inspection operators, and the notion of *equality types* has been borrowed from Standard ML.

Top-level declarations are now subject to a dependency analysis and re-ordering phase before type checking, as in Haskell [129, Section 4.5.11].

More techniques for implementing tailcalls in C have been tested, including one used by two Scheme compilers [63]. However, no real performance improvements have been achieved to date.

The RML compiler has been made much more user-friendly. The type checker now gives accurate and relevant error messages, and a new compiler driver automates the many steps involved in compiling and linking code. Work is underway to support debugging and profiling [139].

Students at Linköping University have used the system to construct compilers for real-world languages, including Java and Modelica [95]. The experience has been positive, but a simplified foreign C code interface, a debugger, and support for more traditional programming are sometimes requested.

The Swedish National Board for Industrial and Technical Development (NUTEK) and the Center for Industrial Information Technology (CENIIT) supported my research at Linköping University. Recent developments were implemented during my postdoc at INRIA Sophia-Antipolis 1997–98, funded by the Swedish Research Council for Engineering Sciences (TFR).

Uppsala, April 1999
Mikael Pettersson

Contents

List of Figures

List of Tables

Chapter 1

Introduction

This short introductory chapter starts by presenting the problem we are trying to solve, followed by a summary of our suggested solution to it, and a brief overview of the remaining chapters. At the end we relate this thesis to our previous work.

1.1 The Problem

Natural semantics has become a popular tool among programming language researchers. It is used for specifying many aspects of programming languages, including type systems, operational semantics, translations between representations, and static analyses.

The formalism has so far largely been limited to theoretical applications, due to the absence of practical tools for its implementation. Those who try to use it in applications have had to translate their specifications by hand into existing programming languages, which can be tedious and error-prone. Hence, natural semantics is rarely used in applications.

Compiling high-level languages to correct and efficient code is non-trivial, hence implementing compilers is difficult and time-consuming. It has become customary to specify *parts* of compilers using special-purpose specification languages, and to *compile* these specifications to executable code. While this has simplified the construction of compiler front-ends, and to some extent their back-ends, little is available to help construct those parts that deal with *semantics* and translations between higher-level and lower-level representations. This is especially true for the Natural Semantics formalism.

This state of affairs is unsatisfactory. If a widely-used semantics formalism, such as natural semantics, had high-quality compilers available, then many advantages would ensue. Language theoreticians and designers would be able to execute their specifications, and thus acquire valuable feedback. Compiler writers would be able to specify semantics-oriented compilation phases in a high-level formalism, and automatically generate those phases. Ideally, a language would have an official formal semantics, whose components could all be compiled to form large parts of a compiler's implementation.

1.2   Our Solution

In this thesis we introduce the Relational Meta-Language, RML, which is intended as a practical language for natural semantics specifications. Runtime efficiency is a prerequisite if natural semantics is to be generally accepted as a *practical* tool. Hence, the main parts of this thesis deal with the problem of *compiling* natural semantics, actually RML, to *highly efficient* code.

We have designed an effective compilation strategy for RML and implemented it in the rml2c compiler. The strategy is as follows:

1. Specifications are first translated to a high-level representation, reminiscent of First-Order Logic. To this structure we apply a *term-rewriting system* whose rules perform a kind of *left-factoring* transformation. Natural semantics specifications tend to be written in a style that calls for non-deterministic search among their inference rules. The purpose of the rewriting system is to transform specifications to a less non-deterministic form. In fact, many specifications become completely deterministic.

2. Large and complicated pattern-matching constructs are expanded using a so-called *pattern-match compiler* to combinations of data shape tests and data field accesses.

3. The high-level logical representation is translated to a medium-level functional *continuation-passing style* representation. To this, various standard optimizations such as constant and copy propagation and inlining are applied.

4. The medium-level functional representation is translated to a low-level imperative representation in which memory management, data construction, and control flow is explicit.

5. The low-level imperative representation is output as portable ANSI-C code which can then be compiled by a C compiler, linked with a small runtime system, and executed.

1.3   Overview of this Thesis

Chapter 2 starts with a discussion about the use of formal specifications for programming languages, and motivates why executable specifications are desirable. It then briefly surveys a number of existing formalisms, before presenting Natural Semantics in more detail.

Chapter 3 discusses the design of the Relational Meta-Language, RML, which is our specification language for Natural Semantics. It also presents a continuation-passing style semantics for backtracking, suitable for languages like Prolog and RML, and analyses its operational properties.

Chapter 4 presents examples from concrete RML specifications. These specifications are also the benchmarks we have used when evaluating the code generated by our rml2c compiler.

Chapter 5 provides an overview of the implementation strategy employed by our rml2c compiler. It also discusses some possible alternative implementation choices, and why they were not chosen.

Chapter 6 describes in detail the first compilation phase. Specifications are encoded as logical formulae, to which rewriting rules are applied in order to discover and utilize possibilities for deterministic execution.

Chapter 7 describes an important sub-system in the compiler, namely the pattern match compiler. It compiles complex pattern matching constructs to efficient matching *automata*, which are then mapped to the compiler's intermediate code.

Chapter 8 describes the compiler's continuation-passing style intermediate language, the optimizations applied, and how it can be translated to low-level but portable C code.

Chapter 9 discusses the practical problems involved when compiling *tailcalls* to C code. Many high-level languages, including RML, SML, Scheme, and Prolog, require sequences of tailcalls to be implemented without net stack growth. Compilers that emit C code must therefore *emulate* tailcalls. This chapter surveys a number of more or less known techniques, and introduces a new one which has proven superior in our compiler.

Chapter 10 presents results from the large number of benchmarks we have run. It evaluates different strategies for tailcalls (Chapter 9), as well as the effectiveness of the different optimizations available in the compiler. It also compares the quality of the code generated by rml2c with code from several other compilers.

Chapter 11 finally summarizes the thesis and our contributions, and discusses possibilities for future work.

Appendix A contains a complete natural semantics definition for RML itself.

1.4 Relation to our Previous Work

This thesis is a continuation of our previous work in Denotational Semantics. That work lead to a code generation method for continuation-passing style denotational semantics, a method for incorporating user-defined syntactic objects in ML in much the same way as user-defined datatypes are, and a pattern-match compiler [61, 130–133, 140, 141].

It was during this time that we became familiar with Natural Semantics. Based on our experiences with denotational semantics, both from using and implementing it, natural semantics seemed a much more viable alternative for the types of applications we are interested in. That observation lead us to the work reported in this thesis.

Chapter 2

Preliminaries

The use of formal specifications in general, and for programming languages in particular, is based on the assumption that formal specifications have practical value, perhaps for a number of user categories. This chapter starts with a small section that motivates this assumption, followed by an overview of some of the formalisms that have been used for programming languages to date. It ends with a more detailed overview of our formalism of choice, viz. Natural Semantics.

2.1 Use of Formal Specifications

A formal specification can find uses in any of a number of areas:

- End users can use it as a *contract* defining how the defined entity may be used, and how it is to behave. If the entity is a programming language, the formal semantics may be consulted to determine whether a program misbehaves because of a programming error or a compiler error.

- An implementor, for instance a compiler writer, can use it as a *requirement* of exactly what to implement.

- A designer may construct clear, precise, and concise documents using high-level specification techniques. This may also reduce the time needed to produce and validate these documents.

- Theoreticians may use formal specification tools as a common well-defined ground for analysis and comparison of definitions.

For programming languages, these observations apply equally well to lexical, syntactic, and semantic levels of descriptions.

While a formalism need not be suitable for *all* categories of users, it is clearly advantageous if it is suitable for more than one category.

2.1.1   Why Generate Compilers?

Compiling a high-level programming language to efficient machine code is
a decidedly complex process. This naturally makes implementing a correct
compiler difficult and time-consuming. There are two main issues involved:
determining *exactly what* the implemented language is, and designing the
mapping to machine code.

Formal specifications of languages solve the first problem, making compiler front-ends easier to implement. Even more is gained if these specifications are *executable*, i.e. if high-quality *specification compilers* are available.
In these cases the specifications *are* implementations, rather than just guide-
lines for manual programming.

Consider the great success of regular expressions for specifying lexical
structures, and context-free grammars for specifying syntax. This is due in
part to their technical merits, but also to the availability of practical tools
that implement such specifications: `lex`, `yacc`, and many more. These tools
not only make front-ends easier to implement correctly, but have also had
a positive effect on language design itself, since prototype compilers can be
implemented with little effort.

Largely absent from this picture are tools for implementing a language's
static semantics, i.e. processing of declarations and type checking. This is
mainly due to the lack of formal semantics for most programming languages,
but also to the lack of suitable tools. The only formalism that seems to have
found some use in this area is *attribute grammars*, described later in this
chapter.

This is where our work comes in. *Natural semantics* has become popular
among language theoreticians and some designers. Our work with the RML
language and the `rml2c` compiler aims to prove that natural semantics can be
a practical specification tool for compiler writers as well as language designers.

2.2   Ways to Specify Semantics

2.2.1   Interpreters

An early approach, but still common, is to write an interpreter for the defined
language D in a known language K. For instance, assuming that Lisp is
widely understood, a Prolog interpreter written in Lisp could be used to
explain/define Prolog's operational semantics.

An immediate advantage of this method is that specifications, being executable, can be used as prototype implementations. A specification is necessarily implementation-oriented, which helps to explain the defined language's
execution mechanisms.

On the other hand, irrelevant details pertaining to the known language K
are likely to be present in the interpreter. This can obscure the specification,
making it unclear whether some detail is K-specific or an actual part of the

defined language. For this reason, interpretive specifications are not very useful for language designers and theoreticians.

One mistake frequently made in the Lisp and Prolog communities is to write the interpreter in the defined language itself; this is called a *meta-circular* interpreter. The problem, as pointed out by Reynolds [153], is that the interpreter might make use of some specific feature, for instance argument evaluation order, when defining that same feature. The end result is $\perp$: the feature remains undefined. Special specification techniques must be applied if such an interpreter is to be well-defined.

2.2.2 Abstract Machines

A more formal way to describe an operational semantics is to make use of a formally well-defined *abstract machine*. The state of such a machine is typically described as a complex mathematical[1] object, together with rewriting rules that define possible state transitions.

A well-known example of this technique is Landin's SECD machine, which has been used as a model for functional languages [106]. Another example is the *interpreting automata* used by the Vienna Definition Language (VDL) [127]. This style of definition was developed during an effort to formalize PL/I. More recent designs include the Categorical Abstract Machine (CAM), the G-machine, Warren's Abstract Machine (WAM), Pascal's P-code, and many other.

Using an abstract machine has several advantages. In contrast to using an interpreter in a 'known' language, the machine is usually reasonably simple, and defined in terms of mathematical values rather than (concrete) machine objects. However, it is still usually concrete enough that it can be implemented straightforwardly.

Like interpreters, abstract machines are essentially algorithmic. They facilitate describing *how* computations can be performed, but are less useful for declarative concepts such as 'what is a well-typed ML program'.

2.2.3 Attribute Grammars

An attribute grammar (AG) is an extension of an ordinary context-free grammar. Every non-terminal can have a number of named values, *attributes*, associated with it. For every production $A \rightarrow \alpha$, there is a set of equations that relate the values of A's attributes with those of terminals and non-terminals in α. Terminals can also have attributes, though their values are not defined by equations but by some external agent.

Attribute evaluation is separate from parsing, at least formally. A parse tree is constructed, and every node is given attributes as determined by its

---

[1]Here, and elsewhere, we use "mathematical" to signify that the objects involved are defined by some formal system, such as set theory or domain theory, as opposed to being composed of bits and storage units in an actual computer.

non-terminal or terminal symbol. Then the attribute equations are expanded
at each non-terminal node. This results in a (large) system of equations
relating all attributes in all nodes. Actual attribute values are determined
by solving this system.

Limited forms of attribute grammars were used in early compiler work in
the 1960s. Knuth [101,102] developed the more general form described above.
Attribute grammars have found much use in compiler construction, as a tool
for specifying type checking and generating intermediate code [3, Chapter 5;
94]. In practice, it is often more convenient to use the *abstract* rather than
concrete syntax of a language when defining an AG. For efficiency reasons, it
is desirable to evaluate attributes *during* rather than after parsing, but this
is only possible for certain restricted classes of AGs.

Knuth imposed several conditions on attribute grammars: they must be
free of circular dependencies, no attribute may have multiple definitions (even
if they are the same), and references to undefined attributes are illegal. This
makes sense when describing compilation of simple procedural languages,
but is a severe limitation compared to other formalisms, such as denotational
or natural semantics. For instance, type systems for functional languages
typically *infer* type declarations for variables, rather than requiring explicit
declarations. These systems compute with partially undefined values, which
is quite straightforward in natural semantics.

2.2.4 Denotational Semantics

In denotational semantics a mathematical mapping is given from every syntactic object to its *denotation*, a mathematical value [160,167]. The mathematical machinery used, Scott's *domain* theory, is much more complex than
the simple objects used in the other formalisms. The complexity is necessary since denotational semantics allows both undefined values and recursive
equations. Typically a sugared λ-calculus is used as the specification language.

Denotational semantics has the advantage of a well-developed repertoire
of specification techniques, enabling straightforward descriptions of many
language features.

There are also disadvantages: the mathematical machinery is complex,
and the syntax is usually very cryptic. The generality of the formalism and
the λ-calculus meta-language cause tremendous overheads when interpreted
or compiled. To achieve acceptable efficiency, compiler-generators have had
to impose restrictions on the way specifications may be written. For instance,
by enforcing continuation-passing style definitions, an implementation may
use call-by-value instead of call-by-name evaluation.

Like interpreters and abstract machines, denotational semantics is useful
for describing *computations*, including implementations of static analyses. It
is less suited for type checking or type inference.

Denotational semantics currently seems to have found its niche in the partial evaluation and abstract interpretation application domains.

2.2.5   Action Semantics

Peter Mosses identified two problems with denotational specifications. The first and less serious one is their usually cryptic notation. The second and more serious problem is that changing some detail of the defined language may require a complete rewrite of the specification. For instance, if statements are added to a pure expression language, two things happen: new equations have to be written to define the new syntactic forms, and the original equations are changed in order to deal with the new concept of *state*. Then, if sufficiently flexible control structures are added to this statement language, *another* global modification is needed to convert existing equations to a continuation-passing style. In essence, denotational semantics has poor *engineering* properties.

Mosses then developed *action semantics* as an alternative formalism with better properties [122]. The core of the formalism is a large number of predefined algebraic operators for expressing computations, side-effects, control flow, and declarations. An operator can have effects in one or several of these *facets*, for instance it might both produce a value and cause a side effect. In other facets, it typically acts as an identity function, e.g. an assignment operator would leave the current declarations unchanged.

Specifications are expressed as functions from syntactic objects to *terms* composed of these algebraic operators. The meaning of a program is the resulting *action term*, which must then be interpreted using the definitions of the primitives.

The formalism is quite verbose, with long alphabetic operator names, and a somewhat English-like syntax. This is a deliberate design choice, but some, this author included, find it too verbose.

Since any operator can have effects in any of the different facets, adding features becomes easy. Adding side-effects would not require any changes to the action terms for expression evaluation, except in the case of variables. This flexibility comes at considerable cost, though. Since any operator can have any effect, it is difficult to see *exactly what* a term actually does. A detailed understanding of *all* action operators is required; the problem is that action notation has a larger number of core primitives (about 20) than the λ-calculus, and an even greater number of derived forms.

Action semantics has attracted some interest since the mid-80s, and recently a few compilers for the notation have been built. Although action notation is more suited for efficient compilation than denotational semantics, these compilers still generate very slow code compared to conventional compilers. The emphasis seems to be on provable correctness rather than efficiency.

As far as we know, action semantics has been applied mostly to procedural languages, including Pascal. We know of no specifications for Scheme with its powerful `call/cc`, Prolog's backtracking, or Standard ML's polymorphic type system.

2.2.6 Evolving Algebras

The *evolving algebras* approach [30, 73] is essentially operational. States are represented by first-order structures (sets with operations). Specifications consist of a (usually large) number of transition rules, each being a *conditional update*: if *Guard* then $f(\vec{a}) := e$. Execution proceeds as follows: The guards are evaluated and a subset of the updates is selected. Then the argument tuples $\vec{a}$ are evaluated (giving values $\vec{x}$), as are the new values e (giving y). Each resulting pair $(f, \vec{x})$ is a *location*. If the set of update locations is *consistent* (every location has exactly one update), the updates are *fired* by *simultaneously* applying them to the current state. This results in a new state, with the same *signature* as before (set of function symbols with arities), but the domains and ranges of some functions have been changed.

The formalism is being advertised as a general model for computations, much like Turing machines. Regarding applications, it appears the main purpose of existing work is to model algorithms (such as communication protocols), languages (specifications exist for the dynamic semantics of C, WAM, Prolog, and several other logic programming languages), and prove correctness of implementations. The formalism can be interpreted, but efficient compilation of language specifications does not appear to be on the evolving algebra research agenda.

2.2.7 Structural Operational Semantics

In 1981 Plotkin published his seminal report on Structural Operational Semantics (SOS) [144]. This work did much to rehabilitate the use of operational semantics in programming language definitions after the domination of Denotational Semantics in the 70s. SOS is based on automata, with simple rules defining state transitions. Rules take the form

$$before \rightarrow after$$

or

$$\frac{conditions}{before \rightarrow after}$$

The *before/after* parts are *configurations*, i.e. system states typically encoded as tuples of terms describing various parts of the computation. The conditions either express constraints on the applicability of the rules or describe that a component of the *before* configuration is rewritten. In the latter case, the *before* and *after* configurations differ only at the rewritten component. For this reason SOS semantics are sometimes called *small step* semantics.

The following example is from Plotkin [144, page 31]. Let n denote integers, and e expressions composed of integers and sums of expressions. Configurations are expressions. Left-to-right stepwise evaluation is defined by the three rules:

$$\frac{e_0 \rightarrow e_0'}{e_0 + e_1 \rightarrow e_0' + e_1} \tag{1}$$

$$\frac{e_1 \rightarrow e_1'}{n_0 + e_1 \rightarrow n_0 + e_1'} \tag{2}$$

$$\frac{n_2 = n_0 + n_1}{n_0 + n_1 \rightarrow n_2} \tag{3}$$

SOS rules define a one-step rewriting relation between states. To complete a specification, initial and final states must also be defined. By taking the reflexive and transitive closure of the one-step relation, one arrives at a relation from initial to final states.

Like abstract machines, SOS specifications work exclusively with simple mathematical structures such as numbers, sets, and tuples.

SOS specifications, being essentially abstract machines, seem to be popular for describing process calculi and language fragments in textbooks. There is an SOS for the core of Scheme [151], including `call/cc`.

2.3 Natural Semantics

During their work on the Mentor and Centaur programming environments, Gilles Kahn's group at INRIA developed and popularized the style of specification which is called *Natural Semantics* [44,56,57,96]. They were influenced initially by Plotkin's Structural Operational Semantics, and later by Gerhard Gentzen's Sequent Calculus for Natural Deduction Systems [68,148].

2.3.1 Natural Deduction

The word 'natural' in Natural Semantics comes from Natural Deduction Systems, which are formal systems for conducting proofs in various logics. For instance, the inference rule

$$\frac{A \quad B}{A \wedge B} \tag{$\wedge$I}$$

says that if formulas A and B are both true, then so is the formula $A \wedge B$. This is called an *introduction* rule since it defines when the $\wedge$ connective may be introduced. There are also *elimination* rules, which state what may be deduced from composite formulas.

Complications arise when *hypothetical* assumptions are made. In the introduction rule for implication,

$$\frac{\begin{array}{c} (A) \\ B \end{array}}{A \Rightarrow B} \tag{$\Rightarrow$I}$$

A is a hypothesis which is used to prove B. However, it must then be *cancelled* (or *discharged*), which is what (A) means. This is a non-local operation because the discharge is performed somewhere on the fringe of B's proof tree. This formulation of natural deduction is the traditional one [49].

A simpler formulation, due to Gentzen, is the *Sequent Calculus* [68; 148, Appendix A]. The idea is to make the treatment of assumptions explicit, by changing inference rules to deal with propositions of the form $\Gamma \to \Delta$, where Γ and Δ are *sets* or *sequences* of formulas. These propositions are called *sequents*. This eliminates the traditional meta-level treatment of assumptions and simplifies formal manipulations of proofs. For instance, the introduction rule for implication is written

$$\frac{A, \Gamma \to \Delta, B}{\Gamma \to \Delta, A \Rightarrow B} \qquad (\to \Rightarrow)$$

This means that, if we can deduce the set of formulas $\Delta \cup \{B\}$ from the set $\Gamma \cup \{A\}$, then we may deduce $\Delta \cup \{A \Rightarrow B\}$ from Γ. Note that A is both added as an assumption and cancelled by the same rule.

2.3.2   Relation to Programming Languages

To see the relation of the above to programming language specifications, we make two observations:

1. SOS rules and natural deduction rules are similar in appearance, except that deduction rules allow arbitrary propositions as premises. A more significant difference is their (operational) interpretation: SOS rules can be seen as state machines, while deduction systems can be seen as proof procedures.

2. The notion of assumptions in logic is essentially the same as the notions of *bindings* and *scope* in programming languages. Encoding assumptions as *sequents* is similar to passing around *environments* and *stores* for describing bindings and state.

2.3.3   Example

A typical specification in natural semantics consists of two parts: declarations of the syntactic and semantic objects involved, followed by groups of inference rules. Each group defines some particular property (also called *judgement* or *signature*), for instance the value or type of an expression. The rules themselves are applied to instances of the signature. These instances are called *sequents* or *propositions*.

Our example language consists of expressions built from numbers, negations, and additions. To specify its evaluation rules, we start by defining its abstract syntax:

$$
\boxed{\begin{array}{ll}
v \in \text{int} & \text{integers} \\
e \in \text{exp} ::= v \mid -e \mid e_1 + e_2 & \text{expressions}
\end{array}}
$$

Then we present the inference rules. They define the judgement $e \Rightarrow v$, which is read as 'the expression e evaluates to value v'. By convention, we write the signature of the relation in a box before the first rule.[2] The rules are also numbered to allow references to be made to them.

$$\boxed{e \Rightarrow v}$$

$$v \Rightarrow v \tag{1}$$

$$\frac{e \Rightarrow v \quad v' = -v}{-e \Rightarrow v'} \tag{2}$$

$$\frac{e_1 \Rightarrow v_1 \quad e_2 \Rightarrow v_2 \quad v_3 = v_1 + v_2}{e_1 + e_2 \Rightarrow v_3} \tag{3}$$

The concrete syntax used by RML naturally differs from that depicted here. See Section 3.1 and Chapter 4 for examples of actual RML syntax.

2.3.4 Meaning

To assign meaning to a specification like the one above, we typically give it a procedural, or proof-theoretic, interpretation.[3] That is, we interpret inference rules as recipes for constructing proofs for the propositions of interest. This construction can be defined formally [148, section 1.2], but here an informal account will suffice. (This section is very informal. See for instance Lloyd [112] for a much more thorough treatment in the context of logic programming.)

Suppose we wish to prove that there is a value v such that $(-1)+3 \Rightarrow v$ holds in the example specification.

In general, to prove a proposition we need an inference rule whose conclusion can be instantiated to the proposition. Rule (3) is the only rule that could prove proposition 1, so we instantiate (3).

$$\frac{-1 \Rightarrow_2 v_1 \quad 3 \Rightarrow_3 v_2 \quad v = v_1 + v_2}{(-1)+3 \Rightarrow_1 v}$$

To complete the proof, we must now prove the new propositions. Proposition 2 can only be proved by an instance of rule (2), so we augment the proof tree with an instance of (2).

$$\frac{\dfrac{1 \Rightarrow_4 v' \quad v_1 = -v'}{-1 \Rightarrow_2 v_1} \quad 3 \Rightarrow_3 v_2 \quad v = v_1 + v_2}{(-1)+3 \Rightarrow_1 v}$$

---

[2]Inspired by the definition of SML [120].

[3]Model-theoretic interpretations are almost never used for natural semantics.

Proposition 4 can be proved by instantiating axiom (1), replacing v' with 1, and replacing v_1 with -1.

$$\frac{\dfrac{1 \Rightarrow_4 1 \quad -1 = -1}{-1 \Rightarrow_2 -1} \quad 3 \Rightarrow_3 v_2 \quad v = -1 + v_2}{(-1)+3 \Rightarrow_1 v}$$

Similarly, proposition 3 can also be proved by instantiating axiom (1), but now replacing v_2 with 3, and v with 2.

$$\frac{\dfrac{1 \Rightarrow_4 1 \quad v_1 = -1}{-1 \Rightarrow_2 v_1} \quad 3 \Rightarrow_3 3 \quad 2 = -1 + 3}{(-1)+3 \Rightarrow_1 2}$$

Now there are no remaining propositions to prove, so this is a complete proof tree for proposition 1. Additionally, a witness $v = 2$ has been computed.

From this example of proof construction, we make the following observations/assumptions:

- A judgement is interpreted as a proof procedure, the parameters of which are the variables in its signature.

- A proposition is interpreted as a call to the corresponding procedure.

- A proof procedure executes a call by choosing one of its rules, instantiating it to match the parameters of the call, and then executing all the premises. If this is successful, the call succeeds. If there is no rule for which the call can succeed, it fails.

- A negated premise $\neg goal$ is interpreted by the negation-as-failure rule: if the sub-goal succeeds, the negation fails, and if the sub-goal fails, the negation succeeds.

Since proofs in natural semantics are tree-shaped rather than sequences of configurations, this style of semantics is sometimes called a *big step* semantics. The term *relational semantics* is also used.

2.3.5 Pragmatics

Natural semantics has several valuable properties:

1. Because of its foundation in logic, specifications are often amenable to formal proof.

2. Most of the specification techniques developed for other formalisms, such as environments, states, locations, etc., are directly applicable.

3. It also adds a few features, primarily the ability to reason about *unknowns*, which are difficult to express in other formalisms.

4. Objects are simple structures. It includes nothing like the complex domains of denotational semantics.

5. A specification usually has a straightforward operational interpretation: the rules are seen as specifying a proof procedure. In many cases, the proof search is deterministic.

6. It has proven its suitability for a wide range of applications, including static semantics, simple type systems, ML-style polymorphic type systems, operational semantics, static analysis, various kinds of translations, and compilation [75,81,114]. (This is just the tip of the iceberg. There are an *immense* number of papers on type systems including interesting language features, or modified type systems used for performing static analysis, and they are almost invariably specified in natural semantics.)

On the negative side, there have been very few direct implementations of the formalism. Before our work on the rml2c compiler, users had a choice of either using the Typol compiler, or to translate their specifications by hand to some programming language.

2.3.6 Recent Extensions

The introduction of the higher-order λProlog language [60,117] has inspired some researchers to abandon environments, using instead higher-order terms, embedded implications (→), and embedded ∀ quantifiers to achieve bindings [76,77,154]. This is essentially a move away from the sequent calculus to ordinary natural deduction. Their motivation for this change is to 'simplify' specifications, and for someone with a strong background in formal logic, the implicit treatment of assumptions in traditional natural deduction is perhaps simpler than explicit mechanisms.

In my view, however, the resulting formalism is much less attractive than traditional natural semantics. Moving away from sequent-style specifications makes their interpretation much more complex, which is unfortunate since only a minority among current and prospective users of natural semantics are likely to be experts in formal logic. From an implementation point of view, λProlog's implication operator is significantly more difficult to realize than are explicit environments. The treatment of equality also becomes more complex, since it needs higher-order unification, which is semi-decidable [60, 90]. Finally, since environments are explicit objects, they are inherently more flexible than the higher-order operators. For instance, Standard ML makes non-trivial use of explicit environments in the specification of its module system [119,120].

Chapter 3

The Design of RML

$\mathcal{D}$ esigning a computer language, whether a general-purpose programming language or a special-purpose language like RML, is non-trivial. A successful language is often influenced by several different sources: intended application areas, existing languages, experiences from early implementation efforts, and experiences from attempting to (perhaps formally) specify it. Ignoring any one of these influences can lead to serious deficiencies in the language.

In this chapter we describe the design of RML. In Sections 3.1 and 3.2 we cover the relatively straightforward design of the syntax and static semantics. Section 3.3 discusses the backtracking model of control flow used by RML, its backgrounds and pragmatic properties. Section 3.4 discusses the reasons for, and consequences of, restricting control flow to be *determinate*. Section 3.5 discusses the evolution of RML's design. Finally, in Section 3.6 we discuss some of the differences between RML and SML, and their implications.

Our design goals include:

Simplicity Unwarranted complexity was to be avoided, both in the language and its definition.

Compatibility RML should be as close as possible to 'typical' natural semantics and, where applicable, Standard ML.

Effectiveness Limitations that inhibit the use of RML in typical applications were to be avoided.

Efficiency A major goal. Efficient implementation should not only be possible, but also not *require* user annotations or global analysis. Global analysis should be optional.

3.1   Syntax

The syntax of RML is based mainly on the style of natural semantics used in type systems and language definitions similar to the one for Standard ML [120], and on SML itself.

The notation for propositions in natural semantics, and natural deduction in general, is often quite complex: any sequence of meta-variables and auxiliary symbols can be a proposition. Examples:

$$\Gamma \vdash e : \tau \tag{1}$$

$$VE, \sigma \vdash e \Rightarrow v, \sigma' \tag{2}$$

$$\vdash e \tag{3}$$

(1) may be read as: with type assumptions Γ, the expression e has type τ. (2) may be read as: given a variable environment VE and state σ, the expression e evaluates to value v and yields an updated state σ'. (3) may be read as: the expression e is well-formed.

In these and many other applications of natural semantics, there is usually a distinction between 'arguments' and 'results' of sequents. In (1), Γ and e are usually intended as arguments, with τ being the result. Similarly, in (2), VE, σ, and e are typically arguments, and v and σ' results. In (3), e is the only argument. The result is implicit in the truth or falsity of the sequent.

RML does away with the plethora of auxiliary symbols, choosing instead simple alphanumeric identifiers to name propositions. Furthermore, RML syntactically separates arguments and results by placing the => symbol between them. (Hannan [76, Definition 7.2] also syntactically separates arguments from results. The attribute-grammar approach of Attali et al. [11–13] depends on arguments being separate from results, but in their case, the property is proved by analysis.)

The above examples could be written in RML as:

$$\texttt{typeof(Gamma,e) => tau} \tag{1}$$

$$\texttt{eval(VE,s,e) => (v,s')} \tag{2}$$

$$\texttt{well\_formed e} \tag{3}$$

RML views propositions as *relations* from inputs to outputs. Relations are declared by the `relation` keyword, followed by the individual rules, and terminated by `end`. For instance, a simple relation for negating a boolean might be written as follows in natural semantics:

$$\boxed{\neg b \Rightarrow b'}$$

$$\neg true \Rightarrow false \tag{1}$$

$$\neg false \Rightarrow true \tag{2}$$

In RML it would be written

```
relation negate: bool => bool =
  axiom negate true => false
  axiom negate false => true
end
```

The declaration of the relation itself, written in a box before, follows immediately after the `relation` keyword. RML will actually *infer* the signature of a relation, so it is not necessary to write the types explicitly. Thus, this examples would usually simply be written as:

```
relation negate =
  axiom negate true => false
  axiom negate false => true
end
```

From natural semantics, RML also borrowed the visual layout of inference rules. A rule with premises is introduced by the `rule` keyword, followed by the premises, a sequence of dashes (at least two), and the conclusion.

```
rule   premise1 & premise2
       ----------------
       conclusion
```

The syntax for lexical elements, such as literals[1], identifiers, and comments, closely follows that in SML. The main omission is SML's *symbolic* identifiers (+, <>, :=, etc.).

The syntax for expressions, patterns, types, and type declarations also follows that in SML, where applicable. Since RML expressions only denote simple values, the syntax for anonymous functions and local bindings is absent. Applications in expressions may only involve data constructors.

The type of an n-to-m-ary RML relation is written[2]

$$(ty_1, \cdots, ty_n) \text{ => } (ty'_1, \cdots, ty'_m)$$

which is similar to the SML type

$$ty_1 * \cdots * ty_n \text{ -> } ty'_1 * \cdots * ty'_m$$

Contrary to languages like Prolog and Haskell, whether an identifier starts with an upper- or lower-case letter has no semantic significance. (But RML is still case-sensitive: X and x are different identifiers.)

---

[1] The notation for character literals is the same as in recent (≥ 107) versions of the SML of New Jersey implementation.

[2] $\cdots$ is a meta-symbol denoting repetition, *not* a literal token.

3.2   Static Semantics

The static semantics is based on two main premises:

1. Strong static typing is required. Specifications are often intended to be precise, formal descriptions of programming languages. It is therefore important that specifications are free of errors. With a strong static type system, errors such as inconsistent types and misspelled names can be detected by the compiler.

2. A module system should be present to allow specifications to be grouped into related and manageable pieces. It should be possible to compile these pieces separately.

The type system is based on the popular Hindley-Milner-Damas polymorphic type system for ML-like languages [50, 86, 118, 120]. This system combines several desirable features:

- It is strong and static: all type errors are detected by the compiler. No runtime type checks are necessary.

- Types can be *inferred*. Declaring the types of relations and variables is not necessary.

- It allows types to be *polymorphic*. Data structures, such as lists or trees, can be parametrized by one or several types, leading to lists of integers, trees of booleans and so on. Relations operating upon these data structures can be written once, and then applied to all instances.

- It is well-understood, easy to specify, and not difficult to implement [38, 152, 155].

The module system allows the description of a flat collection of modules, where each module consists of a public interface and a private implementation section. Modules may import the interfaces of other modules. The module system is essentially just a name space management tool.

In contrast, the SML module system is considerably more flexible, but also more complex. RML trades this flexibility, basically by not having functors or multiple views of structures, for a *much* simplified formal definition and implementation.

The RML module system has one pragmatic advantage over SML's module system. If an SML signature describes a `datatype`, then that description has to be repeated in any structure that is to match the signature. In RML, all type declarations made in the interface of a module are visible in the remainder of the module.

3.2.1 Bindings and Unknowns

Unknowns play an important part in some applications, especially in specifications of polymorphic type systems. Contrary to Prolog, RML does not equate unbound *identifiers* with logical variables (unknowns). Instead, RML defines precisely when variables are bound, and to what. First, since RML executes premises from left to right, it also binds variables in that order. In a call

$$r(e_1, \cdots, e_n) \texttt{ => } (p_1, \cdots, p_n)$$

patterns in the right-hand side are matched against the actual results from the call, and pattern variables become bound. This is just as in a SML `let` binding, except that no variable may have multiple bindings in an inference rule.

Unknowns are introduced explicitly by `exists` x. Here x is a previously unbound variable which becomes bound to some unknown value in the rest of the inference rule.

The construction $x = e$ is interpreted as a `let` binding if x is unbound, and as an equality constraint (unification) if x is bound.

3.2.2 Technicalities

In this section we comment on some technical aspects of the definition of RML's static semantics (in Section A.5), especially in comparison with the definition of SML. It may safely be skipped by those unfamiliar with the details of these specifications.

The technical design of the static semantics is very close to that for Standard ML [119,120]. There are just a few main differences on which we comment here.

SML has local polymorphic definitions via the `let` keyword. This requires the construction of type schemes using a type *generalization* operation that takes into account the surrounding variable environment. RML inference rules only bind local variables to types, not type schemes. This means that type generalization in RML is always trivial: in local bindings no type variables are generalized, while in top-level bindings all type variables are generalized.

Both SML and RML are sensitive to whether an identifier is bound as a `datatype` constructor or whether it denotes a plain variable. This difference is essential in patterns. The definition of SML glosses over this issue, leaving it to a few informal sentences [120, Section 2.4] to describe identifier classification. In the commentary [119, Appendix B], the idea is presented of using a *status* environment. It parallels the variable environment, but maps identifiers to tokens describing their status as constructors or plain variables. (Kahrs [97] also discusses this and other problems with the definition of SML.)

RML uses the status map idea, but integrates it with the ordinary variable environment. An identifier is mapped to a *pair* of a status token and a type scheme. The inference rules both produce correctly tagged bindings, and check that identifiers have correct status when required. This technique could easily be adapted for SML.

One technical advantage of the simple module system is that *generativity* of module and type names is trivial. In RML, a datatype t in module m uses the pair (m, t) as its *type name*. This pair is guaranteed to be unique since module names may not be redefined, and types may not be multiply defined within a module.

3.3   Modelling Backtracking

Natural semantics, like logic, has a declarative rather than operational semantics. The declarative semantics can be model-theoretic, i.e. defining the universe of true ground propositions. Or it can be proof-theoretic, describing how correct proofs are constructed. Programming languages for logic are typically based on the proof-theoretic semantics. To execute a goal is to prove it using a concrete proof search procedure, such as SLD resolution in Prolog. These proof search procedures are generally sound but not complete: if they find a proof for a proposition, then that proposition is indeed true. For some goals however, they may fail to terminate.

RML initially used the same proof procedure as Prolog, viz. a top-down left-right search with backtracking [136]. There are different models of this procedure, including proof streams, abstract machines, and continuation-passing style (CPS). We chose to use a CPS model because of its attractive pragmatic properties: it can be viewed simultaneously as a high-level declarative model, being a mapping to the λ-calculus, and as a low-level imperative model, where continuations are closures and control flow are simple jumps with arguments. Chapter 8 describes more of the pragmatic advantages of CPS, and how a compiler for it can be implemented.

3.3.1   Intuition

Before proceeding with the actual operational semantics for RML, we will discuss the intuitions of CPS models for Prolog-like languages. They are quite simple, as we shall illustrate with a small example. Consider the following Prolog program:[3]

```
one   :- write('1').
two   :- write('2').
three :- write('3').
q     :- one ; two.
```

---

[3]In Prolog , denotes conjunction and ; disjunction.

```
p :- q, three.
```

If p is called to deliver all its solutions (at a Prolog top-level, this can be done with the goal p, fail), it will output 1323. We observe that during the execution of q, a backtracking point (called a choice-point in Prolog parlance) was set up. After three had delivered its answer, backtracking took the execution back to the second disjunct in q, which called two, after which three was called again.

This program can readily be converted to a deterministic program in a procedural or functional language that supports procedure closures and procedure parameters;[4] we will use SML. The idea, which we call the *single-continuation* model, uses *success continuations* (sc) for sequencing. Each predicate becomes a procedure with a single argument, a success continuation sc, which is a procedure with no arguments. When the predicate wants to 'succeed', it invokes its sc. At a conjunction, a new sc is defined to call the right conjunct with the original sc. Then the left conjunct is called with this new sc. As long as no failures occur, no procedure ever returns.

A disjunction is encoded as *the sequence* of first calling its left disjunct, and then calling its right disjunct. It is easy to see that the call stack contains exactly the disjunctions seen but not backtracked into, in chronological order. So backtracking to the youngest choice point is just a matter of *returning*.

Here is the single-continuation version of the example program:

```
fun one sc = (print "1"; sc())
fun two sc = (print "2"; sc())
fun three sc = (print "3"; sc())
fun q sc = (one sc; two sc)
fun p sc =
  let fun sc'() = three sc
  in q sc' end
fun main() =
  let fun sc() = ()   (* force more answers *)
  in p sc; print "\n" end
```

To *this* form one can apply the usual continuation models developed for procedural and functional languages. We then arrive at the *double-continuation* model, in which sequencing and recursion are replaced by parameterless *failure continuations* (fc). Every procedure and every sc must now take a failure continuation fc as an argument. If some operation fails, the current fc is invoked. To 'succeed' is to invoke the current sc with the current fc. Failure continuations are extended at disjunctions, similarly to how success continuations are extended at conjunctions.

Here is the double-continuation version of the example program:

```
fun one sc fc = (print "1"; sc fc)
```

---

[4]That is, the language must have *downwards funargs*.

```
fun two sc fc = (print "2"; sc fc)
fun three sc fc = (print "3"; sc fc)
fun q sc fc =
  let fun fc'() = two sc fc
  in one sc fc' end
fun p sc fc =
  let fun sc' fc' = three sc fc'
  in q sc' fc end
fun main() =
  let fun fc() = print "\n"
      fun sc fc' = fc'()   (* force more answers *)
  in p sc fc end
```

The double-continuation model also admits a concise description of Prolog's ! operation, which removes all choice points created since the entry to the current procedure. Suppose that the q predicate had been written as follows:

```
q :- (one, !) ; two.
```

This is easily expressed in the double-continuation model as follows:

```
fun q sc fc =
  let fun fc'() = two sc fc
      fun sc' fc'' = sc fc
  in one sc' fc' end
```

That is, one is called not with the original sc, but with an sc' that reinstates q's original fc.

3.3.2   Origins

The technique of using continuations to model top-down search with backtracking has been invented and reinvented many times.

In the Prolog community, the single-continuation model is usually attributed to Mellish and Hardy [116] or to Carlsson [39], both published in 1984. It is used, for instance, by [46] and [60] to describe compilation schemes for logic programming languages in some detail.

Sandewall proposed the same technique, using different terminology, already in 1973, although his paper was not published until 1976 [158]. Only Nilsson [125] seems to have previously realized the connection between Sandewall's paper and compiling Prolog.

Koster described the exact same idea in 1974 (published in 1975) [103], as a technique for implementing top-down parsing of non-left-recursive ambiguous grammars. In a later paper [104], he claims to have developed the technique as early as in 1966.

Recently, Tarau and coworkers [170] have built an implementation of Prolog called BinProlog. Their implementation is based on source-to-source transformations that add constructs to mimic success continuations.[5]

The double-continuation model is much less used. In the Prolog community, it is usually attributed to Nicholson and Foo's denotational semantics for Prolog [124], published in 1989. In the same year, de Bruin published a similar semantics [34]. Nicholson and Foo's semantics was later extended to describe features of the λProlog language [33]. Similar to the source-level transformations used by Tarau et al., Lindgren [111] has recently proposed using a source-to-source double-continuation transformation as a means for analysis and compilation of Prolog.

In a combined artificial intelligence and parsing context, Charniak et al. [41] used the double-continuation model to describe how chronological backtracking can be elegantly implemented. Backtracking using continuations is also briefly described in Schmidt's book on denotational semantics [160].

The very first document on the Scheme language [168], published in 1975, contains two programming examples that use procedures as continuations. Generators are implemented using single continuations, and backtracking is implemented using two continuations. From the terseness of the surrounding text, it appears the authors considered the techniques completely obvious and well-known.

Giegerich and Wilhelm [69] presented an attribute grammar for compiling boolean expressions to short-circuit code. The core of their idea is to pass, as inherited attributes, two code labels *tsucc* and *fsucc* to every boolean expression, and emit a jump to the appropriate label as soon as an expression's value is known. The way their AG uses these labels and augments them in **and/or** expressions is very similar to the double-continuation model for backtracking. (This is a simplified picture; see their paper for details.)

3.3.3 Denotational Semantics of Backtracking

We now turn to a denotational semantics, in continuation-passing style, for RML. At this point we are only interested in the control flow of the language, so we present the semantics for a simplified language DNF, so named because procedure bodies are in *disjunctive normal form*. The semantic definitions, in Figures 3.1 to 3.3, simply formalize what was described in the previous section. The purpose of this idealized definition is to facilitate the discussion of some of its important operational properties.[6]

The details of expression evaluation, parameter passing, and pattern-matching are straightforward and can be found in the full natural semantics definition of RML in Appendix A.6.

---

[5]Prolog is a first-order language, so continuations have to be *encoded* as plain terms, which are then *interpreted* accordingly. Reynolds [153] provides an excellent discussion about this and related issues.

[6]This section is closely based on [136].

Strict Evaluation

As a consequence of the continuation-passing style used in the semantic functions shown in Figure 3.3, most argument expressions in the right-hand sides are in weak head normal form. Those that are not (the **let** forms), can be evaluated trivially and reduce in one step to expressions with arguments in weak head normal form. This implies that strict evaluation (call-by-value) can be used. The need to point this out stems from the fact that denotational semantics, being based on λ-calculus, must normally be given a *call-by-name* (or lazy) interpretation. This generally implies overheads that can be avoided when call-by-value is possible.

Implicit Global Procedure Environment

Once $\mathcal{P}$ has iterated through a program's declarations and augmented pe_0 with bindings for user-defined procedures, there is a single pe that is passed around in the semantic equations. Hence, pe can be viewed as a global constant, the bindings can be compiled statically, and the pe arguments can be omitted. This assumes that there are no primitives like Prolog's **assert** and **retract**, or λProlog's implication =>, that can change the pe dynamically.

Stack-Allocation of Continuations

Continuations are λ-abstractions and normally such values are represented as dynamically allocated closures. Here we describe why DNF's continuations may be allocated on a global stack. A precondition is that continuations do not 'escape', i.e. there are no primitive procedures that, like Scheme's call/cc, reify continuations into first-class values.

Since the specification is in continuation-passing style, at any given point there is either *exactly* one redex or the program has reduced to its final answer. Let the first reduction occur at time 1, the second at time 2, and so on. A continuation's *birth-time* is the time at which the reduction occurred that created the continuation. A continuation c_1 is *older than* (*younger than*) a continuation c_2 if c_1's birth-time is strictly less (greater or equal) than c_2's birth-time.

First note that failure continuations do not themselves take continuation arguments; hence, when a particular *FCont* is applied, all younger continuations, including itself, become inaccessible.

Success continuations take failure continuations as arguments. Thus, both continuations in existence when the *SCont* was created and continuations reachable via the argument *FCont*, are reachable. However, suppose a success continuation sc is applied to a failure continuation fc that is older than sc. Then, just as when failure continuations are called, all continuations younger than sc, including itself, become inaccessible.

Abstract syntax

$p \in Proc$		procedure names
$c \in Conj \longrightarrow c_1$ and $c_2 \mid$ *not* $c \mid p$		conjunctions
$d \in Disj \longrightarrow d_1$ *or* $d_2 \mid c$		disjunctions
$P \in Prog \longrightarrow p = d; P \mid \varepsilon$		programs

Semantic domains

$l \in Loc$	(some countable set)	locations
$x \in EVal$	(unspecified)	expressible values
$SVal$	$= EVal + \{unbound, unallocated\}$	storable values
$s \in State$	$= Loc \to SVal$	states
$m \in Marker$	$= State$	state markers
$Answer$	$= \{Yes, No\}_\perp$	answers
$fc \in FCont$	$= State \to Answer$	failure continuations
$sc \in SCont$	$= FCont \to State \to Answer$	success continuations
$pe \in PEnv$	$= Proc \to PVal$	procedure environments
$pv \in PVal$	$= PEnv \to FCont \to SCont \to State \to Answer$	
		procedure values

State auxiliaries

$s_0 : State$ initial state
$s_0 = \lambda l.\ unallocated$
$new : State \to (Loc \times State)$
$new\ s = \langle l, s' \rangle$ **where** $s\ l = unallocated\ \wedge\ s' = s[l \mapsto unbound]$
$bind : State \to Loc \to EVal \to State$
$bind\ s\ l\ x =$ **if** $s\ l = unbound$ **then** $s[l \mapsto x]$ **else** $\perp$
$marker : State \to Marker$
$marker\ s = s$
$restore : Marker \to State \to State$
$restore\ m\ s = m$
$pe_0 : PEnv$ primitive procedures (unspecified)

Figure 3.1: Denotational semantics of DNF, part 1

Control auxiliaries

$fc_0 : FCont$ initial failure continuation
$fc_0 = \lambda s.No$
$sc_0 : SCont$ initial success continuation
$sc_0 = \lambda fc.\lambda s.Yes$
$proceed : SCont \rightarrow FCont \rightarrow SCont$
$proceed_{Prolog} \; sc \; fc_{ignore} = sc$
$proceed_{RML} \; sc \; fc = \lambda fc_{ignore}.\lambda s. \; sc \; fc \; s$

Figure 3.2: Denotational semantics of DNF, part 2

Semantic functions

$C : Conj \rightarrow PEnv \rightarrow FCont \rightarrow SCont \rightarrow State \rightarrow Answer$
$C \; [\![c_1 \; and \; c_2]\!] \; pe \; fc \; sc \; s = C \; [\![c_1]\!] \; pe \; fc \; \{\lambda fc'.\lambda s'. \; C \; [\![c_2]\!] \; pe \; fc' \; sc \; s'\} \; s$
$C \; [\![not \; c]\!] \; pe \; fc \; sc \; s =$
    let $m = marker \; s$
    in $C \; [\![c]\!] \; pe \; \{\lambda s'. \; sc \; fc \; (restore \; m \; s')\} \; \{\lambda fc'.\lambda s'. \; fc \; s'\} \; s$
$C \; [\![p]\!] \; pe \; fc \; sc \; s = pe \; p \; pe \; fc \; (proceed \; sc \; fc) \; s$

$D : Disj \rightarrow PEnv \rightarrow FCont \rightarrow SCont \rightarrow State \rightarrow Answer$
$D \; [\![d_1 \; or \; d_2]\!] \; pe \; fc \; sc \; s =$
    let $m = marker \; s$
    in $D \; [\![d_1]\!] \; pe \; \{\lambda s'. \; D \; [\![d_2]\!] \; pe \; fc \; sc \; (restore \; m \; s')\} \; sc \; s$
$D \; [\![c]\!] \; pe \; fc \; sc \; s = C \; [\![c]\!] \; pe \; fc \; sc \; s$

$P : Prog \rightarrow PEnv \rightarrow PEnv$
$P \; [\![p = d; P]\!] \; pe =$
    let $pv = \lambda pe.\lambda fc.\lambda sc.\lambda s. \; D \; [\![d]\!] \; pe \; fc \; sc \; s$
    in $P \; [\![P]\!] \; (pe[p \mapsto pv])$
$P \; [\![\varepsilon]\!] \; pe = pe$

$M : Prog \rightarrow Answer$
$M \; [\![P]\!] = $ **let** $pe = P \; [\![P]\!] \; pe_0$ **in** $pe \; [\![main]\!] \; pe \; fc_0 \; sc_0 \; s_0$

Figure 3.3: Denotational semantics of DNF, part 3

These observations imply that stack-allocation and controlled dealloca-
tion of continuations are possible. When a failure continuation is called,
i.e. backtracking occurs, everything below and including the choice point becomes inaccessible. Thus the stack pointer can be reset to the position just
before the choice point. When a success continuation is called, i.e. when a
procedure call succeeds, one of two things can happen:

1. The current *FCont* is older than the *SCont*. Then this is the last
   possible return to this *SCont*, and the stack pointer is reset to the
   position just before it.

2. The current *FCont* is younger than the *SCont*. The *FCont* may be
   backtracked into, eventually causing this *SCont* to be returned to several times. Hence the stack pointer cannot be reset to the *SCont*, but
   it *can* be reset to the position of the *FCont*.

Every time a continuation is created, its representation (a record containing a
code pointer and the values of its free variables [153]) is pushed onto a global
stack. When it is invoked, the stack pointer is reset as indicated above.

Finally note that the WAM manages its control stack in a very similar
way to what has been described here [4, 178].

State Single-Threading and Trailing

As indicated in Figure 3.1, we assume that potentially 'unknown' values
are represented as logical variables. These are locations, which the state
then either maps to an actual value or to a token *unbound*. The equations
dealing with backtracking ($\mathcal{D} [\![d_1 \; or \; g_2]\!]$ and $\mathcal{C} [\![not \; c]\!]$) clearly illustrate that
backtracking must restore the state (i.e. the bindings of logical variables)
to the state at the time the failure continuation (a.k.a. choice point) was
initially created.

As currently specified, the *marker* and *restore* primitives are trivial:
marker s saves the current state, and *restore m s'* recovers the one saved in
the marker. This unfortunately means that the state is not *single-threaded*:
at any given time there may exist a number of different states. This has
the disastrous effect of preventing state modifications being implemented by
side-effects to an implicit global state [159].

However, in the equations for disjunction and negation, the states m
(original s) and s' in the expression *restore m s'* are not completely unrelated.
The following can be seen to hold:

1. *Dom m* $\subseteq$ *Dom s'*
   Since the first state was recorded in m, *new* may have been applied a
   number of times to allocate new locations. This does not in any way
   affect the previously allocated locations.

2. $\forall l \in Dom\ m : lookup\ m\ l \neq unbound \Rightarrow lookup\ m\ l = lookup\ s'\ l$

   Since m was created, *bind* may have been called to update some previously *unbound* locations. Note that *bind* expresses a *write-once* semantics of logical variables.

The most important action of *restore* is to unbind those locations that
have been bound since the state was saved in the marker. An obvious way
of accomplishing this is to log side-effects: every time *bind* binds a location,
this location is saved in a global stack known as the *trail*. *marker s* need then
just record the current position of the trail, while *restore m s'* unbinds those
locations pushed between the current trail position and the one recorded in
the marker, before finally resetting the trail position.

Let locations be allocated in some deterministic order and let the state
record its current 'next' location. Then it suffices for *marker s* to record the
current next location and for *restore m s'* to reset it to also achieve the effect
of resetting the state's domain.

Reducing Trailing

The specification, with these operational modifications, is still sub-optimal,
as a comparison with the WAM shows [4]. The difference is that the DNF
specification trails *all* bound locations, whereas the WAM only records those
older than the 'current' failure continuation (a.k.a. choice point).

Since *marker* records the current next free location for use by *restore*, it
can also store this value in a global *trailing boundary* variable. Then *bind*
would only have to trail bindings of locations *previous* to the current trailing
boundary, since later locations are discarded automatically as the domain
of the state is reset. (Here *previous* and *later* refer to the order in which
the state allocates locations.) The trailing boundary must 'track' the *FCont*
that recorded it. This entails that whenever an older *FCont* is made current,
its trailing boundary must also be made current. This can be achieved by
requiring the trailing boundary to be stored at a fixed position in the *FCont*.

With these modifications, the runtime structure of DNF/RML has been
made very similar to that of the WAM.

3.4   Determinacy

As mentioned before, the initial version of RML used the same search procedure as Prolog. This entailed that relations could, as in Prolog, return many
times. Prolog programmers can use this either to their advantage, in so-called
generate-and-test style programs or they can make procedures determinate
by the use of cuts or `if`s.

RML specification writers cannot exercise such detailed control over the
search procedure. Furthermore, natural semantics specifications are over-
whelmingly often completely deterministic even though their formulations

may seem to call for non-deterministic proof search. That is, natural semantics relations are generally *determinate*: for any sequent, at most one actual inference rule in the called relation can be applicable in a proof of that sequent.

This meant that RML specifications tended to backtrack only locally within relations, but the original proof procedure would create many choice points that would never be backtracked into. This caused *serious* memory management problems during execution. (See Section 6.1.)

The first solution was to implement a new phase in the compiler, the First-Order Logic optimizer, described in detail in Chapter 6. This was very successful, and absolutely mandatory for pragmatic reasons, but unfortunately incompatible with the original proof search procedure. The very purpose of the optimizer is to eliminate redundant calls, but this is inconsistent with a Prolog-like search if calls may have visible side-effects.

However, several researchers have already worked on determinate or even *deterministic* (never any choices) formalisms. Both da Silva [48] and Hannan [76, Definition 7.4] used determinate or deterministic specifications, and devised methods to transform determinate specifications to deterministic ones. This was followed up by Hannan [79], Diehl [58], and McKeever [115]. Independently, Berry [22] made the same assumptions. (Some of our colleagues who are using natural semantics as a design and documentation tool also write only deterministic specifications.[7])

Following the precedent set by these researchers, we therefore decided to specify a *determinate* proof search procedure for RML. In the DNF semantics, it suffices to use the $proceed_{\text{RML}}$ combinator instead of $proceed_{\text{Prolog}}$ to describe this change.

3.5 History

3.5.1 Static Semantics

The very first implementation of the type checker was made before the static semantics had been written. It was based on a rather free-wheeling notion of 'anything goes'. It allowed type and relation declarations to be placed in any order in a module. As a consequence (since inferring polymorphic types for mutually recursive relations is undecidable [84]), explicit typing of relations was required. The type checker, not being able to use the lexical order as the order in which to elaborate declarations, emulated a kind of lazy evaluation to defer elaboration until absolutely necessary.

Although somewhat elegant from the user's perspective, this turned out to be difficult to formalize when the type system was written. The usual rule that declarations should precede any uses of the types (or relations) declared

---

[7]L. Viklund, Aug. 1995. Personal communication about the use of deterministic and ground natural semantics when specifying parts of the ObjectMath language.

was therefore adopted. As in SML, the and keyword had to be introduced to signify mutual recursion among type or relation declarations.

This simplified not only the implementation but more significantly the formal static semantics. It also meant that relations no longer needed explicit type declarations, since types could be inferred.

The initial design did not have the exists keyword. Instead, the first reference of an unbound identifier would automatically bind it to a logical variable. This had the disadvantage of complicating the formal semantics, as well as making the determinacy-improving transformations described in Chapter 6 much more difficult to implement. Hence exists x was introduced, acting as an explicit $\exists$ quantifier.

3.5.2 Dynamic Semantics

The initial design called for a full Prolog-like search rule. The disadvantages were soon apparent, so after struggling with different control models and possible optimizations, we settled for the ones described in Chapter 6. The presence of the optimizations necessitated changing the official definition of RML to be determinate.

The very first prototype included Prolog's 'cut' operation. This was done not because it was needed, or even desirable, but because the CPS model made it easy to describe. Discussions during our visit to INRIA Sophia-Antipolis in June 1994 [135] made it clear that cuts have no place in natural semantics. Furthermore, their presence hindered our attempts to find high-level control models with useful axiomatizations. For these reasons cuts were removed from RML. (Unfortunately, they were still present when [136] was written.)

3.6 Differences from SML

One of the design goals was compatibility with SML, another was efficiency. In the interest of the second goal, the importance of the first was occasionally diminished. This had impacts on syntax, and on static and dynamic semantics.

Functions in SML always take a single argument and return a single result. When the analogue of an n-ary function is needed, the function is either defined to take a single n-tuple argument or it is defined in *curried* style. A similar situation holds for datatype constructors: they are either constant or have a single argument. While this is elegant and leads to great uniformity, there are also significant runtime costs.

A great majority of value-carrying data constructors have values that are tuples or records. However, the SML module system can cause one piece of code using a particular datatype not to see the exact same declarations of the constructors as other parts of the program. In particular, whether a value-carrying constructor takes a tuple or not is not always known. At the implementation level, this forces a constructor applied to an n-tuple to be represented as a pair, consisting of a tag and a pointer to the n-tuple [6]. The *flat* $n + 1$ tuple representation, with the tag in the first element, would usually be more efficient.

By design, RML with its simpler module system does not have this problem. All code using a particular data constructor sees the exact same declaration. This allows the implementation to use the more efficient flat representation.

Similarly, RML intrinsically views relations as n-to-m-ary. This allows arguments to be passed as separate values rather than being combined as heap-allocated tuples. It also allows multiple results, a *very* common feature of natural semantics specifications, to be returned as separate values. A possible drawback of this approach is that some extra coding is necessary when a tuple is to be passed as an 'argument' tuple to a relation. In SML this is the normal situation, but in RML the tuple has to be separated into its components first.

Some of these advantages of flat constructor representation and non-unary functions could be achieved in SML by sufficiently clever static analysis and compilation methods [81, 107, 173]. These techniques are still very much in the development stage.

Chapter 4

Examples

$\mathfrak{D}$ eveloping applications in a new language is a worthwhile exercise. It can be used both to expose weaknesses in the language and to demonstrate the effectiveness of its (new) features.

This chapter has two purposes. The first is simply to introduce RML, by way of concrete examples, and show how some typical specification may be written and organized. The second is to describe the 'test-bed' applications we have written in RML, and some of the experiences gained from writing them. They have also been used for benchmarking the compiler and runtime system(s); these results are presented in Chapter 10.

4.1 A Small Example

In Section 2.3.3 a small language of arithmetic expressions was used to illustrate natural semantics. Here we show how that example is expressed in RML, in order to clarify RML's syntax and operational semantics.

4.1.1 Abstract Syntax

First we convert the abstract syntax of the example to RML types. This is done most conveniently using a datatype declaration.

```
datatype exp = INT of int
             | NEG of exp
             | ADD of exp * exp
```

The new type, exp, is a union type. For every production in the abstract syntax, there is an alternative in the datatype declaration. Every alternative starts with the name of its *constructor*, followed by the of keyword and the types of its components. If there are multiple components, they are combined into a tuple type. (The * above is the infix operator for tuple types.) If there are are no components in an alternative, only the constructor is written.

Although we used uppercase letters in the names of the constructors, this is just a *convention*. Constructor names may be written as arbitrary alphanumeric identifiers.

4.1.2   Inference Rules

Next we convert the inference rules of the $e \Rightarrow v$ judgement. As described in Chapter 3, RML uses a simpler notation for judgements and sequents. Choosing to call this judgement eval, its declaration becomes as follows.

```
relation eval =
  axiom eval INT v => v

  rule   eval e => v & int_neg v => v'
         ----------------
         eval NEG e => v'

  rule   eval e1 => v1 & eval e2 => v2 &
         int_add(v1, v2) => v3
         ----------------
         eval ADD(e1,e2) => v3
end
```

The relation keyword introduces the declaration, followed by the name of the relation, its rules, terminated by end. RML views judgements operationally as relations from inputs to outputs, which is why we often use the term 'relation' instead of 'judgement'.

The first rule is the translation of axiom (1) in the example. In this case, the translation only involves adding the name of the relation to the axiom, and adding the name of the constructor used for this particular case in the exp type. The arrow, =>, is RML's syntax for separating arguments from results.

The next rule corresponds to rule (2) in the example. The two premises of that rule are written side-by-side here, separated by the & symbol. As RML does not have infix arithmetic operators, the arithmetic negation in rule (2) is converted to a call to the standard relation int_neg.

The last rule corresponds to rule (3) in the example. Note that when a constructor has multiple components, they are written, separated by commas, between a pair of parentheses. The same applies when relations have multiple arguments or results. Although not necessary, parentheses *may* also be written when there are only single arguments.

4.1.3   Operational Interpretation

As described in Section 2.3.4, logical relations may be interpreted operationally as procedures for performing proofs.

The `eval` relation is viewed as a procedure from the type `exp` to the type `int`. There are no explicit proof trees. Instead, a successful proof (call to `eval`) is indicated by a successful return from `eval` together with the corresponding return value. A failed proof is indicated by a 'failed' call.

The first rule in `eval` is interpreted as the sequence of actions: *match* the argument against the `INT v` pattern, and then succeed, returning v to `eval`'s caller.

The second rule is interpreted as: match the argument against `NEG e`, then call `eval` with e as argument. The return value from that call is then *matched* against the v pattern, which just binds v to the value. Then call `int_neg` with v and match the result against v'. Finally succeed, returning v' to `eval`'s caller. The third rule is analogous.

The `eval` procedure will, when called, execute each of its inference rules in the order written, until one of them succeeds. If all fail, then so does the call to `eval`.

4.2 Mini-Freja

Mini-Freja is a call-by-name pure functional language.[1] Its definition was written initially by two fellow graduate students, H. Nilsson and L. Viklund, using the tools of the Centaur 1.2 programming environment [91]: Metal (for syntax), PPML (for visualization), and Typol (for evaluation). It was converted/rewritten by this author to RML.

4.2.1 Abstract Syntax

In written texts we typically define abstract syntax using some extended BNF. RML follows the modern functional school in having general algebraic datatypes. In particular, RML's type system is very close to that of Standard ML.

An official abstract syntax for Mini-Freja might look as shown in Figure 4.1. In RML (and SML), we can encode this using a few `type` and

$x \in$ var	variables
$c \in$ con	constants
$e \in$ exp ::= c	constant expression
$\quad\mid \lambda x.\, e$	abstraction
$\quad\mid x$	variable
$\quad\mid e_1\, e_2$	application

Figure 4.1: Textbook style syntax for Mini-Freja

---

[1]Freja is a goddess in Nordic mythology.

datatype declarations. (We make a separate type of lambda expressions because we will use it later on.)

```
(* Mini-Freja abstract syntax *)
type var = string
type con = int
datatype exp = CON of con
             | LAM of lam
             | VAR of var
             | APP of exp * exp
and lam      = LAMBDA of var * exp
```

The type declarations just add new names to existing types. The exp and lam types are mutually recursive, which is the reason for the and keyword.

4.2.2 Values

Before we describe the evaluation rules, we need to know what the possible kinds of values are. For a functional language we typically have constants, function values, suspended expressions (due to call-by-name), and various kinds of structures such as tuples, lists, etc. Here we concentrate on functions and suspensions.

Functional values can be modelled in at least two different ways: as closures of expressions and environments, or as expressions whose free variables have been substituted by actual values. We prefer the first model, for its simplicity. However, it does force us to introduce explicit environments mapping free variables to their values. Suspended expressions can, like functions, be modelled as closures.

To get any real work done, one usually also has a set of *primitive* functions for arithmetic and various data-structure manipulations. We make an enumerated type for the primitives, and add this type as a new kind of value.

Putting this together, we have the following declarations:

```
datatype prim  = ADD1
datatype value = CONST of con
               | PRIM of prim
               | FUNC of env * lam
               | SUSP of env * exp
withtype env   = (var * value) list
```

For simplicity, we just have a single primitive, which is why the declaration for prim only has a single alternative. The withtype declaration is used to introduce type aliases simultaneously with one (or several) datatypes.

4.2.3 Environments

Environments are formally speaking partial functions, but they are frequently encoded as association lists: lists of pairs of variables and values. Adding a binding is easy, but looking up a binding requires an auxiliary relation. We define it as follows in RML:

```
relation lookup: (env, var) => value =
  rule  x = x'
        ----------------
        lookup((x,v)::_, x') => v

  rule  not x = x' & lookup(env, x') => v
        ----------------
        lookup((x,_)::env, x') => v
end
```

The first rule deals with the case where the variable is bound in the leftmost (most recent) binding in the list. In this case, the associated value is the value of lookup. (:: is the infix 'cons' operator for lists. _ is a 'wildcard' pattern that matches anything.)

The other rule deals with the case where the first binding is for a *different* variable. In this case, if there is an associated value in the remainder of the list, then that is the value of lookup.

If there is no binding for the variable, lookup will *fail*. Formally, this means that the sequent lookup(env,x) => v has no proof.

In this example we gave an explicit type for the lookup relation. RML, like SML, uses type inference. The above example is therefore typically written without the explicit types:

```
relation lookup =
  ..
end
```

If written this way, RML will infer the type ((`'a * `'b) list, `'a) => `'b for lookup, of which the previous type is an instance.

4.2.4 Evaluation

We now turn to the actual evaluation rules. They are expressed as propositions describing the relationships between environments, expressions, and values.

Evaluating an expression should result in a proper (non-suspended) value. In applications, due to call-by-name, argument expressions are suspended, causing formal variables to be bound to suspensions. We therefore need to *force* the evaluation of suspensions when referencing variables.

Applications of primitives also need to be described. We assume here that all primitives are strict and so force their arguments before invoking an auxiliary relation for evaluating the primop.

```
relation primapp =
  rule  int_add(i, 1) => j
        ----------------
        primapp(ADD1, CONST i) => CONST j
end

relation apply = (* v,v' => v'' *)
  rule  force arg => v & primapp(p, v) => v'
        ----------------
        apply(PRIM p, arg) => v'

  rule  env' = (var,arg)::env & eval(env',exp) => v
        ----------------
        apply(FUNC(env,LAMBDA(var,exp)), arg) => v
end

and eval = (* env |- exp => val *)
  axiom eval(env, CON c) => CONST c
  axiom eval(env, LAM lam) => FUNC(env,lam)

  rule  lookup(env, x) => v & force v => v'
        ----------------
        eval(env, VAR x) => v'

  rule  eval(env, f) => f' & apply(f', SUSP(env,arg)) => v'
        ----------------
        eval(env, APP(f,arg)) => v'
end

and force = (* v => v' *)
  axiom force(CONST c) => CONST c
  axiom force(v as PRIM _) => v
  axiom force(v as FUNC(_,_)) => v

  rule  eval(env, exp) => v
        ----------------
        force(SUSP(env,exp)) => v
end
```

The apply, eval, and force relations are mutually recursive, which is the reason for the and keywords. The pattern v as PRIM _ (in the second axiom for force) behaves just like PRIM _, except that v also becomes bound to the matched value. This feature (borrowed from SML) allows laborious details to be omitted when the whole value is to be used again in some other context.

4.2.5 Modularity

Good software engineering practices apply equally well to executable specifications as they do to ordinary programs. One of these practices is to use
modules to group closely-related entities together. *Interfaces* declare entities
that are to be visible outside their home modules: other entities are by default
private.

RML has a simple flat module system, which identifies files with modules.
Every module consists of three components: a name, an interface, and a
private section containing RML declarations.

Mini-Freja's abstract syntax should be placed in a module of its own, since
it can have several clients apart from the evaluator (parser, type checker,
static analyser, etc.).

```
(* absyn.rml *)
module Absyn:
  (* Mini-Freja abstract syntax *)
  type var = string
  type con = int
  datatype exp = CON of con
               | LAM of lam
               | VAR of var
               | APP of exp * exp
  and lam      = LAMBDA of var * exp
end
(* empty module body *)
```

Note that no change was necessary to the type declarations. Contrary to
SML, RML allows all forms of type declarations, including a kind of `abstype`,
in interfaces.

A client of the `Absyn` module needs to do two things: first the interface
must be imported using a `with` declaration, then the imported names must
be prefixed by the module name, similarly to SML.

```
(* eval.rml *)
module Eval:
  with "absyn.rml"
  datatype prim  = ADD1
  datatype value = CONST of Absyn.con
                 | PRIM of prim
                 | FUNC of env * lam
                 | SUSP of env * Absyn.exp
  withtype env   = (Absyn.var * value) list
  relation eval: (env, Absyn.exp) => value
end
(* declarations of eval etc. *)
```

In the interface we only listed the `eval` relation and its type. The other relations will not be accessible from the outside.

4.2.6   Adding Recursion

At this stage, Mini-Freja is a very primitive language. Extending it with composite data types and more primitives present no problems. Conditionals and recursive definitions can be added as primitives, or they can be defined in the language itself using combinators. We show here two ways of adding (single) recursive functions as a primitive construct.

First we augment the abstract syntax with a fix-point operator:

```
datatype exp = CON of con
             | LAM of lam
             | FIX of var * lam
             | VAR of var
             | APP of exp * exp
and lam      = LAMBDA of var * exp
```

A recursive function $f\ x = E$, sometimes written $fix\ \lambda f.\lambda x.E$, would be encoded as `FIX(f,LAMBDA(x,E))`.

For the evaluation rules, there are two possible approaches: one that follows Typol [44, 56] and one that follows SML [120].

The Typol approach is to model recursive definitions using recursive objects. This is formally nonsense since objects in natural semantics are finite *terms*, but it works in Typol and RML thanks to logical variables and unification without occur-check.

The value of a recursive function is a function closure where the environment of that closure contains a binding for the function's name to the closure itself. The evaluation rule can be expressed as:

```
relation eval =
  ..
  rule  exists v &
        env' = (f,v)::env &
        v' = FUNC(env',lam) &
        v = v'
        -----------------
        eval(env, FIX(f,lam as LAMBDA(x,e))) => v
  ..
end
```

Read operationally, this assumes the existence of some value v, then binds f to that value in the environment, constructs a closure, and finally asserts the identity of the closure and the assumed value.

A formally acceptable technique is that of *finite unfolding*. It is based
on encoding recursions as special values which are unfolded *one* level when
accessed, giving rise to values that can be unfolded again when needed. Since
the unfolding is controlled, all values remain finite. This technique is used in
the definitions of both SML and RML.

We first change the type of function values by adding an optional name,
which is only present for recursive functions:

```
datatype clo   = CLO of var option * env * lam
datatype value = ..
                 | FUNC of clo

                 ..
```

Then we define an auxiliary relation to unfold recursive closures one level,
while leaving non-recursive closures unchanged.

```
relation unfold =
  axiom unfold(clo as CLO(NONE,_,_)) => clo

  rule   env' = (var, FUNC(CLO clo)) :: env &
         clo' = CLO(SOME var,env',lam)
         ----------------
         unfold(clo as CLO(SOME var,env,lam)) => clo'
end
```

Then we change apply to unfold a closure before invoking it:

```
relation apply =
  ..
  rule   unfold clo => CLO(_,env,LAMBDA(var,exp)) &
         env' = (var,arg)::env &
         eval(env',exp) => v
         ----------------
         apply(FUNC(CLO clo), arg) => v
end
```

The last step is to modify the rule for plain abstractions and add a rule for
recursive abstractions:

```
relation eval =
  ..
  axiom eval(env, LAM lam) => FUNC(CLO(NONE,env,lam))
  axiom eval(env, FIX(f,lam)) => FUNC(CLO(SOME f,env,lam))
  ..
end
```

4.2.7 Summary

The real version of Mini-Freja is somewhat richer than shown here. It operates on more types (booleans, strings, lists), has more primitives (15), functions defined by pattern-matching rules, and allows groups of mutually recursive functions. The Mini-Freja specification is 298 lines, of which about one third concern evaluation proper, one third realize primitive operators, and the rest deal with environments and pattern matching. To this is added a module with pre-compiled test cases, the `absyn` module that just declares the abstract syntax, and the `main` module. It totals 542 lines of RML. There is no C code, apart from that in the runtime system.

4.3 Diesel

Another application of natural semantics is for high-level descriptions of *translators* or *compilers*, and abstract machines [56, 78, 96].

Diesel is a simple Pascal-like language with nested procedure declarations, integer and real scalar and array variables, and overloaded arithmetic and comparison operators allowing integers in real-typed contexts. Diesel has been used in our department's undergraduate compilers course since 1987, where the students are given a skeleton of the Diesel compiler and have to implement the missing pieces.

The RML specification maps Diesel to low-level C code in three steps. It uses no new features of the RML language, being 'just' larger and more complex. We describe here the high-level structure of the Diesel specification.

4.3.1 Static Elaboration

Static checking and evaluation is often referred to as static *elaboration*. The elaborator applies the static semantics to Diesel programs (abstract syntax) to verify static conditions (definition before use, type consistency), and to resolve overloaded operators. The result is a program in a slightly different representation which we call *TCode* (for Tree Code). This representation is identical to the abstract syntax, except for a few details:

- Overloaded operators, such as arithmetic and assignments, have been replaced by type-specific operators. Implicit integer-to-real conversions have been replaced by an explicit operator.

- The context-sensitive interpretation of variables as *l-values* or *r-values* has been eliminated. Scalar variables have been replaced by an address-of-object operator. Subscripted arrays use a combination of the address operator and a type-specific indexing operator to produce the location of the array element. In r-value contexts, a type-specific *load* operator is applied to fetch the value; in l-value contexts (assignments), a type-specific *store* operator is used.

- Syntactic types in variable declarations have been replaced by (representations of) semantic types.

- No distinction is made between syntactic operators and functions, they all become calls to functions.

The core of the static elaboration consists of two judgements

```
elab_exp(env, exp) => (ty, exp')
elab_stmt(ty_opt, env, stmt) => stmt'
```

where the left-hand-side expressions and statements are from the abstract syntax, and the right-hand-side ones are from *TCode*. The optional type in `elab_stmt` is the return type of functions. It is present so that `return` statements can be checked.

Other important judgements include:

```
widen(exp, ty_exp, ty_ctx) => exp
lub_ty(ty_1, ty_2) => ty_3
choose(ty, x_int, x_real) => x
```

The first inserts the integer-to-real conversion if an integer expression occurs in a real-typed context; other cases remain unchanged. The second computes the least upper bound of two types, which is trivial in this type system which only has integers and reals. The third selects either the integer x or the real x, depending on the type.

Given these, elaboration of operators is quite simple. To elaborate an addition expression one elaborates the arguments, computes the least upper bound (lub) of their types, widens the translated expressions to the lub, chooses the appropriate integer or real addition *function*, and finally assembles a call to that function.

Real division is similar, except widening is always to real, not the lub. Integer modulus, too, is similar, except no widening takes place. Instead pattern matching is used to verify that the arguments are integer-typed.

Comparison and relation operators are much like addition, except that the result type is always integer.

4.3.2 Flattening

The *TCode* representation is still very high-level. The *flattening* phase reduces its complexity by flattening procedures to a single scope level. The resulting *FCode* (for flattened code) representation uses record-like *frames* to describe the activation records of procedures, and an implicit *display* to access activation records at runtime. The original structure of expressions and statements is kept, except that the address operator now uses a frame descriptor and a name in that frame.

A real compiler should here also flatten control structures to combinations of labels, gotos, and conditional gotos.

4.3.3   Emitting Code

The *FCode* representation corresponds closely to a simple subset of C. We therefore chose to emit it as C, treating C as a portable assembly language.

The *fcemit* phase corresponds to a simple back-end. There is nothing declarative about it, being essentially just a series of traversals of the representation. Each traversal generates C code on the standard output file.

We could have coded this phase in C, however we coded it in RML for two reasons:

1. Accessing RML's algebraic data structures in hand-written C code is awkward and error-prone.

2. We wished to demonstrate that algorithmic code *can* be written in RML, its control flow being reasonably predictable (like Prolog's).

The following excerpt shows the rule for converting the *FCode* representation of while-loops to text. print is a built-in RML relation for printing strings and other objects to the standard output file.

```
relation emit_stmt =
  ..
  rule  print "\twhile( " &
        emit_exp exp &
        print " ) {\n" &
        emit_stmt stmt &
        print "\t}\n"
        ----------------
        emit_stmt(FCode.WHILE(exp,stmt))
  ..
end
```

4.3.4   C Glue

The Diesel compiler also uses a lexical analyser generated by Lex, and a parser generated by Yacc. These are interfaced to the rest of the compiler through a set of C functions for constructing abstract syntax objects in the representation expected by RML. The objects are allocated in the C heap, and then passed to the RML code *en masse* when parsing has been completed. We mention this only to assure the reader that RML can peacefully co-exist with code of other origins.

4.3.5   Summary

The complete Diesel compiler uses 1036 lines of RML, spread over 6 modules. To this it adds a Lex scanner specification, a Yacc parser specification, and some C glue code. The total, 1900 lines, can be compared with the original Diesel compiler's 3453 lines of Pascal code.

4.4 Petrol

The Diesel specification introduced several general mechanisms in its intermediate forms, viz. pointers, displays, and records (frames). We therefore defined an extension of Diesel, called Petrol, which adds Pascal-like type declarations, records, and pointers; from C it has pointer arithmetic, array parameters, casts, and a constant 0 overloaded at all pointer and numeric types.

The added complexity is concentrated in the static elaborator, which was split into two modules: a 513-line module responsible for elaborating declarations and doing type-less translations to *TCode*, and a 469-line module dealing exclusively with type conversions and overloaded operators.

Recursive record types are dealt with in a manner completely analogous to the finite unfolding technique described earlier. Unfolding takes place in the elaboration of field accesses: in `node.field`, the left operand must have a record type; that type is unfolded to allow access to potentially recursive components.

Some complexity also spilled over to the C code emitter: it became necessary to add an additional traversal for scanning out and emitting record declarations, and general type expressions have to be converted to C declaration syntax.

The last point can be illustrated by an example. We have the following three representations for the same declaration:

```
Petrol     var x : array[5] of pointer to int
internal   x ↦ ARR(5,PTR(INT))
C          int *x[5]
```

In particular, the abstract syntax for a C *declarator* is essentially an inverted form of the internal type. Dealing with this required additional types for representing C types, relations for printing them, and 'inversion' relations for converting internal types to C types.

4.4.1 Summary

The Petrol specification uses 2047 lines of RML, in 10 modules. When the usual Lex, Yacc, and C glue is added, the total is 3150 lines. This is still less than the original Diesel compiler's 3453 lines, even though the language has been significantly extended.

4.5 Mini-ML

The next example concerns another common use of natural semantics, viz. to specify type systems for functional languages. These systems often contain features such as parametric polymorphism, implicit typing, overloading, or subtyping. We describe here the specification of a type system close to the

SML core language, in which we have integrated Rémy's ranked generalization condition [152], Wright's simple imperative polymorphism [181], SML's equality types [120], and a technique of our own for SML's overloading.

The reader who is unfamiliar with polymorphic type systems may want to skip directly to the summary in Section 4.5.6. Providing a gentle introduction to these non-trivial systems is unfortunately outside the scope of this text; interested readers may wish to read any of the following for a start [38,50,120].

In the sequel, we assume familiarity with ML-style type systems, in particular the use of *type schemes* and let-polymorphism.

We note that several of the ideas presented below are based on type variables having *attributes* that serve to prevent illegal substitutions from occurring. This mechanism seems to be very close to that used in the implementation of Constraint-Logic Programming languages [92, 126].

4.5.1 Rémy-Style let-Polymorphism

ML introduces polymorphic type schemes through the construct let $x = e_1$ in e_2. It is operationally equivalent to $(\lambda x.e_2)e_1$, but the type system allows x to be polymorphic in the first form, but not in the second.

In the type system, this is mainly visible in two places: the rule for let, and the rule for variables.[2] When type checking let $x = e_1$ in e_2, e_1 is type checked and its type is *generalized* to a type scheme. Generalization is traditionally defined as:

$$Gen(\Gamma, \tau) = \forall \alpha^*.\tau \text{ where } \alpha^* = FV(\tau) \setminus FV(\Gamma)$$

That is, those free variables in τ that are not also free in the typing context Γ are bound by $\forall$. The complementary action occurs when type checking a variable reference. Then the variable's type scheme in Γ is instantiated by substituting types for the $\forall$-bound type variables.

To work properly, the type system must be constrained to infer *principal types*, i.e. maximally general types. This condition is difficult to encode in formal systems [80], so it is usually specified informally, or even left implicit.

Implementing this type system is quite straightforward, using type variables to represent unknown types, and unification to enforce type constraints [50; 38; 3, sections 6.6 and 6.7].

The one problematic issue concerns the type generalization operation which must ensure that free variables in Γ are not generalized. Implementing the definition literally as a search through Γ becomes very costly, since Γ is typically very large.

Cardelli [38] described a simple improvement in which all λ-bound types are maintained in a separate set (called the *non-generic vars*). Since any free variable in the context must have been λ-bound, this allows the scope of the search to be limited to this set.

---

[2]We assume a syntax-directed system with no separate Gen/Inst rules.

Recently, Rémy [152] has described a much simpler and cheaper mechanism for deciding which variables to generalize; we summarize his type system in Figure 4.2.

$$\frac{\Gamma(x) \succ_n \tau}{\Gamma \vdash_n x : \tau} \qquad (1)$$

$$\frac{\Gamma + \{x \mapsto \forall().\tau_1\} \vdash_n e : \tau_2}{\Gamma \vdash_n \lambda x.e : \tau_1 \to \tau_2} \qquad (2)$$

$$\frac{\Gamma \vdash_n e_1 : \tau_1 \to \tau_2 \quad \Gamma \vdash_n e_2 : \tau_1}{\Gamma \vdash_n e_1\ e_2 : \tau_2} \qquad (3)$$

$$\frac{\Gamma \vdash_{n+1} e_1 : \tau_1 \quad \Gamma + \{x \mapsto Gen_{n+1}(\tau_1)\} \vdash_n e_2 : \tau_2}{\Gamma \vdash_n \text{let } x = e_1 \text{ in } e_2 : \tau_2} \qquad (4)$$

$$Gen_n(\tau) = \forall \alpha^*.\tau \text{ where } \alpha^* = FV(\tau) \cap \mathcal{V}^n$$

Figure 4.2: Rémy-style let-polymorphism

Every type variable is associated with a *rank* n, a natural number. They are partitioned into sets $\mathcal{V}^n$ containing exactly the variables of rank n. The instantiation operation $\sigma \succ_n \tau$ is rank preserving: bound type variables can only be instantiated by types of equal or less rank. Finally, the generalization operation binds only those variables of the given rank n.

In propositions $\Gamma \vdash_n e : \tau$, n is the maximum rank of any free type variables in τ and Γ. Now consider rule (4) for let. The right-hand side e_1 is elaborated at maximum rank $n + 1$. If its type τ_1 contains a type variable which is free in Γ, then that variable *must* have rank less than $n + 1$, and so will not be generalized.

The benefit of this formulation is that is allows type generalization to be implemented in time $\Theta(|\tau|)$, since the test for generalization takes constant time for every type variable in τ. The exact bound for the traditional formulation depends on implementation details, but at least one traversal of Γ seems necessary.

To ensure that substitutions are rank-preserving, unification of two variables replaces the one of greater rank with the one of lesser rank. Also, when a variable α is unified with a type, it is verified that no variable in this type has rank greater than α's, if necessary by substituting fresh variables of correct rank for any variable with rank greater than α's.

4.5.2   Equality Types

SML has a polymorphic equality operator which is applicable to all objects, except functions and certain other types that do not admit equality. To model this, the definition of SML [120] makes use of an *equality attribute* of type variables, and gives the = operator type ''a * ''a -> bool, where ''a requires equality.

In much the same way as in the previous case, the equality attribute serves to control instantiations of this variable. An equality type variable may only be instantiated by types that *admit equality*. They are:

- Type variables with the equality attribute set.

- Records/tuples whose components all admit equality.

- A constructed type, such as int or 'a list, if both the *type name* and all type parameters admit equality.

- All types 'a ref.

Most base types admit equality. User-defined datatypes admit equality if every alternative does so (under the assumption that the parameters admit equality). Abstract datatypes, exceptions, and functions never admit equality. (This and other issues are discussed in more depth in [119].)

In our specification we let type variables have an equality attribute which is set if equality is required. When a variable is bound to a type, we verify that the type admits equality. In the type, type variables (except under ref) that do not require equality are substituted by fresh variables that do.

Without attributes, unification of type variables is easy since it does not matter which variable is bound to the other. With only one attribute, one can compare their constraints and bind the one with weaker constraints to the one with stronger constraints. With multiple attributes, there is no guarantee that such an ordering exists. One alternative is to *update* the attributes of one of the variables and bind the other to it. Instead, we chose to use the ordinary substitution mechanism to substitute a fresh variable with correct attributes for both of the other variables.

To keep these details separate from the main typing rules, we have split the specification into three components: a module containing only the inference rules of the type system, a module responsible for generalization and instantiation, and a module responsible for unification and constraints.

4.5.3   Wright's Simple Imperative Polymorphism

ML adds imperative features, including updateable reference cells, to an otherwise side-effect-free functional language. It has been long known that full polymorphism combined with references can subvert the safety of the type system, and a number of type systems have been proposed to deal with the problem [70, 87, 108, 109, 174, 180, 181].

Standard ML uses a solution devised by Tofte [174]. It involves adding an *imperative* attribute to type variables and restricting the generalization operation to not generalize imperative type variables.

The specification and implementation of this is straightforward, but the system has a pragmatic disadvantage: a polymorphic function that happens to use references internally, cannot be given a fully polymorphic type in the module system.

Wright later found a simpler type system which both makes imperative polymorphism safe and allows fully polymorphic types for functions with imperative implementations [181]. This system does not use imperative type variables, but limits the type generalization operation slightly. In

$$\texttt{let } x = e_1 \texttt{ in } e_2$$

the type of e_1 is generalized only if e_1 is a *syntactic value*, i.e. variable, constant, function, or a record composed only of values. If e_1 is a function application, then it is not a syntactic value, and its type will not be generalized. Wright has found that this limitation very rarely causes problems in practice.[3]

Our type checker uses Wright's idea. There are two judgements:

```
pure exp
gen(exp,τ,rank) => σ
```

The first describes those expressions that are pure syntactic values. The second is used by the rule for `let` to generalize *exp*'s type τ, but only if *exp* is pure.

4.5.4   Overloading

SML defines several arithmetic and comparison functions to be overloaded on integer or real arguments. (But contrary to typical imperative languages, `int` is not a subtype of `real`.) SML/NJ furthermore overloads the comparison functions on strings, and adds `print` and `makestring` functions, overloaded on most base types.[4]

The formal definition of overloading in SML says that

$$\texttt{+} : \texttt{num} \times \texttt{num} \to \texttt{num}$$

stands for two functions, corresponding to replacing `num` by `int` or `real`. It then says that 'the surrounding text', essentially the whole of the current

---

[3]The recent revision of Standard ML [121] uses Wright's generalization rule instead of imperative type variables.

[4]Recent releases of SML/NJ no longer overload `print` or `makestring`.

top-level declaration, determines which is intended. Explicit type constraints are sometimes necessary.

A simple way of modelling this is by using *bounded* polymorphism, where we give + the type scheme:

$$\forall \alpha \in \{\texttt{int}, \texttt{real}\}.\alpha \times \alpha \to \alpha$$

This limits instantiations of α to just those monomorphic types listed.

We noted that all overloadings in SML and the SML/NJ implementation could be expressed using constraints consisting of sets of monomorphic atomic types. We therefore chose to specify overloading by adding an *overload* attribute to type variables. This attribute is an optional set of type names. When absent, no constraints are implied. When present, it restricts instantiations to just those types whose type names are in the set.

As in the previous examples of attributed type variables, we realize unification of two type variables by appropriately combining their attributes, assigning them to a fresh variable, and substituting it for the original ones. If both variables have overload sets, they are intersected. If the empty set results, a type error has occurred.

Overloading adds another problem, viz. that all overloaded type variables *must* be properly instantiated. The following is wrong since it does not instantiate the overloaded type variable for +.

```
fun f x = x + x
```

In a formal system, this is not a problem since the type rules by definition must 'guess' the correct type substitution when polymorphic variables are referenced. However, most if not all implementations are based on the use of unification [155] to gradually enforce contextual constraints. The absence of a constraint simply leaves a type less instantiated.

We deal with this by restructuring the typing rules slightly. Our new rules take the form:

```
elab_exp(Γ, rank, C, exp) => (τ, C')
check_constraints C
```

where the C's are sets of constraints that must be solved. At the end of the current top-level declaration, a second phase checks that all constraints indeed have been solved. In essence, the constraint sets are a way of realizing suspended goals, as found in some Prolog systems' `freeze` primitive [40,126].

Our specification only has to deal with constraints for overloaded type variables: when an overloaded variable is instantiated, its type variables are added to the constraint set. The second phase just checks that all those type variable have been instantiated.

4.5.5 Specification Fragments

The miniml specification makes use of some new RML features, viz. unknown values and the isvar primitive procedure. Since type variables have attributes they are not encoded as featureless RML logical variables. Instead, a type variable is a tuple of attribute values and a logical variable. This also forces us to encode the substitution, dereferencing, and unification mechanisms in RML as well.[5]

We represent types using the following structures:

```
type tag = int
type attributes = ... (* rank,equality,overload *)
type tyname = string
datatype ty = VAR of alpha
            | CONSTR of ty list * tyname
and alpha = ALPHA of tag * attributes * ty
```

Constructed types are general enough to encode all non-variable types, as exemplified in the following table.

int	CONSTR([], "int")
int list	CONSTR([CONSTR([], "int")], "list")
t_1 -> t_2	CONSTR([t_1, t_2], "->")

A type variable is a term

$$VAR(ALPHA(tag, attrs, ty))$$

where *ty* is an unbound RML logical variable. To construct an unknown type, we use the exists operator to construct a new RML logical variable, and the tick standard relation to acquire a fresh tag, and then construct a type variable with appropriate attributes:

```
relation mkUnknown =
  rule  tick => tag & exists ty
        ----------------
        mkUnknown attrs => VAR(ALPHA(tag,attrs,ty))
end
```

The unifier uses deref as a subroutine to dereference chains of instantiated type variables. deref uses the isvar standard relation to determine when it has found the end of the chain.

```
relation deref =
  rule  isvar var => true
        ----------------
        deref(ty as VAR(ALPHA(_,_,var))) => ty
```

---

[5]The same also tends to happen when Prolog is extended [126].

```
  rule   isvar var => false & deref var => ty
         ----------------
         deref(VAR(ALPHA(_,_,var))) => ty

  axiom deref(ty as CONSTR(_,_)) => ty
end
```

The unifier itself is standard. The only noteworthy feature is that before a type variable can be bound to a type, its attributes are verified with respect to that type. This includes performing an *occur-check*, in addition to the *rank*, *equality*, and *overloading* checks.

```
relation check_attrs =
  rule   check_occur(alpha, ty) &
         check_rank(rank, ty) &
         check_equality(eq, ty) &
         check_overload(ovld, ty)
         ----------------
         check_attrs(alpha as ALPHA(_,(rank,eq,ovld),_), ty)
end

relation bind_alpha = (* alpha = type *)
  rule   check_attrs(alpha, ty) & var = ty
         ----------------
         bind_alpha(alpha as ALPHA(_,_,var), ty)
end
```

Before two type variables can be unified, their attributes are combined, a new unknown type is introduced to contain the combined attributes, and the two type variables are bound to the new unknown type.

```
relation join_alphas = (* alpha1 = alpha2 *)
  rule   join_attrs(attrs1, attrs2) => attrs3 &
         mkUnknown attrs3 => ty &
         v1 = ty &
         v2 = ty
         ----------------
         join_alphas(ALPHA(_,attrs1,v1), ALPHA(_,attrs2,v2))
end
```

This particular part of the specification is not terribly high-level. However, these representation-oriented operations can easily be hidden from the typing rules proper, which need only know the existence of a relation mkUnknown for assuming an unknown type, and a relation unify for enforcing equality between types.

4.5.6 Summary

The previous applications were all fairly simple, in that they always computed with *known* values. The Mini-ML type checker has shown that RML has enough built-in mechanisms to compute with (partially) unknown values. Typical applications include ML-style polymorphic type systems.

The Mini-ML specification uses 620 lines of RML for its static semantics, spread over 4 modules. To this is added the usual Lex, Yacc, and C glue, and RML modules for the abstract syntax and the actual interpreter. The complete Mini-ML interpreter totals 1834 lines.

4.6 Problematic Issues

4.6.1 Environments

The use of partial functions or association lists for environments is traditional in most formalisms for programming language semantics. However, typical language implementations often use other data structures, for instance hash tables [2, 134], to make identifier lookups more efficient.

Replacing environments in specifications with hash tables is not easy. The problem is that hash tables are objects with state, while formal semantics tend to work with pure values. Entering a binding or opening a new scope in a hash table changes the table, while the same operation in formal semantics would create a new object, leaving the old one unchanged. Hash tables typically require *explicit* operations to delete bindings or close scopes. In formal semantics, one would just revert to an earlier environment instead. Hash tables typically enforce either a flat or a block-structured (stack-like) name space, while environments are frequently composed from smaller environments in various ways. (Both the definitions of SML and RML use this flexibility extensively.)

The problem of designing efficient data structures with purely functional interfaces is studied under the name of *fully persistent data structures* [59]. Structures such as lists, stacks, arrays, and binary search trees have been studied extensively, but we do not know of any successful results for hash tables.

4.6.2 Default Rules

The coding of the *fcemit* module for Diesel unearthed a major flaw in the design of RML: the absence of *default* rules. It is not uncommon to have a situation where some objects may have many possible shapes. One action is to be performed for a few of those, leaving another (default) action for all other cases. Consider a judgement operating on two lists, such that the case where both lists are empty is special. A naïve coding

```
relation r =
  rule  proveA
        ----------------

        r([], [])


  rule  proveB
        ----------------

        r(_, _)
end
```

is both logically incorrect (the second rule also covers the first case) and
causes performance problems in the generated code (accumulation of redundant choice points).[6]

Explicitly enumerating all 'default' cases wherever similar situations arise
is not an attractive solution. We eventually settled for an approach that relies
on an auxiliary predicate for the case analysis, leaving only the two cases in
the real relation:

```
relation both_null =
  axiom both_null([],[])
end


relation r =
  rule  both_null(xs, ys) & proveA
        ----------------

        r(xs, ys)


  rule  not both_null(xs, ys) & proveB
        ----------------

        r(xs, ys)
end
```

If the language had had explicitly-declared default rules, something like the
first solution could have been used instead, leading to cleaner specifications.

4.7 Summary

We have introduced most of RML through a number of examples. We have
also indicated how typical applications, in three different domains, may be
structured, and the specification techniques that may be used. We believe
these examples show that RML is indeed suitable for writing executable specifications in natural semantics.

---

[6]RML has recently been changed to have *determinate* semantics, which eliminates the
second problem. The first remains though.

Chapter 5

Implementation Overview

> *Compilers for high-level languages are generally constructed to give*
> *the complete translation of the programs into machine language.*
> *As machines merely juggle bit patterns, the concepts of the original*
> *language may be lost or at least obscured during this passage.*
> – Dana Scott and Christopher Strachey [162]

In this chapter we present a summary of the implementation strategy, discuss some alternative approaches, and describe the current implementation's status. The next four chapters treat specific parts of the implementation in detail. A summary of this part of the thesis was published as [138].

5.1 Compilation Strategy

The compiler is organized as a multi-stage pipeline that step-by-step translates specifications from high-level abstract syntax to low-level C code. Appropriate optimizations are applied at each representation level.

1. Source code is translated to a form reminiscent of first-order logic, FOL. A left-factoring transformation is applied to reduce the usually enormous amount of non-determinism present in natural semantics specifications. (Chapter 6.)

2. Then the FOL form is translated, with the aid of a pattern-match compiler, to a continuation-passing style functional form, CPS. Inlining of procedures and continuations is performed, as are constant propagation and other simple optimizations. (Chapters 7 and 8.)

3. A low-level *Code* form is produced in which continuations are replaced by concrete data structures, and creation of composite data structures is made explicit. A *copy-propagation* optimization is applied to remove

some redundancies introduced by the low-level code for parameter passing (caused by the mechanism for emulating tailcalls). (Chapter 8.)

4. The final step prints the low-level representation as C code. (Chapter 9.)

5.1.1 Development

This strategy did not materialize at once, but in two distinct steps as we gained better understanding of the problems involved.

Initially, we wrote a denotational semantics for Prolog restricted to procedure definitions and control operators (see Section 3.3). We used continuations in this specification, both because they provided a natural means for encoding control flow and because such a specification can almost trivially be seen as a *compiler* from abstract syntax to a CPS-based representation.

Upon investigation of this semantics [136], we found that it had operational properties close to those of Warren's Abstract Machine (WAM). In particular, we found that stack allocation of continuations was possible in exactly the same way as the WAM manages choice points and environments in its (local) stack.

Using this semantics a very simple prototype compiler was written. It performed a direct translation from syntax to CPS, applied some simple CPS optimizations, and then emitted C code using a straightforward implementation of tailcalls (the technique we call 'plain' dispatching labels in Chapter 9). The runtime system was crude and completely non-tuned. Even so, our benchmarks at this time [136] indicated a 2-4 orders of magnitude advantage over Typol, and a factor of two advantage over SICStus and Quintus Prolog.

However, our benchmarking exposed a very serious problem with this simplistic compiler: excessive stack consumption. Just about every specification would cause stack overflow after a few seconds of execution. (The stack at this time was 2 megabytes.)

We noted that backtracking was only used *locally* in procedures when selecting the correct rule; afterwards execution would be mostly deterministic. This, however, usually left a redundant choice point (failure continuation) on the stack, making it grow indefinitely.

At this point we became aware of Billaud's work on axiomatizations of Prolog's control flow [26]. Although different in scope, it led us to believe that a suitable algebra for RML's control flow could be found, and that useful optimizations could be derived from it. We also noted the similarity between our problem and the problem of top-down parsing of context-free grammars, and its solution, viz. left-factoring. (Only later did we learn of the similar transformations devised by da Silva [48].)

This led to the introduction of the FOL-translation and optimization phase first in the compiler. The FOL optimizations cause small pattern-matches to be combined into larger `case` constructs, so we implemented a real pattern-match compiler [133] to take advantage of this fact. (This match compiling algorithm was originally developed in a completely different context, but was easily adapted to RML.)

5.2 Alternatives

Although our compilation strategy seems natural to us, and its effectiveness is supported by our performance evaluation discussed in Chapter 10, there *are* several plausible alternative strategies. Below, we comment on some of these and explain why we rejected them.

5.2.1 Prolog

Translating Natural Semantics to Prolog has been done before; it is exactly what the Typol implementation in the Centaur system does. However, such a translation necessarily loses important information. RML is a statically strongly typed language with parametric polymorphism, while Prolog is dynamically typed. RML uses pattern-matching as its primary data inspection mechanism while Prolog uses unification. We believe, and this is supported by our benchmarks, that a specialized compiler is likely to generate significantly better code than would a Prolog compiler on a translated specification.

5.2.2 Warren's Abstract Machine

The WAM is a common, almost default, starting place for many implementations of new logic programming languages, especially extensions of Prolog. We have three objections against it:

1. The instruction set is very low-level and imperative, with global registers and side-effects. To perform high-level transformations, e.g. to improve determinacy, could be difficult, and their effectiveness would be uncertain.

2. The instructions are also too high-level and complex, since they hide many implicit operations. Making hidden operations *explicit* enables more opportunities for optimizations, as noted by Van Roy [175].

3. At the start of our project, it was not clear exactly what kind of model would be suitable for RML. We did not want to commit ourselves to an implementation model that might have turned out to be inappropriate.

Having said this, we *do* note that RML's denotational semantics admits an operational interpretation that essentially coincides with the WAM. Our strategy makes use of a WAM-like model for the control and trail stacks, but ignores its instruction set.

5.2.3　Attribute Grammars

Attali and co-workers [11–13] have pursued a different approach. The observation is that there exists a class of attribute grammars (Strongly Non-Circular) for which efficient evaluators can be mechanically constructed. Then sufficient conditions for Typol specifications to be equivalent to this class are identified and a translation algorithm is given. In their recent Minotaur system, they use the facilities of the FNC-2 system to provide an implementation of translated Typol programs. They claim a performance improvement of about a factor of 10.

While this approach does allow *some* Typol specifications to be given more efficient implementations, it is not a general compilation strategy. Any specification outside the designated subset will be implemented in the old way.

5.2.4　SML

Standard ML has all the language features necessary to implement the intermediate CPS representation: first-class functions, automatic memory management, and proper tailcalls. So why did we not skip the entire back-end and write a translator to SML instead?

We once attempted to write a translator from our CPS form to SML, but it quickly became apparent that the translated code would be very inefficient. There were two causes for this. First, our pattern-match compiler outputs CPS expressions that access data at a low representation-oriented level. Second, logical variables are always potentially present, so values must be dereferenced before inspection. This forced us to map all values to a single 'union' type in SML, and map all accesses to 'projections' followed by the actual accesses, causing significant overhead. A complete redesign of the front-end and pattern-match compiler would have been necessary to avoid this overhead, so we abandoned the idea.

5.3　Implementation Status

The rml2c compiler is operational, implements the entire RML language, and implements all the transformations and optimizations mentioned in Chapters 6 to 8. It has four different back-ends and runtime systems, corresponding to the four tailcall techniques 'plain', 'switch', 'pushy', and 'warped' discussed in Chapter 9. A command-line flag to the compiler is used to select the desired back-end.

The compiler is written entirely in Standard ML:[1] ml-lex was used for the scanner, and ml-yacc for the parser. The source code totals 11569 lines. We use the SML/NJ compiler in its most recent versions, and its compilation

---

[1] Technically, we use the revised SML'97 dialect [121].

manager CM. The rml2c compiler can be built on any machine supported by SML/NJ; so far it has been built on machines based on Alpha, HP-PA, Intel x86, MIPS, PowerPC, and SPARC processors, under various Unix and Unix-like operating systems.

The runtime system is written in C. No assembly code is used, except as an optional performance enhancement in one obscure case (Section 9.7.1). It is easily portable to clean byte-addressable 32 and 64-bit machines. Chapter 10 details the targets used when developing and benchmarking the rml2c system.

From a practical point of view, the main limitations of rml2c are its overly terse error messages and the absence of runtime support for debugging or tracing.

Chapter 6

Reducing Nondeterminism

$\mathfrak{M}$ any natural semantics specifications are intended to be deterministic: type systems, interpreters, and compilers usually have just one expected result. In contrast, specifications usually contain relations with several, often partially overlapping, rules. Executing a specification involves searching among rules for those that contribute to a successful completion. Much control information (choice points) is therefore created on a control stack to guide this search.

Since many specifications in fact *are* deterministic, they tend to rarely backtrack among alternative rules. This results in the control stack growing rapidly. There is also significant overhead involved with the manipulations of the control stack.

To deal with these problems we have devised transformations that rewrite specifications to expose possibilities for deterministic execution. Tightly coupled with these transformations is a representation of specifications in which high-level control flow, both deterministic and non-deterministic, is made explicit.

In this chapter we describe the representation and transformations in detail, and give examples demonstrating their usefulness. Some of the content of this chapter was included in our presentation at PLILP'94 [136], but was not ready in time for inclusion in the proceedings.

Section 6.1 starts with giving a background to the problem and its solution. Section 6.2 describes the intermediate representation used (FOL), and Section 6.3 outlines the mapping from RML source to FOL. Section 6.4 then presents the term rewriting system used to simplify FOL terms (FOL-TRS), followed by a discussion of its properties in Section 6.5. Section 6.6 then gives some examples, showing the effectiveness of FOL-TRS. Section 6.7 discusses why FOL-TRS considers negations important. The implementation is described in Section 6.8, followed by a discussion of some limitations in Section 6.9. Finally, Section 6.10 discusses related work.

6.1   Background

The first version of the RML-to-C compiler, described in [136, 137], did not have a proper pattern-match compiler, nor did it attempt to analyse and optimize high-level control flow. It just followed the simple strategy: translate to CPS, apply local optimizations, translate to a low-level representation, output C code.

Despite of this simple approach, the first benchmarks were very encouraging. The generated code ran about 2.5 times faster than the equivalent Prolog code in Quintus or SICStus Prolog using native machine code, and it ran up to 20000 times faster than the equivalent Typol code.

However, it had a very serious limitation: since no attempts were made to optimize for deterministic execution, the generated code would continuously push failure continuations (choice points) onto the control stack. These would almost never be popped, leading very quickly to stack overflow.

It was obvious that some form of high-level transformation *had* to be introduced to eliminate, or at least greatly reduce, the amount of unnecessary nondeterminism.

6.1.1   Grammars

Our solution is based on two observations: The first is that executing a natural semantics specification is very much like performing top-down left-right parsing of a context-free grammar. The second observation is that the problem of non-deterministic search was identified long ago in the parsing context, and a practical solution has been devised: *left-factoring.*

Consider the following productions, where b and c are terminals, and A, D, and E are non-terminals:

$$A \ ::= \ b\,c\,D$$
$$A \ ::= \ b\,c\,E$$

The problem here is that the non-terminal A has several productions with common prefixes. A top-down parser faced with parsing A cannot make a deterministic choice of which production to try. Technically, this is because the intersection of the *FIRST* sets of the right-hand-sides is non-empty.

Equally well-known is the standard solution, namely to *left-factor* the grammar [3, Algorithm 4.2]. Left-factoring would transform the above to:

$$A \ ::= \ b\,c\,A'$$
$$A' \ ::= \ D$$
$$A' \ ::= \ E$$

Further factoring would be needed if there is a symbol that can start both D and E, i.e. $FIRST(D) \cap FIRST(E) \neq \emptyset$.

Languages in the $LL(1)$ class have the property that left-factoring results in grammars that can be parsed deterministically. Operationally, any choice can be postponed until the next input symbol makes the outcome obvious. This greatly improves the performance of the parsing process.

6.2 FOL Representation

The representation we use is somewhat inspired by First-Order Logic, hence we call it FOL. The front-end represents a rule as the conjunction of its actions, and a relation as the disjunction of (the representations of) its rules. The atomic actions are: call relation, match patterns, unify terms, bind variable, introduce 'unknown', return to caller. The composite actions are: negation, conjunction, disjunction, case analysis. The structure is such that the 'return' action is always the last one executed.

Transformations change this structure: conjunctions can occur before disjunctions, a disjunction of matches can be replaced by a special **case** operator, and a disjunction of mutually exclusive parts can be replaced by a conditional.

We want a representation with a 'no nonsense' property: only those (syntactic) objects that occur as the results of our transformations are to be representable. Figure 6.1 shows the representation we use.

$id \in Ident$		global identifiers
$v \in Var$		variables
$p \in Pat$	(defined later)	patterns
$e \in Exp$		expressions
$c \in Conj ::=$	$(\text{call } id \ (e^*) \ (v^*))$	conjunctive forms
	$\mid (\text{match } (v \ p)^*)$	
	$\mid (\text{unify } v \ e)$	
	$\mid (\text{bind } v \ e)$	
	$\mid (\text{exists } v)$	
	$\mid (\text{not } c)$	
	$\mid (\text{and } c_1 \ c_2)$	
$d \in Disj ::=$	$(\text{return } e^*)$	disjunctive forms
	$\mid (\text{orelse } d_1 \ d_2)$	
	$\mid (\text{andthen } c \ d)$	
	$\mid (\text{cond } c \ d_1 \ d_2)$	
	$\mid (\text{case } v^k \ (p^k \ d)^n)$	$k \geq 0, n \geq 1$
$r \in Rel ::=$	$(\text{define } (id \ v^*) \ d)$	relations

Figure 6.1: Syntax of FOL

The interpretation of these operators is as follows:

$(\text{call } id \ (e^*) \ (v^*))$ Call the named relation with the expressions as arguments. On return, bind the variables to the results.

(match $(v\ p)^*$) Match patterns against the values bound to the given variables. Also bind variables in the patterns.

(unify v e) Unify the value of the variable with that of the expression.

(bind v e) Bind v to the value of the expression.

(exists v) Bind v to a new logical variable.

(not c) Succeed if c fails, fail otherwise.

(and c_1 c_2) Execute c_1 before c_2.

(return e^*) Return values to the caller of this relation.

(orelse d_1 d_2) Execute d_1, on failure execute d_2. Operationally, push a new choice point referring to d_2, then execute d_1.

(andthen c d) Execute c before d.

(cond c d_1 d_2) Execute d_1 if c succeeded, d_2 otherwise. Operationally, a choice point referring to d_2 is introduced before c is executed, but removed when (if) c succeeds, before d_1 is executed.

(case v^k $(p^k\ d)^*$) Search left-to-right for a rule whose patterns match the values of the variables, and execute its right hand side. On failure, try to find another rule.

The cond and case forms are not produced by the front-end, but may be introduced by the rewriting rules.

The exact structure of patterns is not important for the discussion about the rewriting rules. It is described later in Section 6.8.

6.3   The Front-End

The front-end translates relations as follows.

- A relation r with k parameters becomes (define $(r\ v_1 \cdots v_k)\ d$), where the variables v_i are new and d is the disjunction (orelse) of the translations of the individual inference rules and axioms.

- Given argument variables v_i, an inference rule

$$\frac{premises}{id\,(pat_1 \cdots pat_n) \Rightarrow exps}$$

becomes the conjunction:

> (andthen   (match $(v_1\ pat_1) \cdots$)
>   (andthen *premises* (return *exps*)))

In our representation, this is actually treated as a disjunctive form.

- Similarly, an axiom $id(pat_1 \cdots) \Rightarrow exps$ becomes the conjunction:

  (andthen (match (v_1 pat_1) $\cdots$) (return *exps*))

- A goal $id\ exps \Rightarrow (pat_1 \cdots)$ becomes:

  (and (call *id exps* ($v_1 \cdots$)) (match (v_1 pat_1) $\cdots$))

  where the variables v_i are new. For example, the call

  eval *e* => *v*

  would be translated to

  (and (call eval (e) (tmp)) (match (tmp v)))

- *var = exp* becomes (bind *var exp*) if *var* was not previously bound, and (unify *var exp*) otherwise.

- exists *var* becomes (exists *var*).

- not *goal* becomes (not *c*), where *c* is the translation of *goal*.

- $goal_1$ & $goal_2$ becomes (and c_1 c_2), where c_1 (c_2) is the translation of $goal_1$ ($goal_2$).

6.4 The FOL-TRS Rewriting System

To simplify FOL terms, we use three sets of transformation rules. The first two, for disjunctive ((1) to (9)) and conjunctive ((10) to (11)) forms, are 'context-free', and hence described as rewriting rules in an ordinary term-rewriting system.

Negated actions never produce any visible bindings. For this reason, there is a third group of rules that are applicable *only* to certain parts of negated actions, viz. the path from the not operator down to the last executed action. Their purpose is to simplify negated goals that are known to succeed without visible side-effects. For notational convenience, we let true denote an effect-free succeeding conjunctive goal. It is defined as (match).

Unfortunately, these *context-dependent* transformations are difficult to express in a plain TRS. We therefore introduce the following extension: There is a separate group of rewrite rules (12) to (17), denoted by $\stackrel{not}{\Rightarrow}$, and a few *trigger rules* (our terminology) (11), (15) and (17). The trigger rules are specified as inference rules in natural semantics. They essentially traverse parts of negated goals and mark visited nodes. For the visited nodes, but no others, the restricted rules ($\stackrel{not}{\Rightarrow}$) may be applied.

Some important rules, viz. (6), (7), and (8), reduce the number of times a conjunct is executed during backtracking. This can be observed if the conjunct has a visible non-idempotent side-effect (such as I/O, but not unification). Specifications are not supposed to have such side-effects so, in the interest of performance, we keep these transformations.

Disjunctions $\boxed{d \Rightarrow d'}$

$$\text{(andthen (match } (v_1\ p_1) \cdots)\ d)$$
$$\Rightarrow \quad \text{(case } (v_1 \cdots)\ ((p_1 \cdots)\ d)) \tag{1}$$

Rule (1) serves to expose the matching operation.

$$\text{(andthen (and } c_1\ c_2)\ d)$$
$$\Rightarrow \quad \text{(andthen } c_1\ \text{(andthen } c_2\ d)) \tag{2}$$

Rule (2) is a linearization to expose c_1 for further inspection.

$$\text{(case () (() } d))$$
$$\Rightarrow \quad d \tag{3}$$

Rule (3) replaces an empty case by its only disjunct.

$$\frac{p_0^k \not\sim p_i^k \quad (1 \le i \le j)}{\begin{array}{l}\text{(case } v^k\ \cdots (p_0^k\ d)\,(p_1^k\ \_) \cdots (p_j^k\ \_)\,(p_0^k\ d') \cdots) \\ \Rightarrow \quad \text{(case } v^k\ \cdots (p_0^k\ \text{(orelse } d\ d'))\,(p_1^k\ \_) \cdots (p_j^k\ \_) \cdots)\end{array}} \tag{4}$$

If the same set of patterns occurs in two match rules, rule (4) combines them to one match rule whose right-hand-side is the disjunction of the original right-hand sides, when it is safe to do so.

Two patterns p and p' are *similar*, written $p \sim p'$, if there exists input values v that match both p and p'. This notion is extended in the obvious way to sequences of patterns. Since the case operator is defined to search from left to right, it would be incorrect to float a match rule past, i.e. to the left of, any other match rule with similar patterns. The precondition prevents such illegal rewrites.

$$\text{(orelse (orelse } d_1\ d_2)\ d_3)$$
$$\Rightarrow \quad \text{(orelse } d_1\ \text{(orelse } d_2\ d_3)) \tag{5}$$

Rule (5) is a linearization to expose d_1 for further inspection.

$$\text{(orelse (andthen } c\ d_1)\ \text{(andthen } c\ d_2))$$
$$\Rightarrow \quad \text{(andthen } c\ \text{(orelse } d_1\ d_2)) \tag{6}$$

Rule (6) is a left-factoring transformation. If c succeeds in the first disjunct, then it is unnecessary to re-prove c should backtracking occur. If c

failed, then it will obviously fail again in the second disjunct. Operationally, this delays the creation of a choice point. Furthermore, it limits the 'scope' of the choice point so that any failure in d_1 will branch directly to d_2.

$$\text{(orelse (andthen } c\ d_1\text{) (andthen (not } c\text{) } d_2\text{))} \qquad (7)$$
$$\Rightarrow\quad \text{(cond } c\ d_1\ d_2\text{)}$$

If c succeeds in the first disjunct, then the second disjunct cannot succeed. If c fails in the first disjunct, then (not c) will succeed in the second disjunct. Rule (7) introduces a conditional which expresses this directly, without the need to re-execute c.

$$\text{(orelse (andthen (not } c\text{) } d_1\text{) (andthen } c\ d_2\text{))} \qquad (8)$$
$$\Rightarrow\quad \text{(cond } c\ d_2\ d_1\text{)}$$

Rule (8) is an obvious analogue of the previous rule.

$$\text{(orelse (case } v^k\ (\_\ d_1)\cdots(\_\ d_n))$$
$$\text{(case } v^k\ (\_\ d_1')\cdots(\_\ d_m'))) \qquad (9)$$
$$\Rightarrow\quad \text{(case } v^k\ (\_\ d_1)\cdots(\_\ d_n)\ (\_\ d_1')\cdots(\_\ d_m'))$$

Rule (9) combines two matchings if they inspect the same set of variables. Doing so allows the pattern-match compiler to consider a larger set of match rules, and may also allow (4) to perform further rewrites.

Conjunctions $\boxed{c \Rightarrow c'}$

$$\text{(and (and } c_1\ c_2\text{) } c_3\text{)} \Rightarrow \text{(and } c_1\ \text{(and } c_2\ c_3\text{))} \qquad (10)$$

Rule (10) is a linearization to expose c_1 for further inspection.

$$\frac{c \overset{not}{\Rightarrow} c'}{\text{(not } c\text{)} \Rightarrow \text{(not } c'\text{)}} \qquad (11)$$

Rule (11) triggers the stricter set of rules (12) to (17) that apply to negated conjunctions.

Negated Conjunctions $\boxed{c \overset{not}{\Rightarrow} c'}$

$$\text{(bind } \_\ \_\text{)} \overset{not}{\Rightarrow} \text{true} \qquad (12)$$

The binding will always succeed, but the negation will throw away the new binding. Rule (12) replaces it with the simplest succeeding goal.

$$\text{(exists } \_\text{)} \overset{not}{\Rightarrow} \text{true} \qquad (13)$$

Rule (13) is similar to the previous rule.

$$(\texttt{match} \ (v_1 \ \_) \ (v_2 \ \_) \cdots) \overset{not}{\Rightarrow} \texttt{true} \tag{14}$$

If all patterns are wildcards, then the match is just a sequence of bindings. The sequence has to be non-empty for rule (14) to apply.

$$\frac{c_2 \overset{not}{\Rightarrow} c_2'}{(\texttt{and} \ c_1 \ c_2) \overset{not}{\Rightarrow} (\texttt{and} \ c_1 \ c_2')} \tag{15}$$

Rule (15) is a trigger rule. Since the second conjunct is the last item to execute under the negation, binding operations in it can be simplified.

$$(\texttt{and} \ c \ \texttt{true}) \overset{not}{\Rightarrow} c \tag{16}$$

As a result of the previous rule, the second conjunct may be reduced to true. In that case, rule (16) reduces the conjunction to its first conjunct.

$$\frac{c \overset{not}{\Rightarrow} c'}{(\texttt{not} \ c) \overset{not}{\Rightarrow} (\texttt{not} \ c')} \tag{17}$$

Rule (17) is a trigger rule, analogous to rule (11).

6.5 Properties

In this section we analyse important properties of FOL-TRS. We will show that the system is terminating, but, alas, not confluent.

We assume standard terminology and results in the theory of term rewriting systems [54, 55, 100].

6.5.1 Termination

A *normal form* is a term for which no rewrite rule is applicable. A rewriting system is *terminating* (*strongly normalizing* or *noetherian*) if, for any given term, only a finite number of rewrite rules can be applied to it before a normal form is produced.

This is obviously an important property for some systems, such as simplification rules such as those in FOL-TRS, because it guarantees that no input can cause the system to loop indefinitely.

Since term rewriting systems have universal computing power, termination is in general undecidable. Hence various heuristics have to be applied when attempting termination proofs. (See Dershowitz' [54] survey article on termination of TRSs.)

Definition 6.1 A set S is *well-founded* by a partial order $\succ$ if there are no *infinite* descending sequences $s_1 \succ s_2 \succ s_3 \succ \cdots$ of elements in S. $\succ$ is then said to be a well-founded ordering over S.

Suppose that we define an ordering relation $\succ$ over the terms of a TRS, and then prove that the application of a rewrite rule always leads to a smaller (in $\succ$) term. If $\succ$ is well-founded, then termination follows.

It is often convenient to define such an ordering in terms of simpler orderings by constructing a mapping from terms to some other set, and then use an existing well-founded ordering on that set. In particular, one can often map terms to natural numbers, ordered by $>$. In some cases it is not easy to define a *single* mapping that leads to 'smaller' terms for all rewrite rules. One can sometimes combine simpler mappings to form a more complex one. One technique is to *lexicographically* combine two orders $\succ_1$ and $\succ_2$.

Suppose we have two functions f and g from terms to natural numbers, and let the two orders simply be $>$. Suppose term x is rewritten to y. If $f(x) > f(y)$, then y is 'smaller' than x, i.e. $x \succ y$. Alternatively, if $f(x) = f(y)$ but $g(x) > g(y)$, we also consider y to be smaller than x. In all other cases, i.e. $f(x) < f(y)$, or $f(x) = f(y)$ and $g(x) \le g(y)$, x and y are *not* ordered. The idea is that some rewrite rules $x \Rightarrow y$ will lead to $\succ_1$-smaller terms $(f(x) > f(y))$, while the other rules will lead to no change for $\succ_1$ $(f(x) = f(y))$, but then the terms should be ordered by $\succ_2$ $(g(x) > g(y))$.

Definition 6.2 The *termination* functions s and l on FOL terms are defined in Table 6.1.

Both s and l compute size measures for terms, as positive integers. s is a normal measuring function designed to decrease whenever its argument becomes 'smaller'. Some rewriting rules, however, just rearrange terms by pushing 'heavy' arguments to the right. Consequently, l assigns more weight to the left subterms of the relevant constructors.

term	$s(term)$	$l(term)$
(call _ _ _)	3	1
(match $(v\ p)^k$)	$k + 2$	$k + 1$
(unify _ _)	3	1
(bind _ _)	3	1
(exists _)	3	1
(not c)	$s(c) + 1$	$l(c) + 1$
(and c_1 c_2)	$s(c_1) + s(c_2)$	$2l(c_1) + l(c_2)$
(return _)	1	1
(orelse d_1 d_2)	$s(d_1) + s(d_2)$	$2l(d_1) + l(d_2)$
(andthen c d)	$s(c) + s(d)$	$2l(c) + l(d)$
(cond c d_1 d_2)	$s(c) + s(d_1) + s(d_2)$	$l(c) + l(d_1) + l(d_2)$
(case _ (_ d_1) $\cdots$ (_ d_n))	$(\sum_{i=1}^{n} s(d_i)) + n$	$(\sum_{i=1}^{n} l(d_i)) + 1$

Table 6.1: Termination functions for FOL-TRS

Definition 6.3 The $\succ$ ordering relation on FOL terms is defined by:

$$t \succ t' \quad \text{if } s(t) > s(t')$$
$$t \succ t' \quad \text{if } s(t) = s(t') \text{ and } l(t) > l(t')$$
$$t \not\succ t' \quad \text{otherwise}$$

Theorem 6.4 $\succ$ is a monotonic well-founded order over FOL terms.

Proof: From the definition of s it is obvious that:

1. s is *monotonic*, i.e. s has the *replacement property*: reducing $s(t)$ also reduces $s(u)$ for any term u that has t as a subterm.

2. s has the *subterm property*: $s(u)$ is greater than $s(t)$ whenever t is a subterm of u.

3. s has the *deletion property*: deleting a immediate subterm from a variadic constructor (`match` or `case`) reduces the value of s for the containing term.

From this it follows that s is a *simplification ordering*. Those are known to be well-founded.

By inspection, the same properties also hold for l, i.e. l is a monotonic well-founded ordering.

It is known that composing orderings lexicographically preserves these properties. Hence, $\succ$ is monotonic and well-founded. $\square$

Theorem 6.5 For every rewrite rule $lhs \Rightarrow rhs$ in FOL-TRS, $lhs \succ rhs$.

Proof: For each rule $lhs \Rightarrow rhs$ we show that $s(lhs) > s(rhs)$, or $s(lhs) = s(rhs)$ and $l(lhs) > l(rhs)$.

(1) $s(lhs) - s(rhs) = (k+2) + s(d) - (s(d) + 1) = k + 1 > 0$.

(2) $s(lhs) - s(rhs) = s(c_1) + s(c_2) + s(d) - (s(c_1) + s(c_2) + s(d)) = 0$.
$l(lhs) - l(rhs) = 2(2l(c_1) + l(c_2)) + l(d) - (2l(c_2) + 2l(c_2) + l(d)) = 2l(c_1) > 0$.

(4) $s(lhs) - s(rhs) = \sum_{i=1}^{n} s(d_i) + n - (s(d_1) + \cdots + (s(d_i) + s(d_j)) + \cdots + s(d_n) + (n-1)) = 1 > 0$.

(5) $s(lhs) - s(rhs) = s(d_1) + s(d_2) + s(d_3) - (s(d_1) + s(d_2) + s(d_3)) = 0$.
$l(lhs) - l(rhs) = 2(2l(d_1) + l(d_2)) + l(d_3) - (2l(d_1) + 2l(d_2) + l(d_3)) = 2l(d_1) > 0$.

(6) $s(lhs) - s(rhs) = s(c) + s(d_1) + s(c) + s(d_2) - (s(c) + s(d_1) + s(d_2)) = s(c) > 0$.

(7) $s(lhs) - s(rhs) = s(c) + s(d_1) + s(c) + 1 + s(d_2) - (s(c) + s(d_1) + s(d_2)) = s(c) + 1 > 0$.

(9) $s(lhs) - s(rhs) = \sum_{i=1}^{n} s(d_i) + n + \sum_{i=1}^{m} s(d'_i) + m - (\sum_{i=1}^{n} s(d_i) + \sum_{i=1}^{m} s(d'_i) + n + m) = 0.$
$l(lhs) - l(rhs) = 2(\sum_{i=1}^{n} l(d_i) + 1) + \sum_{i=1}^{m} l(d'_i) + 1 - (\sum_{i=1}^{m} l(d_i) + \sum_{i=1}^{m} l(d'_i) + 1) = \sum_{i=1}^{n} l(d_i) + 2 > 0.$

(10) $s(lhs) - s(rhs) = s(c_1) + s(c_2) + s(c_3) - (s(c_1) + s(c_2) + s(c_3)) = 0.$
$l(lhs) - l(rhs) = 2(2l(c_1) + l(c_2)) + l(c_3) - (2l(c_1) + 2l(c_2) + l(c_3)) = 2l(c_1) > 0.$

(12) $s(lhs) - s(rhs) = 3 - (0 + 2) = 1 > 0.$

The remaining cases are trivial: (3) and (16) follow from the subterm property, (11), (15) and (17) follow from the replacement property, the calculations for (8) are the same as for (7), and likewise (13) and (14) are similar to (12). □

Corollary 6.6 FOL-TRS is terminating (strongly-normalizing).

6.5.2 Confluence

For a rewriting system to be *confluent*, or *Church-Rosser*, means that every term has at most one normal form. This is a desirable property, because it means that the choice of reduction strategy does not affect the final result. If the system also is terminating, then every reduction strategy *will* find 'the' result.

Definition 6.7 A *context* is a term with a hole in it. The hole is denoted by the symbol □, and the context itself is written as $C[]$. $C[t]$ instantiates the context by replacing the hole with the term t.

Definition 6.8 Let $l_1 \Rightarrow r_1$ and $l_2 \Rightarrow r_2$ be two rewrite rules, with no common variables, $C[]$ a context, and t a non-variable term, such that $l_2 = C[t]$ and l_1 and t are unifiable with a most general unifier σ. Then l_1 and l_2 are said to *overlap*. A term $t' = \sigma(C[t])$ can be rewritten in two distinct ways, namely $t' \Rightarrow \sigma(C[r_1])$ under the first rule, or $t' \Rightarrow \sigma(r_2)$ under the second rule. The pair $\langle (\sigma(C[t]), \sigma(r_2) \rangle$ is called a *critical pair*. A critical pair $\langle t_1, t_2 \rangle$ is *convergent* if t_1 and t_2 have a common reduct.

For example, using Peano numerals, we might have the rules:

$$add(A,\ A) \quad \Rightarrow \quad mul(A,\ s(s(zero)))$$
$$add(s(B),\ C) \quad \Rightarrow \quad add(B,\ s(C))$$

It is easy to see that $\sigma = \{A \mapsto s(B), C \mapsto s(B)\}$ is a unifier for the two left-hand sides. Any term $add(s(B),\ s(B))$ can be rewritten either as $mul(s(B),\ s(s(zero)))$ or as $add(B,\ s(s(B)))$.

The presence of critical pairs in a rewriting system is a strong indication that the system may be non-confluent. If all critical pairs are convergent, then the system is known to be *weakly* Church-Rosser. If it also is terminating, then confluence follows.

Alas, there are many non-convergent critical pairs in FOL-TRS, making the system grossly non-confluent. In this situation, one may attempt to regain confluence by adding rules to make (previously non-convergent) critical pairs convergent. When we attempted to do this for FOL-TRS, we found several problems.

The most serious practical problem was that for every new rule, several new critical pairs would arise. Then *they* would have to be dealt with by creating even more rules.[1] A less serious problem was that the termination proof had to be revised for each new rule.

At this point one should ask oneself whether non-confluence is such a disaster for FOL-TRS. FOL-TRS performs the task of *simplifying* terms in accord with our desire to reduce non-determinism. In this rôle, finding *most* but not always *all* redexes is usually acceptable. In contrast, confluence is much more important for TRSs that describe evaluation or semantics.

Another issue is the chosen *reduction strategy*. A formal system may be non-confluent because it cannot mandate any particular reduction order. However, fixing the order makes an *implementation* confluent. FOL-TRS was developed hand-in-hand with the implementation, which uses a leftmost-innermost (i.e. left-right bottom-up) order.

6.5.3　Alternatives for Rewriting Negations

The rewrite rules for negations use a non-standard extension of term rewriting systems, namely natural-semantics-style inference rules to selectively 'trigger' a group ($\stackrel{not}{\Rightarrow}$) of rules for certain terms. We considered several alternative formulations:

- Use natural semantics throughout. However, then both reduction order and *absence* of rewrites would have to be made explicit in the inference rules, making the resulting system bulkier.

- Encode the 'trigger' rules in plain TRS notation. This can be done in at least two different ways:

  - Add a few unary constructors to encode context:

    $$\text{(not } c) \quad\quad\quad\quad\quad \Rightarrow \quad \text{(not (special } c))$$
    $$\text{(special (and } c_1\ c_2)) \quad \Rightarrow \quad \text{(and } c_1 \text{ (special } c_2))$$

    When (6), (7) and (8) unify conjunctions, these special markers have to be ignored. This can be done, at considerable complexity, by adding more markers, each encoding a particular notion of

---

[1] We did this by hand. If we had had an implementation of Knuth-Bendix completion available, then maybe we *would* have found a confluent system.

'state' of its argument. It also means that many rules have to be added to manipulate the markers.

Placing a marker onto a previously unmarked term actually makes it larger, so some entirely different approach to proving termination would have had to be taken.

– Encode context in the name of a constructor. When a 'plain' constructor occurs under a negation, it can be replaced by a special one:

$$(\text{not } (\text{and } c_1 \ c_2)) \Rightarrow (\text{not } (\text{special-and } c_1 \ c_2))$$

A rule like this would have to written for *every* constructor that can occur in this context. The ordinary rules would have to be extended to recognize all new constructors as well. As in the previous approach, there would be problems for rules (6), (7) and (8).

In conclusion, neither alternative seemed worthwhile.

6.6 Examples

6.6.1 append

```
relation append =
  axiom append([], ys) => ys

  rule   append(xs, ys) => zs
         ----------------
         append(x::xs, ys) => x::zs
end
```

The initial representation produced by the front-end is shown below. We have renamed variables and used a simple notation for patterns, to improve readability. The WILD pattern matches any value; CONS and NIL match the ordinary list constructors; PAIR matches 2-tuples. When a rewrite rule matches some term, we indicate this by writing a comment last on the first line of the term. For instance, ;(1) in line 3 in the figure below means that rule (1) is applicable to the term starting on line 3.

```
(define (append xs' ys)
  (orelse
    (andthen (match (xs' NIL) (ys WILD)) ;(1)
             (return ys))
    (andthen (match (xs' (CONS x xs)) (ys WILD)) ;(1)
             (andthen (and (call append (xs ys) (zs)) ;(2)
                           (match (zs WILD)))
                      (return (CONS x zs)))))))
```

Rule (1) is applicable in two places, and rule (2) is applicable in one place. Applying these rewrites results in the following.

```
(define (append xs' ys)
  (orelse ;(9)
    (case (xs' ys)
      ((NIL WILD)
        (return ys)))
    (case (xs' ys)
      (((CONS x xs) WILD)
        (andthen (call append (xs ys) (zs))
                (andthen (match (zs WILD)) ;(1)
                        (return (CONS x zs)))))))))
```

Now, rule (1) is again applicable, and rule (9) is applicable to the disjunction of the two cases. This results in:

```
(define (append xs' ys)
  (case (xs' ys)
    ((NIL WILD)
      (return ys))
    (((CONS x xs) WILD)
      (andthen (call append (xs ys) (zs))
              (case (zs)
                ((WILD) (return (CONS x zs))))))))
```

And this is the final result. The seemingly-redundant **case** after the recursive call to **append** will be treated by the pattern-match compiler as a no-op. The two match rules in the first **case** are non-overlapping, so the pattern-match compiler will not introduce a choice point. The end result is that **append** is completely deterministic.

6.6.2   lookup

```
relation lookup =
  rule  key = key'
        -----------------
        lookup((key,attr)::_, key') => attr

  rule  not key = key' &
        lookup(alist, key') => attr
        -----------------
        lookup((key,_)::alist, key') => attr
end
```

This relation expresses the usual idiom for looking up the most recent binding stored in an association-list. The initial representation is:

```
(define (lookup v2 v1)
  (orelse ;(6)
    (andthen ;(1)
      (match (v2 (CONS (PAIR v3 v4) WILD)) ;line 4
             (v1 WILD))
      (andthen (unify v3 v1)
               (return v4)))
    (andthen ;(1)
      (match (v2 (CONS (PAIR v5 WILD) v6)) ;line 9
             (v1 WILD))
      (andthen (and (not (unify v5 v1)) ;(2)
                    (and (call lookup (v6 v1) (v7))
                         (match (v7 WILD))))
               (return v7)))))
```

Rule (6) is applicable since the disjunction has two conjunctions with 'equal' first conjuncts. It is apparent here that equality is not a trivial syntactic equality, but equality under α-conversion, i.e. renaming of bound variables and wildcards. By renaming v3 to v5, changing (PAIR v5 WILD) to (PAIR v5 v4) on line 9, and changing (CONS (PAIR v3 v4) WILD) to (CONS (PAIR v5 v4) v6) on line 4, the two matchings become syntactically equal. (We have more to say about these renamings later on.) There is also an opportunity to apply rule (2).

Alternatively, we could apply rule (1) twice. It turns out that doing so, and then applying rule (6) in the next step, would give the same result.

Applying (6) and (2) results in:

```
(define (lookup v2 v1)
  (andthen ;(1)
    (match (v2 (CONS (PAIR v5 v4) v6))
           (v1 WILD))
    (orelse ;(7)
      (andthen (unify v5 v1)
               (return v4))
      (andthen (not (unify v5 v1))
               (andthen ;(2)
                 (and (call lookup (v6 v1) (v7))
                      (match (v7 WILD)))
                 (return v7))))))
```

Now, rule (1) may convert the matching into a case. Rule (2) is applicable to further linearize the conjunctions after the negated unification. Finally, rule (7) is applicable at the disjunction to turn it into a conditional.

The result is:

```
(define (lookup v2 v1)
  (case (v2 v1)
    (((CONS (PAIR v5 v4) v6) WILD)
     (cond (unify v5 v1)
           (return v4)
           (andthen
             (call lookup (v6 v1) (v7))
             (andthen (match (v7 WILD))  ;(1)
                      (return v7))))))))
```

Again, rule (1) is applicable, which results in:

```
(define (lookup v2 v1)
  (case (v2 v1)
    (((CONS (PAIR v5 v4) v6) WILD)
     (cond (unify v5 v1)
           (return v4)
           (andthen
             (call lookup (v6 v1) (v7))
             (case (v7)
               ((WILD) (return v7)))))))))
```

This is the final result. Note how only one pattern-matching operation is applied on the first argument, and how a conditional was introduced. As in the previous example, the **case** after the recursive call to lookup is treated by the pattern-match compiler as a no-op. The CPS optimizer is then able to η-reduce the return continuation in the recursive call, and thus turn it into a tailcall.

6.7   Missed Conditionals

Our initial set of rules did not include the stricter rules for negated conjunctions. This sometimes caused the compiler to miss opportunities for converting disjunctions to conditionals, as the following example shows.

Assume for now that the $\overset{not}{\Rightarrow}$ relation and rule (11) do not exist, and consider the following relation:

```
relation r =
  rule  q x => z
        ----------------
        r(x::xs) => z

  rule  not q x => z & r xs => z'
        ----------------
        r(x::xs) => z'
end
```

This relation expresses a choice based on the outcome of some other relation. The front-end will represent it as:

```
(define (r xs')
  (orelse ;(6)
    (andthen
      (match (xs' (CONS x xs)))
      (andthen ;(2)
        (and (call q (x) (z))
             (match (z WILD)))
        (return z)))
    (andthen
      (match (xs' (CONS x xs)))
      (andthen ;(2)
        (and (not (and (call q (x) (z))
                       (match (z WILD)))))
             (and (call r (xs) (z'))
                  (match (z' WILD))))
        (return z')))))
```

After applying rule (6) once and (2) twice, we have:

```
(define (r xs')
  (case (xs')
    (((CONS x xs))
     (orelse
       (andthen
         (call q (x) (z))
         (andthen ;(1)
           (match (z WILD))
           (return z)))
       (andthen
         (not (and (call q (x) (z))
                   (match (z WILD))))
         (andthen ;(2)
           (and (call r (xs) (z'))
                (match (z' WILD)))
           (return z')))))))
```

Apart from the opportunity to apply rules (1) and (2), we are stuck. In particular, the heads of the two disjuncts do *not* enable rule (7) to introduce a conditional.

When this problem initially was discovered, we first considered adding rules to simplify match conjunctions. In particular, one can remove matchings of variables against wildcards. Unfortunately, rule (9) relies on individual matchings having *identical* sets of variables if it is to combine them to form larger matchings. So simplifying individual matchings may inhibit rule (9) to combine them.

It would seem that we had a choice: adding rules to allow more disjunctions to be converted to conditionals, at the expense of more backtracking and pattern-matching, or leave things as they were and miss some opportunities for introducing conditionals.

The solution to this dilemma was to realize that negated conjunctions never produce visible bindings. We can then introduce a set of rules to simplify negated conjunctions. In particular, bind and exists can always be removed, and match can be removed if all patterns are wildcards. This led to the rules in the $\stackrel{not}{\Rightarrow}$ relation.

Now, let us reconsider the negated conjunction:

```
(not (and (call q (x) (z))
          (match (z WILD))))
```

First, rule (11) causes the $\stackrel{not}{\Rightarrow}$ rules to be considered, and rule (15) applies $\stackrel{not}{\Rightarrow}$ to the second conjunct, the match. We find that rule (14) allows the match to be rewritten as true.

```
(not (and (call q (x) (z)) true))
```

Now rule (16) will simplify the and:

```
(not (call q (x) (z)))
```

The full example has now become:

```
(define (r xs')
  (case (xs')
    (((CONS x xs))
     (orelse ;(7)
       (andthen
         (call q (x) (z))
         (case (z)
           ((WILD) (return z))))
       (andthen
         (not (call q (x) (z)))
         (andthen
           (call r (xs) (z'))
           (andthen ;(1)
             (match (z' WILD))
             (return z')))))))))
```

Now we find that rule (7) *is* able to introduce the conditional. Also, rule (1) is applicable.

```
(define (r xs')
  (case (xs')
    (((CONS x xs))
     (cond (call q (x) (z))
           (case (z)
             ((WILD) (return z)))
           (andthen
             (call r (xs) (z'))
             (case (z')
               ((WILD) (return z'))))))))))
```

This is the final result. As in the `lookup` example, the `case` after the recursive call to r is a no-op and the call eventually becomes a proper tailcall.

6.8 Implementation Notes

To implement the rewriting rules, we need to be able to

- unify lists of patterns, in rule (4),

- test lists of patterns for similarity, in rule (4),

- unify conjunctions, in rules (6), (7) and (8), and

- compare lists of variables, in rule (9).

As mentioned before in the `lookup` example, equality is taken to be syntactic equality after renaming of bound variables. Furthermore, we may need to change some wildcard patterns to variables.

First, we represent patterns using a notation where describing the *shape* of a pattern has been made orthogonal to describing the variables that are bound in various positions of the pattern. The purpose of separating shapes from bindings is to simplify the implementation of unification of patterns. Figure 6.2 describes the representation.

$lit \in Lit$	literals
$con \in Con$	constructors
$p' \in Pat' ::= \texttt{wild}$	wildcard
$\mid (\texttt{lit } lit)$	literal
$\mid (\texttt{con } con)$	constant
$\mid (\texttt{struct } con \; p^*)$	constructor application
$p \in Pat \; ::= (\texttt{as } v \; p')$	patterns

Figure 6.2: Syntax of FOL patterns

In this representation, a pattern binds a variable to *every* position within it. The construction (`as` v p') means that a term is matched against p'. If the match succeeded, v is bound to the entire term.[2] All forms of aggregate objects, i.e. cons cells, tuples, or constructors applied to arguments, are represented as structs with appropriate tags. A source pattern x::xs would be represented as (as xs' (struct CONS (as x wild) (as xs wild))).

Patterns are compared for equality by treating as as λ. To compare (as v_1 p_1') with (as v_2 p_2'), we first substitute v_1 for v_2 in p_2' giving p_2'', and then compare p_1' with p_2''. The result of a successful comparison of patterns results in a renaming substitution which we have to apply to the conjunction or disjunction p_2' occurred in.

Note that this is a much simpler problem than unification for the full λ-calculus, which was studied by Huet [90]. Huet needed to deal with equality under β-reduction, which made his problem undecidable.

Instead of computing explicit substitutions, and applying them to the terms the patterns occurred in, we implemented destructive unification of variables. Every variable is represented by a cell, which is either unbound or bound to another variable. Both the binding point of a variable, i.e. in an as pattern, bind, exists, or call conjunction, and all its uses refer to the same cell.

During unification of binding operators variables are unified physically by binding one to the other. At the same time, this binding is remembered on a *trail* stack. Should the unification fail later on, the trail is used to undo the bindings. If the initial unification call succeeds, the trail is discarded, thus 'committing' to the renamings made. During unification of *uses* of variables, both variables are first dereferenced and then compared.

The similarity test is simpler, since variable names can be ignored. Two patterns are similar if either is a wildcard, or they are both the same literal or constant, or they are both constructor applications using the same constructor and number of sub-patterns, and the sub-patterns are similar.

6.8.1   Implementation Complexity

The compiler implements the simplification rules given here as an alternating bottom-up / top-down normalization algorithm. The default rules are applied bottom-up in a leftmost-innermost reduction strategy. Upon finding a negation, the additional $\overset{not}{\Rightarrow}$ rules are applied (top-down) as specified by the trigger rules. The code totals 120 lines of SML, not counting blank lines or comments. The additional code to implement unification totals 76 lines of SML.

Chapter 10 gives benchmarking results showing the large performance improvements yielded by the optimizations described here. We see up to 2-3 orders of magnitude less stack usage, and 2-2.5 times faster code due to the reduced memory traffic. These are very encouraging results from what is such a small part of the compiler!

---

[2]The keyword as is taken from SML.

6.9 Limitations

While the benchmarking data indicate that the simplification rules are effective for several applications, we are aware of some serious limitations.

Rules (7) and (8) attempt to turn disjunctions into conditionals. This is possible when the heads of the two disjuncts are mutually exclusive. The problem is that our current rules are purely *syntactic*: they recognize that c and (not c) are mutually exclusive, but miss many other cases.

Consider for instance:

```
relation r =
  rule  int_lt(x, 10) => true
        ----------------
        r x => x

  rule  int_ge(x, 10) => true
        ----------------
        r x => 10
end
```

It is obvious that $x < 10$ and $x \geq 10$ are mutually exclusive, but discovering this requires knowledge of the $<$ and $\geq$ operations, and in general the rules would have to be taught about many of RML's predefined relations.

Replacing the second premise `int_ge(x, 10) => true` with `int_lt(x, 10) => false` will result in completely deterministic code using our current set of transformation rules. This is one of the reasons why built-in predicates return booleans rather than success/failure.

Now consider:

```
relation isnull =
  axiom isnull []
end

relation iscons =
  axiom iscons(_::_)
end

relation r =
  rule  isnull x & ...
        ---------------
        r x

  rule  iscons x & ...
        ---------------
        r x
end
```

The two rules in r are mutually exclusive, but to discover this the compiler would need to analyse the definitions of user-defined relations. Recently, Post has described an analysis technique for doing this analysis for Prolog [146, Chapter 6; 147]. Something similar should definitely be implemented for RML.

6.10   Related Work

Interestingly, several researchers in Natural Semantics have adopted deterministic execution models, and consequently required deterministic specifications. Since many realistic specifications are not obviously deterministic, da Silva [48] devised a *left-factoring* transformation to transform determinate specifications into deterministic ones. This and similar transformations were also used by Hannan [76, 79], Diehl [58], and McKeever [115].

Independently, Berry [22] too required specifications to be determinate. During the execution of a relation (our terminology), several rules may be applicable. However, eventually at most one may remain.

An initial inspiration point for our approach was the work by Billaud [24–28] on axiomatizing Prolog's control flow. Technical differences between the languages he studied, viz. pure Prolog combined with various extensions, and RML meant .that his results could not be transferred directly to RML. However, it hinted that using a 'control' algebra for representing programs and deriving rewriting 'equivalences' for it, was a viable approach.

Chapter 7

Compiling Pattern Matching

attern matching is an integral part of RML. It is the mechanism by
which relations inspect arguments in order to locate relevant inference
rules, and callers use it to inspect results from successful calls. This
chapter presents an algorithm for compiling term pattern-matching. Earlier
algorithms may produce duplicated code, and redundant or sub-optimal discrimination tests for certain combinations of patterns. Our algorithm, which
was inspired by finite automata theory, addresses these problems and solves
them to some extent. It does so by viewing patterns as regular expressions
and optimizing the finite automaton that is built to recognize them. It also
makes checking patterns for *exhaustiveness* and *irredundancy* cheap operations, since this information is apparent in the automaton.

This chapter is based on [133]. The presentation of the algorithm has
been completely revised, but the basic ideas remain the same. An additional
Section 7.9 describes how the approach had to be modified to accommodate
the RML language.

7.1 Introduction

7.1.1 What is Matching?

Pattern matching is a general operation that is used in many different application areas. Abstractly, a *pattern* is a description of a set of values. Matching
a value against a pattern determines whether the value is in the set denoted
by the pattern. Matching problems differ in the kinds of values and patterns
they deal with, and the types of results computed.

In *string matching*, values are finite strings and patterns are regular expressions. The typical application is to search for substrings in larger texts.

String matching is typically implemented using various kinds of augmented finite automata [15, Chapter 5].

In *term matching*, values are terms and patterns are incomplete terms with variables. A variable matches any value. The matching problem is typically stated: given a value v and patterns $p_1, \cdots, p_n$, is v an instance of any of the p_i? At the same time, the variables in p_i become bound to the corresponding parts of the input value v.

Term matching is a built-in feature in modern functional programming languages such as Standard ML [120] and Haskell [89]. It is also an integral part of RML. It is primarily used to define functions by case analysis on their arguments. Term matching is typically implemented by top-down methods; for instance, our algorithm constructs top-down matching automata.

Tree matching is similar to term matching, except that the problem is stated differently: given a tree t and patterns $p_1, \cdots, p_n$, compute all pairs $\langle o, i \rangle$, where p_i matches the subtree of t at position (occurrence) o. Tree matching can be implemented by top-down methods, but the most common approach seems to be to use bottom-up automata. Tree matching is often used in applications based on *rewriting*, such as term-rewriting or code selection [1, 88]. A problem arises in that the constructed automata tend to be quite large. Improved generation algorithms [51, 149] and representation techniques [31, 67] are used to combat this problem.

In the sequel, we deal only with top-down term matching.

7.1.2   Compiling Term Matching

Pattern matching allows complex nested patterns, and also partial overlap between different equations. The purpose of *compiling* pattern matching is to reduce this complexity, making the resulting code more efficient. Consider:

```
fun f(y::nil) = A
  | f(y::_)   = B
  | f(nil)    = C
```

The first two equations use nested patterns. They also overlap. In typical languages, higher priority is given to the topmost pattern.

A naïve implementation could expand each pattern into a sequence of tests and then try these sequences, one at a time, until a match is found. This is wasteful, since many tests will be repeated. For instance, if the argument is (5::6::nil), first the first pattern will fail, and then the second pattern will repeat the initial 'cons' test.

Compiled pattern matchings use only *simple* case expressions. These have (a) no nested patterns, (b) no overlap between different cases, and (c) a single optional default case. Consequently, simple cases have efficient implementations.

There exists a standard algorithm for compiling pattern-matching [14, 176] (these papers describe very similar algorithms). It produces good code for most cases, but has problems with certain combinations of patterns, viz. when it must fall back on the so-called 'mixture rule'.

The algorithm presented here was inspired by finite automata theory: a pattern is now viewed as an alternation and repetition-free regular expression over atomic values, constructor names and wildcards. The pattern-match compiler takes a sequence of patterns and compiles them to an acyclic deterministic finite automaton. Equivalent states are merged, and the automaton is then transformed to an expression in the compiler's intermediate language. This approach has some interesting consequences:

- Since equivalent states are merged, the problem of duplication of the right-hand side expressions is avoided. In some cases, even some of the discrimination code itself can be shared.

- Since automata encode all control information in their states, they never need to backtrack or inspect a particular value more than once.

The rest of this chapter is organized as follows: Section 7.2 presents some examples that are troublesome for the standard algorithm. Section 7.3 presents the basic ideas of the new algorithm, and (informally) illustrates its workings on an example. Then Section 7.4 defines the auxiliary structures and operations used, followed by the algorithm itself in Section 7.5. In Section 7.6, we revisit the previous 'troublesome' examples, illustrating how our algorithm deals with them. Section 7.7 discusses some implementation issues, and Section 7.8 compares this with related work. Section 7.9 describes the adaptations made for RML. Section 7.10 concludes with some comparisons between this algorithm and an earlier implementation of the standard one.

7.2 Troublesome Examples

The well-known pattern-match compilation algorithm in [14,176] works with a matrix of patterns. The algorithm proceeds by analysing the matrix, choosing one of several cases, and recursively solving smaller problems. It often works well, but may produce poor code for certain inputs. This happens when it selects a 'column' of patterns that contains a *mixture* of variable and non-variable patterns. In this case the column is partitioned into alternating sub-sequences of variable and non-variable patterns. The problem is that when a discrimination test is done on a sub-sequence, the original context is lost, and this may lead to redundant or sub-optimal tests. This section presents some examples that illuminate these weak spots. All examples are written in Standard ML, as is the generated code.

7.2.1   Copied Expressions

Consider the following function definition (from [176]):

```
fun unwieldy [] [] = A
  | unwieldy xs ys = B xs ys
```

A naïve implementation of the standard algorithm might generate:

```
fun unwieldy xs ys =
  case xs
    of nil      => (case ys
                      of nil    => A
                       | _      => B xs ys)
     | _        => B xs ys
```

Since there are two ways for the second equation to match, the second expression B xs ys appears two times in the generated code.

To eliminate expression copying, Augustsson proposes a new control operator DEFAULT. If it appears in the right-hand side of some case expression, then control is transferred to the nearest enclosing default entry:[1]

```
fun unwieldy xs ys =
  case xs
    of nil      => (case ys
                      of nil    => A
                       | _      => DEFAULT)
     | _        => B xs ys
```

This has the drawback of being far too low-level for a compiler using a goto-less high-level language as its intermediate code. A much cleaner solution, and no less efficient if the compiler does basic analysis and integration of local procedures [8, 105, 166], is to wrap up shared expressions as local procedures. The above example could then become:

```
fun unwieldy xs ys =
  let fun default() = B xs ys
  in
    case xs
      of nil      => (case ys
                        of nil    => A
                         | _      => default())
       | _        => default()
  end
```

---

[1]I.e. the wildcard entry in the nearest enclosing case that has one. Wadler uses the []
and FAIL operators instead to achieve the same effect.

7.2.2 Repeated and Sub-Optimal Tests

Consider the following definition (again adapted from [176]):

```
fun demo [] ys = A ys
  | demo xs [] = B xs
  | demo (x'::xs') (y'::ys') = C x' xs' y' ys'
```

which would be expanded to:

```
fun demo xs ys =
  case xs
    of nil        => A ys
     | _          =>                      (* 1 *)
         case ys
           of nil => B xs
            | _   =>
                case xs                    (* 2 *)
                  of x'::xs' =>
                     (case ys
                         of y'::ys' => C x' xs' y' ys'
                          | _        => ERROR)
                   | _ => ERROR
```

The problem is that the repeated tests must check for all constructors of the type, even though it is easily seen that only some actually can appear. The nested tests need to test for all constructors *only* if control could come to the default case via some use of the DEFAULT operator. The pattern-match compiler should optimize nested tests when this is not the case. Furthermore, when the repeated test is for a single constructor, it should be eliminated and replaced by a let to directly bind the variables to the components of the value.

The pattern-match compiler *could* do a post-optimization pass on the generated expression. At every simple match *pat* ⇒ *exp*, it would simplify *exp* with the knowledge that the matched variable was *pat*. Consider the line marked *1*. We know that xs is a list, i.e. either nil or a cons cell (::), but at line *1*, xs must be a cons since it cannot be nil. The optimizer propagates this knowledge through the right-hand side expression. The test marked *2* can then be replaced by a let to directly fetch and bind the components of the cons cell, without the need for a runtime test. One of the ERROR cases can also be removed. Our algorithm achieves this optimization directly, without the need for an additional pass.

7.3   Intuitive Operation

A pattern match compiler can be seen as applying a sequence of meaning-preserving and performance-improving transformations on case expressions, until only simple cases remain. Consider a reformulation of our first example:

```
fun f xs =
  case xs
    of cons(y,nil) => A
     | cons(y,_)    => B
     | nil          => C
```

We describe the state of the algorithm by a *matrix of patterns*. The initial state would be the following 3×1 matrix:

$$\begin{pmatrix} \text{cons(y,nil)} \\ \text{cons(y,\_)} \\ \text{nil} \end{pmatrix}$$

We find that column 1 is not in simple form, so we inspect it and find two constructors at the top level, nil and cons. By joining the two first cases to a single one, we arrive at the following (inventing a new variable ys as we go along):

```
case xs
  of cons(y,ys) => ..
   | nil        => ..
```

To determine the right-hand sides of these equations, we *match* the constructors against column 1, and *select* the corresponding rows.

nil matches only row 3. As it has no sub-patterns, it contributes no further work, so its right-hand side is just C.

cons matches rows 1 and 2. We select these rows, and strip away the top-level cons to expose the sub-patterns. This gives us the following 2×2 matrix of new patterns to consider, together with the A and B right-hand sides:

$$\begin{pmatrix} \text{y} & \text{nil} \\ \text{y} & \_ \end{pmatrix}$$

Our top-level case has become:

```
case xs
  of cons(y,ys) =>
       (case (y,ys)
          of (y,nil) => A
           | (y,_)   => B)
   | nil => C
```

Now the inner case, i.e. the 2×2 matrix, is not simple. Column 2 has the constructor nil, which matches rows 1 and 2. If ys was not nil, then only row 2 can apply. First we remove column 2. In the nil case, we select rows 1 and 2 from column 2 and strip away the top-level constructor to expose any sub-patterns (none here). Then we select rows 1 and 2 from the remaining 2×1 matrix, and combine them with the exposed sub-patterns to form a new matrix. The other non-nil case is similar. This results in:

```
case xs
  of cons(y,ys) =>
       (case ys
          of nil =>
               (case y
                  of y => A
                   | y => B)
           | _ =>
               (case y
                  of y => B))
   | nil => C
```

Matchings where all patterns in the topmost row are variables or wildcards are known to succeed. This allows us to replace both of the innermost `cases` with their topmost right-hand sides. The final result is:

```
case xs
  of cons(y,ys) =>
       (case ys
          of nil => A
           | _ => B)
   | nil => C
```

In practice, one operates on a matrix of patterns, a vector of right-hand sides (one for each row in the matrix), and a vector of variables (one for each column in the matrix).

As was evident in the second-last step, there may at some points be several paths leading to the same right-hand side; B above (although here one of those paths could be removed). We deal with this problem by considering each right-hand side expression, and each intermediate `case` expression to be a *state* in an *automaton*. Rather than using nested expressions, control flows through the arcs of that automaton. A final step turns this automaton into an expression that *does not* duplicate the code for shared states.

7.4 Preliminaries

The basic intuition behind our algorithm is that patterns can be viewed as alternation and repetition-free regular expressions consisting of constructor names (possibly with sub-patterns), atomic values and wildcards. These regular expressions are easily mapped to tree-based deterministic finite automata. This in turn implies that backtracking is never needed: all control information is encoded in the states of the automata. These automata are essentially n-ary trees, with arcs labelled by constructors, atomic values or wildcards. Leaf nodes correspond to right-hand side expressions, and non-leaf nodes correspond to discrimination tests.

Two non-leaf nodes are equivalent if their sets of outgoing arcs are the same, and they correspond to the same position in the input patterns. Assuming that these positions – *occurrences* as they are usually called – are computed and recorded in the states, the trees can easily be transformed into DAG-shaped automata in a single bottom-up traversal.

Using the analogy of finite automata makes it possible to directly describe an algorithm that neither needs backtracking nor generates duplicate code. Viewing patterns as regular expressions also makes it quite easy to define the mapping from patterns to states and arcs in the automata.

7.4.1   Objects

Before we describe the algorithm itself, we define the syntax of the objects we manipulate, and some auxiliary operations. See Figure 7.1. For notational clarity, we deviate somewhat from the syntax of SML/RML and write ? instead of _ for wildcard patterns. The x as *pat* notation is the SML/RML way of binding a variable to the term that matched pattern *pat*. An ordinary 'variable' pattern x is shorthand for x as ?.

$$
\begin{array}{lll}
n \in \mathrm{Nat} & & \text{natural numbers} \\
con \in \mathrm{Const} & & \text{constants} \\
ctor \in \mathrm{Ctor} & & \text{constructors} \\
exp \in \mathrm{Exp} & & \text{expressions} \\
x \in \mathrm{Var} & & \text{variables} \\
pat \in \mathrm{SrcPat} & ::= con \mid ctor(pat_1, \cdots, pat_n) & \text{source patterns} \\
& \quad\ \mid\ ?\ \mid\ x \text{ as } pat & \\
mrule \in \mathrm{MRule} & ::= pat^* \Rightarrow exp & \text{match rules} \\
p \in \mathrm{Pat} & ::= ?\ \mid\ con\ \mid\ ctor(p_1, \cdots, p_n) & \text{preprocessed patterns} \\
o \in \mathrm{Occ} & ::= xn^* & \text{occurrences} \\
spat \in \mathrm{SimPat} & ::= con\ \mid\ ctor(o_1, \cdots, o_n) & \text{simple patterns} \\
a \in \mathrm{Arc} & ::= spat \Rightarrow q & \text{arcs} \\
q \in \mathrm{State} & ::= \mathbf{final}\ o^*\ exp & \text{states} \\
& \quad\ \mid\ \mathbf{test}\ o\ a^*\ q_{\mathrm{opt}} & \\
\end{array}
$$

Figure 7.1: Syntax of auxiliary objects

Occurrences are encoded as variable names followed by sequences of natural numbers. An occurrence x denotes the top-level node of x's value; we sometimes call x a *root variable*. The sequence of numbers after x describes the path taken from the root to the particular position in x's value. For instance, $x21$ would be the first sub-tree of the second sub-tree of x. If x is a list, then $x21$ is the second element of that list. In our examples, we ignore the notational ambiguity that might occur should some term have more than 9 sub-terms.

Input: The input to the algorithm is a sequence of *match rules* (*row of n source patterns ⇒ expression*), and a sequence of *n root variables*. At runtime, the root variables should be bound to the input values that are to be pattern-matched. The order of the match rules is significant: the first (or topmost) rule that matches is the one whose expression will be evaluated. For example, the `unwieldy` function shown before would have two match rules, `([] [] => A)` and `(xs ys => B)`, and two root variables, say, `xs` and `ys`.

The intermediate data structure of the algorithm is an acyclic deterministic finite automaton. Each state in the automaton is either a *final* or a *test* state. There is one final state for each expression in the right-hand sides of the match rules, and one for matching failure. A test state corresponds to a simple case-expression that performs a discrimination test on a certain position, and is characterized by that position, a sequence of arcs (simple pattern, new state), and an optional default arc.

7.4.2 Operations

The algorithm makes use of a large number of custom operations; they are defined below.

Definition 7.1 Let $\mathbf{x} = (x_1, \cdots, x_n)$ be a vector. Then $\mathbf{i} = (i_1, \cdots, i_m)$ is an *index vector for x*, if the elements in $\mathbf{i}$ are distinct and increasing, and $1 \le i_j \le n$ for every i_j.

Definition 7.2 Let $\mathbf{x} = (x_1, \cdots, x_n)$ be a vector and $\mathbf{i} = (i_1, \cdots, i_m)$ an index vector for $\mathbf{x}$. Then $\mathbf{x_i} = (x_{i_1}, \cdots, x_{i_m})$. This operation uses the index vector to *select* a sub-vector of $\mathbf{x}$. For instance, $(x, y, z)_{(1,3)} = (x, z)$.

Definition 7.3 Let $\mathbf{x}$ be a vector as above, and $1 \le i \le n$ an index in $\mathbf{x}$. Then $\mathbf{x} \setminus i = (x_1, \cdots, x_{i-1}, x_{i+1}, \cdots, x_n)$. This operation *removes* an element from a vector.

Definition 7.4 Let $\mathbf{A}$ be a matrix with n rows and m columns. We consider $\mathbf{A}$ to be a vector with n elements (rows), each of which is a vector with m elements (a column). Then $\mathbf{A}_{(\cdot, j)} = (\mathbf{A}^T)_j$. This operation *selects* a column from a matrix. ($\mathbf{A}^T$ is $\mathbf{A}$ transposed.)

Definition 7.5 Let $\mathbf{A}$ be a matrix as above. Then $\mathbf{A} \setminus (\cdot, j) = ((\mathbf{A}^T) \setminus j)^T$. This operation *removes* a column from a matrix.

Definition 7.6 Let $\mathbf{x}$ be a vector with m elements, and $\mathbf{y}$ a vector with n elements. Then $\mathbf{x} \mid \mathbf{y} = (x_1, \cdots, x_m, y_1, \cdots, y_n)$. This operation *concatenates* vectors.

Definition 7.7 Let $\mathbf{A}$ be a $k \times n$ matrix and $\mathbf{B}$ be a $k \times m$ matrix. Then $\mathbf{A} \parallel \mathbf{B}$ is a $k \times (n + m)$ matrix defined by:

$$(\mathbf{A} \parallel \mathbf{B})_i = \mathbf{A}_i \mid \mathbf{B}_i$$

i.e., row i in $\mathbf{A} \parallel \mathbf{B}$ is the concatenation of row i in $\mathbf{A}$ and row i in $\mathbf{B}$. This operation *concatenates* matrices by placing them side-by-side.

Definition 7.8 Let $\mathbf{p}$ be a vector of k preprocessed patterns. Then the *n-lifted* $\mathbf{p}$, written $\mathbf{p} \uparrow n$, is a $k \times n$ pattern matrix, defined by:

$$(\mathbf{p} \uparrow n)_i = \begin{cases} (?_1, \cdots, ?_n) & \text{if } \mathbf{p}_i \text{ is ?} \\ (p_1, \cdots, p_n) & \text{if } \mathbf{p}_i \text{ is } ctor(p_1, \cdots, p_n) \\ () & \text{if } n = 0 \text{ and } \mathbf{p}_i \text{ is a constant} \\ error & \text{otherwise} \end{cases}$$

It is an error to supply an n that is different from the arity (number of sub-patterns) of any $\mathbf{p}_i$. It follows that the vector $\mathbf{p}$ cannot contain constructors of different arities.

This operation strips away the topmost constructors in a pattern column and 'lifts' the sub-patterns. This exposes the sub-patterns for further pattern-matching. Any wildcards are expanded by the arity n.

For example, $(?, \texttt{cons}(?,?)) \uparrow 2 = ((?,?), (?,?))$.

Definition 7.9 Let o be an occurrence $xk_1 \cdots k_n$ $(n \geq 0)$ and $m \geq 0$. Then $o_m = xk_1 \cdots k_n m$. Given an occurrence of a term, this operation computes the occurrence of that term's mth sub-term.

Definition 7.10 Let o be an occurrence and n a non-negative integer. Then $o \uparrow n = (o_1, \cdots, o_n)$. This operation computes, from an occurrence of a term with arity n, the occurrences of its n sub-terms.

For example, if a 'cons' has occurrence $x3$, then $x3 \uparrow 2 = (x31, x32)$ are the occurrences of its 'car' and 'cdr'.

Definition 7.11 Let p be a preprocessed non-wildcard pattern and o an occurrence. Then $p \downarrow o$ is a *simple pattern* defined by:

$$\begin{aligned} con \downarrow o &= con \\ ctor(p_1, \cdots, p_n) \downarrow o &= ctor(o_1, \cdots, o_n) \end{aligned}$$

This operation is used when internal (preprocessed) patterns are to be output as simple patterns. For example, if $p = \texttt{cons}(?,?)$ has occurrence x, then $p \downarrow x = \texttt{cons}(x1, x2)$ is the simple pattern that will be output.

Definition 7.12 The *erasure* of a preprocessed pattern p, written $\#p$, summarizes the top-level structure of that pattern. It is defined as:

$$\begin{aligned} \#? &= ? \\ \#con &= con \\ \#ctor(p_1, \cdots, p_n) &= ctor(?_1, \cdots, ?_n) \end{aligned}$$

Definition 7.13 Let $\mathbf{p} = (p_1, \cdots, p_n)$ be a vector of preprocessed patterns. Then the *erasure of* $\mathbf{p}$, written $\#\mathbf{p}$, is defined as $\{\#p_i \mid 1 \leq i \leq n\} \setminus \{?\}$. This operation is used to summarize a column of patterns by computing its set of (erased) top-level patterns, excluding any wildcards.

For example, $\#(\mathtt{nil}, \mathtt{nil}, ?) = \{\mathtt{nil}\}$ would be the erasure of a column containing two $\mathtt{nil}$s and one wildcard.

Definition 7.14 Let p and p' be preprocessed patterns. Then p *matches* p', written $p \geq p'$, if $p = ?$ or if $\#p = \#p'$. By erasing the patterns before comparing them, we ignore any sub-patterns.

Definition 7.15 Let $\mathbf{p}$ be a vector of preprocessed patterns and p a preprocessed pattern. Then p's *matching indices* in $\mathbf{p}$, written $\mathbf{p}/p$, is an index vector $(i_1, \cdots, i_k)$ for $\mathbf{p}$, such that for every i_j, $\mathbf{p}_{i_j} \geq p$, and for every index i not in the index vector, $\mathbf{p}_i \not\geq p$. This operation computes an index vector corresponding to those elements in $\mathbf{p}$ that match p. For example, $(\mathtt{true}, \mathtt{false}, ?)/\mathtt{true} = (1, 3)$.

Definition 7.16 Let p be a non-variable preprocessed pattern. Then the *arity of* p, written $|p|$, is defined as:

$$|p| = \begin{cases} 0 & \text{if } p = con \\ n & \text{if } p = ctor(p_1, \cdots, p_n) \end{cases}$$

7.5 The Algorithm

The algorithm is composed of four logical steps: *preprocessing of patterns, generating the DFA, merging of equivalent states,* and *mapping to intermediate code.* Each of these steps will now be described in detail.

7.5.1 Step 1: Preprocessing

As described in Section 7.3, two non-final states are equivalent if they test the same occurrence in the input, and their sets of outgoing arcs are equivalent. Therefore, the algorithm operates on occurrences rather than random 'temporary' variables.

The preprocessing step takes the sequences of root variables and match rules, and produces a matrix $\mathbf{P}$ of (preprocessed) patterns, a vector $\mathbf{o}$ of occurrences (one for each pattern column), and a vector $\mathbf{q}$ of final states (one for each pattern row).

Source patterns are preprocessed by replacing variable bindings x **as** *pat* with their sub-patterns. At the same time, a substitution is computed that maps these variables to their *occurrences* in the preprocessed patterns.

For every match rule, the patterns are first preprocessed, producing a row of (preprocessed) patterns and a renaming substitution, mapping source-level variable names to names based on occurrences. This renaming is applied to the right-hand side expression which is then turned into a new final state.

7.5.2   Step 2: Generating the DFA

The algorithm *match* operates on an m-vector $\mathbf{o}$ of occurrences, an $n \times m$ pattern matrix $\mathbf{P}$, and an n-vector $\mathbf{q}$ of states. It recursively translates these into states and arcs in a deterministic finite automaton. The value of a call to *match* is a state in this automaton.

match $\mathbf{o}$ $\mathbf{P}$ $\mathbf{q}$ proceeds by analysing the pattern matrix, and choosing one of the two rules in the algorithm.

The Variable Rule

$$match\ \mathbf{o}\ \begin{pmatrix} ? & ? & \cdots \\ & \cdots & \end{pmatrix} \begin{pmatrix} q_1 \\ \cdots \end{pmatrix} \ \Rightarrow\ q_1$$

The topmost pattern row has only wildcard patterns. Therefore, q_1 is the topmost final state to match the input, and the result is simply q_1.[2]

The Mixture Rule

$$match\ \begin{pmatrix} \cdots & \mathbf{o}_k & \cdots \end{pmatrix} \begin{pmatrix} \cdots & p_{(1,k)} & \cdots \\ \cdots & \cdots & \cdots \end{pmatrix} \mathbf{q}$$

There must be a column k such that $\mathbf{P}_{(1,k)}$ is non-variable. Compute the residuals of $\mathbf{o}$ and $\mathbf{P}$ by removing occurrence k and column k, and summarize column k by computing its erasure.

$$
\begin{aligned}
\mathbf{o}' &= \mathbf{o} \setminus k \\
\mathbf{P}' &= \mathbf{P} \setminus (\cdot, k) \\
\mathbf{p} &= \mathbf{P}_{(\cdot, k)} \\
\mathbf{P}_{\#} &= \#\mathbf{p}
\end{aligned}
$$

For each (non-variable) pattern p_i in $\mathbf{p}_{\#}$ (the summary of column k), construct its arc a_i as follows. First compute its matching indices in $\mathbf{p}$ and its arity, select the sub-column for these indices and lift *its* sub-patterns to form a matrix of the sub-patterns. Also lift the occurrence for this column to cover the exposed sub-patterns.

$$
\begin{aligned}
\mathbf{i} &= \mathbf{p}/p_i \\
n &= |p_i| \\
\mathbf{P}'' &= \mathbf{p_i} \uparrow n \\
\mathbf{o}'' &= \mathbf{o}_k \uparrow n
\end{aligned}
$$

Then combine the sub-problem for p_i with the residual $\mathbf{o}'$ and $\mathbf{P}'$, and compute the state corresponding to the continued matching.

$$q' = match\ (\mathbf{o}'' \mid \mathbf{o}')\ (\mathbf{P}'' \parallel \mathbf{P}'_\mathbf{i})\ \mathbf{q_i}$$

---

[2]Note that this rule differs significantly from Augustsson and Wadler's rule of the same name [14, 176].

Finally construct the arc a_i by computing the simple pattern for p_i with respect to $\mathbf{o}_k$, and joining it with the state q'.

$$p' = p_i \downarrow \mathbf{o}_k$$
$$a_i = p' \Rightarrow q'$$

If the set of constructors is exhaustive, then there is no default arc. Otherwise, compute the indices of the wildcards in this column: $\mathbf{w} = \mathbf{p}/?$. If there were none ($\mathbf{w}$ is the empty vector), the default arc goes to the error state. Otherwise, if $\mathbf{w}$ is non-empty, restrict the residual $\mathbf{P}'$ and $\mathbf{q}$ to the wildcard rows, and compute the state for the continued matching of those rows: $q_{\mathrm{def}} = match\ \mathbf{o}'\ \mathbf{P}'_{\mathbf{w}}\ \mathbf{q_w}$.

The result of $match\ \mathbf{o}\ \mathbf{P}\ \mathbf{q}$ is a test state with occurrence $\mathbf{o}_k$, arcs a_i, and default state q_{def} if one was computed.

7.5.3 Step 3: Merging of Equivalent States

The third step is to merge equivalent states. Since the DFAs are acyclic, this process can be efficiently implemented in a bottom-up fashion. Two test states are equivalent if they test the same input position (this is the raison d'être for using occurrences), and their sets of outgoing arcs are equal. Two arcs are equal if their simple patterns are equal and their target states are equal.

Here it has been described as a separate step, but this can easily be integrated into the *match* algorithm itself. *Match* can maintain a set of the states generated so far. Whenever it is about to create a new test state, is first checks whether an equivalent one already exists. If so, that one is used. Otherwise, a new one is created and added to the set.

In an implementation, it can be convenient to associate a unique tag with each state. This makes equivalence checking of arcs more efficient as it suffices to compare the tags of the target states.

7.5.4 Step 4: Generating Intermediate Code

The fourth and final step is to map the automaton to an expression in the intermediate language. Since shared states are to be implemented as local procedures, the notion of the *free variables* of a state becomes important: when following an arc to a shared state, the free variables of that state become parameters in a local procedure tail-call.

- The free variables of a final state are the occurrences from the substitution created in the preprocessing step that created this final state. The error state has no free variables.

- The free variables of an arc *simple pattern* => *state* are the free variables of the state, minus the occurrences bound in the pattern.

- The free variables of a test state are the free variables of the outgoing arcs, plus the occurrence that is tested.

Example: We have the following states:

$q_1 = $ final E_1
$q_2 = $ final $\{o_1, o_2\}$ E_2
$q_3 = $ test o_1 $(ctor(o_2)$ => $q_2)$

Their free variables are $\emptyset$, $\{o_1, o_2\}$, and $\{o_1\}$ respectively.

As for step 3, the free variable computation has been described as a separate step. Again, this is not necessary since a free-variable field can be computed once and for all when a state is initially created.

Starting with the start state, the intermediate language expression is constructed as follows:

- The translation of a final state is the expression it contains.

- The translation of a test state is a simple **case**-expression, whose variable is the occurrence of the state, and whose sequence of match rules is the result of translating its outgoing arcs, while preserving order.

- The translation of an arc *pattern* => *state* is the match rule *pattern* => *expression*, where the expression is the translation of the state reference.

- A reference to a non-shared state is replaced by the translation of the state itself.

- A reference to a shared state is made into a tail-call of a local procedure, the arguments of which are the free variables of the state. The body of the procedure is the translation of the state itself.

The resulting intermediate expression may refer to procedures corresponding to shared states. In this case, the expression is wrapped with bindings for these states/procedures. Either the order of these bindings has to be carefully computed, or a single recursive set of bindings can be used.

In an implementation, it can be convenient to associate a reference count field with each state, to make checking for shared states more efficient. In step 3, whenever a new test state is created, every state reached from its outgoing arcs has its reference count incremented. States initially have a reference count of zero.

7.6 The Examples Revisited

7.6.1 The demo Function

```
fun demo [] ys = E1
  | demo xs [] = E2
  | demo (x'::xs') (y'::ys') = E3
```

Step 1: Preprocessing

We consider demo to have two formal parameters, a and b, so they will be used as root variables. The result of the preprocessing is:

$$\mathbf{o} = (\ a,\ b\ )$$

$$\mathbf{P} = \begin{pmatrix} nil & ? \\ ? & nil \\ cons\,(?,?) & cons\,(?,?) \end{pmatrix}$$

$$\mathbf{q} = \begin{pmatrix} q_1 = \mathtt{final}\ \{b\}\ E1' \\ q_2 = \mathtt{final}\ \{a\}\ E2' \\ q_3 = \mathtt{final}\ \{a1, a2, b1, b2\}\ E3' \end{pmatrix}$$

where

$$E1' = E1[ys \mapsto b]$$
$$E2' = E2[xs \mapsto a]$$
$$E3' = E3[x' \mapsto a1, xs' \mapsto a2, y' \mapsto b1, ys' \mapsto b2]$$

The free variables in the final states are the occurrences that were substituted to replace the pattern variables.

Step 2: Generating the DFA

The initial call to *match* is:

$$match_0\ (\ a,\ b\ )\ \begin{pmatrix} nil & ? \\ ? & nil \\ cons\,(?,?) & cons\,(?,?) \end{pmatrix} \begin{pmatrix} q_1 \\ q_2 \\ q_3 \end{pmatrix}$$

The mixture rule is applicable in the first column. The constructor *nil* matches rows 1 and 2, and *cons* matches rows 2 and 3. The constructors are exhaustive, so there is no default case.

$$q_0 = \mathtt{test}\ a\ (nil \Rightarrow match_1)\ (cons\,(a1, a2) \Rightarrow match_2)$$

and new calls:

$$match_1\ (\ b\ )\ \begin{pmatrix} ? \\ nil \end{pmatrix} \begin{pmatrix} q_1 \\ q_2 \end{pmatrix}$$

$$match_2\ (\ a1,\ a2,\ b\ )\ \begin{pmatrix} ? & ? & nil \\ ? & ? & cons\,(?,?) \end{pmatrix} \begin{pmatrix} q_2 \\ q_3 \end{pmatrix}$$

Notice how the wildcard in column 1, row 2, was split into two wildcards to make it compatible with the two new sub-patterns from the *cons* in row 3.

Considering $match_1$ this is a case for the variable rule. It immediately reduces to q_1.

Considering $match_2$, this is a case for the mixture rule in column 3. The *nil* constructor only matches row 1, and *cons* row 2. Again, there is no default case.

$$q_4 = \texttt{test } b \ (nil => match_3) \ (cons(b1, b2) => match_4)$$

and new calls:

$$match_3 \ (\ a1, \ a2 \ ) \ (\ ? \quad ? \ ) \ (\ q_2 \ )$$

$$match_4 \ (\ b1, \ b2, \ a1, \ a2 \ ) \ (\ ? \quad ? \quad ? \quad ? \ ) \ (\ q_3 \ )$$

For both of the new matches, the variable rule is applicable, and they reduce to their respective first final states.

The final automaton is:

$$q_0 = \texttt{test } a \ (nil => q_1) \ (cons(a1, a2) => q_4)$$
$$q_1 = \texttt{final } \{b\} \ E1'$$
$$q_2 = \texttt{final } \{a\} \ E2'$$
$$q_3 = \texttt{final } \{a1, a2, b1, b2\} \ E3'$$
$$q_4 = \texttt{test } b \ (nil => q_2) \ (cons(b1, b2) => q_3)$$

Step 3: Optimization

In this example, no state merging can be made.

Step 4: Intermediate Code

```
fun demo a b =
  case a
    of nil                => E1'
     | cons(a1, a2)        =>
         case b
           of nil          => E2'
            | cons(b1, b2) => E3'
```

7.6.2   The unwieldy Function

```
fun unwieldy [] [] = E1
  | unwieldy xs ys = E2
```

Step 1: Preprocessing

Again we use a and b as the root variables. The result of preprocessing is:

$$\mathbf{o} = (\; a, \; b \;)$$

$$\mathbf{P} = \begin{pmatrix} nil & nil \\ ? & ? \end{pmatrix}$$

$$\mathbf{q} = \begin{pmatrix} q_1 = \texttt{final E1} \\ q_2 = \texttt{final } \{a, b\} \texttt{ E2'} \end{pmatrix}$$

$$\texttt{E2'} = \texttt{E2}[xs \mapsto a, ys \mapsto b]$$

Step 2: Generating the DFA

$$match_0 \; (\; a, \; b \;) \; \begin{pmatrix} nil & nil \\ ? & ? \end{pmatrix} \begin{pmatrix} q_1 \\ q_2 \end{pmatrix}$$

The mixture rule is applicable in the first column. The constructor *nil* matches rows 1 and 2. As *nil* is not exhaustive, there is a default arc for the wildcard rows (row 2).

$$q_0 = \texttt{test } a \; (nil \; \texttt{=>} \; match_1) \; match_2$$

and new calls:

$$match_1 \; (\; b \;) \; \begin{pmatrix} nil \\ ? \end{pmatrix} \begin{pmatrix} q_1 \\ q_2 \end{pmatrix}$$

$$match_2 \; (\; b \;) \; (\; ? \;) \; (\; q_2 \;)$$

Considering $match_2$ first, this is a case for the variable rule, so it reduces to q_2.

Considering $match_1$, this is a case for the mixture rule in column 1. The *nil* constructor matches rows 1 and 2, but is not exhaustive, so there will be a default arc for the wildcard rows, i.e. row 2.

$$q_3 = \texttt{test } b \; (nil \; \texttt{=>} \; match_3) \; match_4$$

and new calls:

$$match_3 \; (\;) \; (\;) \; \begin{pmatrix} q_1 \\ q_2 \end{pmatrix}$$

$$match_4 \; (\;) \; (\;) \; (\; q_2 \;)$$

The variable rule is applicable in both cases, so $match_3$ reduces to q_1 and $match_4$ to q_2. The final automaton is:

$$q_0 = \texttt{test } a \; (nil \; \texttt{=>} \; q_3) \; q_2$$
$$q_1 = \texttt{final E1}$$
$$q_2 = \texttt{final } \{a, b\} \texttt{ E2'}$$
$$q_3 = \texttt{test } b \; (nil \; \texttt{=>} \; q_1) \; q_2$$

Step 3: Optimization

Note that there are two references to state q_2. No states can be merged.

Step 4: Intermediate Code

State q_2 has multiple references, so it is made into a local procedure. It has free variables $\{a, b\}$ from the renaming in step 1.

```
fun unwieldy a b =
  let fun q2(a,b) = E2'
  in
    case a
      of nil            =>
            (case b
               of nil    => E1
                | _      => q2(a,b))
        | _              => q2(a,b)
  end
```

7.6.3   State Merging

We now show an example where state merging actually occurs. Consider:

```
case (x,y,z)
  of (_::_,true,_    ) => A
   | (_,    _,  SOME _) => B
   | (_,    _,  NONE ) => C
```

Preprocessing

Preprocessing results in:

$$o = \begin{pmatrix} x & y & z \end{pmatrix}$$

$$P = \begin{pmatrix} cons(?,?) & true & ? \\ ? & ? & SOME(?) \\ ? & ? & NONE \end{pmatrix}$$

$$q = \begin{pmatrix} q_1 = \text{final } A \\ q_2 = \text{final } B \\ q_3 = \text{final } C \end{pmatrix}$$

Generating the DFA

$$match_0 \begin{pmatrix} x & y & z \end{pmatrix} \begin{pmatrix} cons(?,?) & true & ? \\ ? & ? & SOME(?) \\ ? & ? & NONE \end{pmatrix} \begin{pmatrix} q_1 \\ q_2 \\ q_3 \end{pmatrix}$$

The mixture rule is applicable in column 1. *cons* matches rows 1, 2, and 3. *cons* is not exhaustive, so there is a default case for rows 2 and 3.

$$q_0 = \text{test } x \ (cons\,(x1\,,x2) \Rightarrow match_1) \ match_2$$

and new calls:

$$match_1 \ (\ x1 \quad x2 \quad y \quad z\ ) \ \begin{pmatrix} ? & ? & true & ? \\ ? & ? & ? & SOME\,(?) \\ ? & ? & ? & NONE \end{pmatrix} \begin{pmatrix} q_1 \\ q_2 \\ q_3 \end{pmatrix}$$

$$match_2 \ (\ y \quad z\ ) \ \begin{pmatrix} ? & SOME\,(?) \\ ? & NONE \end{pmatrix} \begin{pmatrix} q_2 \\ q_3 \end{pmatrix}$$

Considering $match_1$, the mixture rule is applicable in column 3. It becomes:

$$q_4 = \text{test } y \ (true \Rightarrow match_3) \ match_4$$

and new calls:

$$match_3 \ (\ x1 \quad x2 \quad z\ ) \ \begin{pmatrix} ? & ? & ? \\ ? & ? & SOME\,(?) \\ ? & ? & NONE \end{pmatrix} \begin{pmatrix} q_1 \\ q_2 \\ q_3 \end{pmatrix}$$

$$match_4 \ (\ x1 \quad x2 \quad z\ ) \ \begin{pmatrix} ? & ? & SOME\,(?) \\ ? & ? & NONE \end{pmatrix} \begin{pmatrix} q_2 \\ q_3 \end{pmatrix}$$

For $match_3$ the variable rule applies, so it reduces to q_1.
For $match_4$, the mixture rule applies in column 3. It becomes:

$$q_5 = \text{test } z \ (SOME\,(z1) \Rightarrow match_5) \ (NONE \Rightarrow match_6)$$

and new calls:

$$match_5 \ (\ x1 \quad x2 \quad z1\ ) \ (\ ? \quad ? \quad ?\ ) \ (\ q_2\ )$$

$$match_6 \ (\ x1 \quad x2\ ) \ (\ ? \quad ?\ ) \ (\ q_3\ )$$

For both of these, the variable rule applies, and they reduce to q_2 and q_3 respectively.

Going back to $match_2$, the mixture rule applies in column 2. It becomes:

$$q_6 = \text{test } z \ (SOME\,(z1) \Rightarrow match_7) \ (NONE \Rightarrow match_8)$$

and new calls:

$$match_7 \ (\ y \quad z1\ ) \ (\ ? \quad ?\ ) \ (\ q_2\ )$$

$$match_8 \ (\ y\ ) \ (\ ?\ ) \ (\ q_3\ )$$

For both of these, the variable rule applies, and they reduce to q_2 and q_3 respectively. The final automaton is:

$$q_0 = \text{test } x \ (cons(x1,x2) => q_4) \ q_6$$
$$q_1 = \text{final } A$$
$$q_2 = \text{final } B$$
$$q_3 = \text{final } C$$
$$q_4 = \text{test } y \ (true => q_1) \ q_5$$
$$q_5 = \text{test } z \ (SOME(z1) => q_2) \ (NONE => q_3)$$
$$q_6 = \text{test } z \ (SOME(z1) => q_2) \ (NONE => q_3)$$

Optimization

q_6 is equivalent to q_5. We remove q_6 and change q_0 to:

$$q_0 = \text{test } x \ (cons(x1,x2) => q_4) \ q_5$$

The resulting automaton is shown in Figure 7.2.

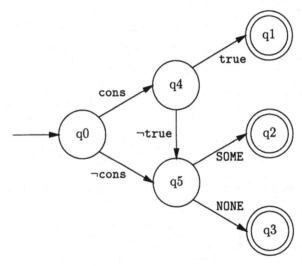

Figure 7.2: Automaton with a shared state

Intermediate Code

q_5, being a shared state, becomes a local procedure. Here we see that our technique not only guarantees non-duplication of right-hand sides, but also sometimes is able to share discrimination code (state q_5).

```
let fun q5() =
        case z
            of SOME z1 => B
```

```
              | NONE => C
    in
      case x
        of (x1::x2) =>
            (case y
                of true => A
                 | _ => q5())
         | _ => q5()
    end
```

7.7 Implementation Notes

7.7.1 Data Representation

Like most published term pattern-matching algorithms, this algorithm compiles complex pattern-matching to simple patterns, i.e. patterns with no nested constructors. An actual implementation should however go one step further and also consider low-level representation issues before emitting the final intermediate code. In particular, the application of a `datatype` constructor can be represented in several different ways depending on the rest of its `datatype` declaration. See [6] and [37] for further information about representation choices. It should be noted though that such representation optimizations are often limited to statically-typed and strict languages like Standard ML or RML. Lazy languages implemented by graph reduction often choose uniform representations in order to speed up the reduction process (see e.g. [142]).

A special case deserves to be mentioned here. Simple `case`-expressions whose patterns are the constructors of a `datatype` can often execute in $O(1)$ time by the use of jump tables. The implementation of simple `case`-expressions has been studied in the context of ordinary imperative languages, see e.g. Bernstein's article [21] and the followup [98].

7.7.2 Compile-Time Warnings

The definition of Standard ML [121, Section 4.11] requires the compiler to emit a warning if a patterm-match is not *exhaustive* and *irredundant*. These conditions are easily checked by inspecting the reference counts of the final states in the automaton. If the failure state has a non-zero reference count, then the match can fail, and the non-exhaustiveness message is triggered. If any final state corresponding to a right-hand side expression has a zero reference count, then that expression can never be evaluated, and the patterns must be redundant.

7.7.3   Matching Exceptions

In Standard ML it is possible to have different names for the same exception constructor. In the following example,

```
exception E1
exception E2 = E1

fun f(E1) = 1
  | f(E2) = 2
  | f(_)  = 3
```

f should never return 2. This implies that a linear sequence of tests is necessary at runtime. In the mixture rule, the order of the generated arcs *must* follow the order of the corresponding patterns in the selected column. And this order must be preserved when the state is mapped to the compiler's intermediate representation.

7.7.4   Guarded Patterns

Some functional languages have patterns with *guards*. For an equation to be selected, the patterns must match and the guard must evaluate to true. For example, in Erlang [9] one can write:

```
func([X|_]) when integer(X) -> E1;
func([_|_]) -> E2;
func([]) -> E3.
```

to distinguish between non-empty lists starting with an integer, other non-empty lists, and the empty list.

Compiling guarded patterns causes no problems for our algorithm. The q parameter to *match* becomes a vector of pairs (*optional guard, state*). The variable rule is augmented as follows:

$$match\ \mathbf{o}\ (\quad)\ (\quad)\ \Rightarrow\ q_{\text{fail}}$$

$$match\ \mathbf{o}\ \begin{pmatrix} ? & ? & \cdots \\ & \cdots & \end{pmatrix} \begin{pmatrix} -, q_1 \\ \cdots \end{pmatrix} \Rightarrow\ q_1$$

$$match\ \mathbf{o}\ \begin{pmatrix} ? & ? & \cdots \\ & \cdots & \end{pmatrix} \begin{pmatrix} guard_1, q_1 \\ \cdots \end{pmatrix} \Rightarrow\ q'$$

where

$$q' = \text{if } quard_1 \text{ then } q_1 \text{ else } q_2$$
$$q_2 = match\ \mathbf{o}\ (\mathbf{P} \setminus 1)\ (\mathbf{q} \setminus 1)$$

The pattern-match compiler simply views the guards as opaque patterns. An if state becomes a conditional, in the obvious way.

7.8 Related Work

There are both interesting similarities and differences between this and the standard algorithm. Both operate on a matrix of patterns, repeatedly choosing a column on which to perform a discrimination test, and continuing with several smaller matches. The primary difference, apart from this algorithm's use of occurrences instead of random temporary variables, and an explicit intermediate data structure, appears to be the treatment of matching failure. The standard algorithm uses a third argument to *match*, which acts as a 'failure continuation'. In the sub-matches generated by the mixture rule, the fail expression is defined by the continued matching on the bottom part of the pattern matrix (from the first variable and downwards) (or DEFAULT if backtracking is used). This is why the same part of the input can be inspected multiple times. In contrast, the algorithm described here always considers *all* the rows that might match at the same time. It is possible that this may cause an exponential increase in the number of states of the DFA (analogously to when nondeterministic finite automata are converted to deterministic ones), although this has not yet been observed in practice.

Our idea that a non-variable pattern is *matched* against the pattern column, producing a set containing both the patterns with the same top-level structure and the wildcard patterns, was also used by Ophel [128]. He, too, attempted to improve upon the standard mixture rule, but did not recognize the connection with regular expressions and finite automata. Therefore, he was only able to deal successfully with the demo function, but not with the unwieldy function.

We have deliberately ignored the issue of how to make *good* choices of columns when the variable rule does not apply. Baudinet and MacQueen have an unpublished paper discussing this [18]. Since the general problem is NP-complete, they present some heuristics, although they have no hard data to back up their particular choices.

Lazy languages sometimes use a predefined top-down left-right inspection ordering to make it easy to see the termination properties of a particular match. Some prefer 'maximally lazy' semantics, and have studied the problem of producing such orderings, see for example [150].

The inspiration for viewing patterns as regular expressions and generating automata from them, came from a classic paper by Hoffman and O'Donnell on *tree* pattern matching [88].

In step 4, we simply make procedures of shared states, bound at the top-level of the generated expression. A different approach would be to bind a shared state in the expression corresponding to its *nearest common dominator*. A dominator for node n in a rooted directed graph, is a node n' such that every path from the root to n passes through n' [3]. The *nearest* dominator in a rooted DAG is a dominator n' such that there is no other dominator n'' on the path from n' to n. Chu has described an optimal algorithm for computing nearest dominators [43].

Using this approach, one may reduce the number of parameters that have to be passed to the procedures corresponding to shared states. This is because some of the state's free variables may already be in scope at the point the procedure is bound. Due to the added implementation complexity, we have not pursued this alternative.

7.9 Modifications for RML

Operationally, RML differs from an ordinary strict functional language in two respects: the use of backtracking and the presence of logical variables.

Backtracking means that several rules may be applicable for some input. For instance, in

$$\frac{\rho \vdash e_1 \Rightarrow true \quad \rho \vdash e_2 \Rightarrow v}{\rho \vdash \text{if } e_1 \text{ then } e_2 \text{ else } e_3 \Rightarrow v} \tag{1}$$

$$\frac{\rho \vdash e_1 \Rightarrow false \quad \rho \vdash e_3 \Rightarrow v}{\rho \vdash \text{if } e_1 \text{ then } e_2 \text{ else } e_3 \Rightarrow v} \tag{2}$$

when the pattern if e_1 then e_2 else e_3 has been matched and the first rule been entered, if e_1 evaluates to non-*true*, then we must backtrack to the next rule whose pattern matched the input, i.e. rule (2).

In the *match* algorithm, this manifests itself in the structure of the DFAs and the variable rule. There is a new kind of state, orelse q_1 q_2, that operationally behaves like a disjunction: a backtracking point is created, and the code for q_1 is executed. Any failures cause backtracking to the code for q_2. The variable rule becomes:

$$match \text{ o } (\quad) (\quad) \quad \Rightarrow \quad q_{\text{fail}}$$

$$match \text{ o } (\text{ ? } \text{ ? } \cdots) (\text{ } q_1 \text{ }) \quad \Rightarrow \quad q_1$$

$$match \text{ o } \begin{pmatrix} \text{ ? } & \text{ ? } & \cdots \\ & \cdots & \end{pmatrix} \begin{pmatrix} q_1 \\ \cdots \end{pmatrix} \quad \Rightarrow \quad q'$$

where

$$q' \quad = \quad \text{orelse } q_1 \ q_2$$
$$q_2 \quad = \quad match \text{ o } (\mathbf{P} \setminus 1) \ (\mathbf{q} \setminus 1)$$

(Note the great similarity with the sketch for compiling guarded patterns in a functional language.)

Note that q_1 is a *final* state corresponding to the 'continuation' after the pattern, for instance the premises of an inference rule. A failed execution of q_1 brings control back into the automaton (q_2) in order to allow other patterns to be considered. The pattern matching code itself never uses backtracking. (Suspending and resuming the automaton is not a problem since rml2c uses CPS in the following phase.)

Logical variables force values to be *dereferenced* before being inspected. We do this by associating *two* occurrences with every non-wildcard pattern. If o is the occurrence of the value, then $o!$ is the occurrence of the dereferenced value. Furthermore, $(o!)_1, \cdots, (o!)_n$ are used as the occurrences of the sub-values. In step 4 of the algorithm, when translating a test state for occurrence o, the generated code will dereference o, bind the result to $o!$, and then use $o!$ for the actual discrimination test.

Since any value can be unbound, and thus fail to match, exhaustiveness testing is not done: every test state will have a default arc.

When the pattern-match compiler dereferences a value, it knows if that value is immediate or boxed. In our RML runtime system, dereferencing a boxed value is simpler and more efficient than dereferencing an immediate value. Because of this, our `rml2c` compiler uses boxed representations for all constructors (including the constants) in a `datatype`, unless there are *only* constants. Using the optimized dereferencing operator whenever possible made the code generated by `rml2c` about 4% faster.

7.10 Experiences and Conclusions

The algorithm presented here, with refinements for exploiting the actual representations of various datatypes, has been implemented six times by this author. First as an initial prototype based on the original presentation [133], followed by implementations in three actual compilers, for Scheme, SML, and RML. Then as a new prototype based on the improved presentation here, followed by an implementation in a compiler for Erlang.

Having previously implemented the Augustsson/Wadler algorithm, we feel that the present algorithm was definitely easier to implement and debug, especially when various optimizations or language-specific modifications were added. We believe this can be attributed both to the simple ideas and operations underlying the algorithm, and the use of an explicit *intermediate* representation.

Chapter 8

Compiling Continuations

$\mathcal{T}$he logical representation, FOL, is useful for very high-level transformations, such as the determinacy-improving ones. It does not, however, expose any of the actual *mechanisms* used to implement specifications. In the final code, these mechanisms are *too* explicit, making optimizations more difficult. A continuation-passing style (CPS) representation sits in between these extremes, allowing operational behaviour to be expressed and manipulated in a declarative framework: the call-by-value λ-calculus.

This chapter describes the CPS representation and the transformations that are applied at this level. Then it turns to the low-level representation, which we call *Code*. (N.B. this is *not* machine code.) The translation from CPS to Code is outlined, as is a simple optimization applied to the Code level. Then a straightforward realization of Code as portable C code is presented. A code generation example displays the CPS and C code representations of a simple RML relation. (Chapter 9 deals with more elaborate techniques for representing low-level code in C.)

This chapter is partially based on an earlier presentation of the rml2c compiler [136].

8.1 Properties of CPS

The λ-calculus is quite simple: it has applications, abstractions (anonymous functions), variables, and usually some set of constants; evaluation is described by the β-reduction rule. CPS is a subset of the λ-calculus whose essential feature is that functions and arguments in applications must be *values*, not expressions. The CPS calculus is summarized in Figure 8.1.

CPS enjoys a number of useful properties, which we summarize below:

- It is *complete*: all λ-expressions can be encoded in CPS.

- Function application in CPS uses call-by-value evaluation, which has

$x \in Var$ variables
$v \in Val ::= x \mid \lambda x.e$ values
$e \in Exp ::= v_1 \, v_2 \mid v$ expressions

$(\lambda x.e) \, v \Rightarrow e[x \mapsto v]$ β_{CPS}

let $x = v$ **in** $e \equiv (\lambda x.e) \, v$ syntactic sugar

Figure 8.1: CPS calculus

a simple and efficient realization. This is in contrast to the plain λ-calculus, whose function application corresponds to call-by-name evaluation.

- Since CPS is a subset of the call-by-value λ-calculus, the reduction rules of the latter apply also to the former. Other representations typically do not have such simple interpretations. To invent, and validate, optimization rules for those representations requires more work by a compiler writer.

- Since evaluation order is explicit and intermediate results are bound to variables, CPS is no more complex than traditional representations using quadruples or register transfers. CPS can be viewed as a kind of assembly language.

- The practicality of using CPS in compilers has been demonstrated several times in the context of (semi-)functional languages [7,8,99,105,166].

Compilers for functional languages sometimes use so-called 'direct-style' (DS) representations that are close in structure to the (abstract) syntax of the languages. Some research has indicated that using CPS instead of DS can produce better results in abstract interpretation and partial evaluation [47, 123].

Recently however, other research has shown that CPS and DS are *incomparable* when performing static analysis [156, 157]: either may lead to better results than the other. In spite of this, the simplicity of CPS and its closeness to the call-by-value λ-calculus make it superior to plain DS. An alternative representation, the *A-normal form*, has been proposed [66]. It has a guaranteed simple structure, like CPS, but does not introduce continuations for function calls.

The original definition of RML made the proof search procedure equivalent to that in Prolog. To allow control flow optimizations, we decided that CPS would be the most appropriate representation. A recent change to RML (see Section 3.4) has simplified control flow slightly. It would now be possible to use a DS representation with SML-like exception operators instead of CPS, although this has not been investigated.

8.2 Translating RML to CPS

The CPS representation of RML programs is a straightforward encoding of the λ-terms occurring in the denotational semantics for backtracking in Section 3.3. Likewise, the translation to CPS follows the denotational semantics closely. The fact that RML specifications are first translated to FOL, and then translated via the pattern-match compiler to CPS, has almost no impact on the CPS representation itself.

For historical reasons, expressions denoting values rather than computations are called *trivial expressions*.

Abstractions (denoted by λ) and applications (denoted by @)[1] are *typed*, as indicated by their fc, sc, or p subscripts. For instance, $@_{sc}$ invokes success continuations. All abstractions and applications are in un-curried form, since partial applications never occur.

Pattern matching must dereference values before inspecting them, this is the reason for the *deref* operators. The untrailing of logical variables during backtracking is realized by the *marker* operator and *restore* expression.

Shared states in pattern matching automata become 'let label' expressions. Control transfers to such states become $@_{lab}$ expressions.

The primitive operators *mkref* and *mkstruct* create logical variables and composite structures respectively.

8.2.1 Data Representation

The CPS form is not *only* about control flow: data representation must also be made more concrete, so that data creation and inspection operations can be suitably optimized. The translation to CPS commits to the following design choices:

1. There are two classes of values, *immediate* and *boxed*. The first is used for integers and enumerated types, while the latter contains all structured values. The *isptr* operator can be used to distinguish between immediate and boxed values.

2. Every boxed value has a header. The header is an integer, but its representation is not specified.

3. Composite values, such as tuples or value-carrying data constructors, become boxed structures. A structure's header has room for a small integer tag, which is used for pattern-matching. A tuple has tag zero.

4. Logical variables are represented as boxed *references*. Unbound references have a special header that is different from any actual value's header. The *deref* operators dereference logical variables; for efficiency

---

[1]The use of @ to denote application seems to be traditional in the lazy functional programming community [142].

Abstract syntax

$i \in Int$ integers

$r \in Real$ reals

$s \in String$ strings

$x \in Var$ variables

$lab \in Lab$ local labels

$proc \in Proc$ procedure names

$w \in Word ::= \textbf{\textit{fixnum}}\ i\ |\ \textbf{\textit{structhdr}}\ i_{\text{len}}\ i_{\text{tag}}$ integer words
$\quad\quad\quad\quad |\ \textbf{\textit{realhdr}}\ |\ \textbf{\textit{stringhdr}}\ i_{\text{len}}$

$c \in Const ::= w\ |\ r\ |\ s$ constants

$lit \in Lit\quad ::= \textbf{\textit{const}}\ c\ |\ \textbf{\textit{struct}}\ i_{\text{tag}}\ lit^*$ literals

$uop \in UOP ::= \textbf{\textit{derefimm}}\ |\ \textbf{\textit{derefbox}}\ |\ \textbf{\textit{isptr}}$ unary operators
$\quad\quad\quad\quad |\ \textbf{\textit{fetch}}\ i_{\text{off}}\ |\ \textbf{\textit{bool\_not}}\ |\ \textbf{\textit{int\_neg}}\ |\ \textbf{\textit{int\_abs}}$

$bop \in BOP\ ::= \textbf{\textit{unify}}\ |\ \textbf{\textit{bool\_and}}\ |\ \textbf{\textit{bool\_or}}$ binary operators
$\quad\quad\quad\quad |\ \textbf{\textit{int\_add}}\ |\ \textbf{\textit{int\_sub}}\ |\ \textbf{\textit{int\_mul}}\ |\ \textbf{\textit{int\_div}}\ |\ \textbf{\textit{int\_mod}}$
$\quad\quad\quad\quad |\ \textbf{\textit{int\_max}}\ |\ \textbf{\textit{int\_min}}\ |\ \textbf{\textit{int\_lt}}\ |\ \textbf{\textit{int\_le}}\ |\ \textbf{\textit{int\_eq}}$
$\quad\quad\quad\quad |\ \textbf{\textit{int\_ne}}\ |\ \textbf{\textit{int\_ne}}\ |\ \textbf{\textit{int\_ge}}\ |\ \textbf{\textit{int\_gt}}$

$o \in POpr ::= \textbf{\textit{marker}}$ primitive operations
$\quad\quad\quad\quad |\ \textbf{\textit{mkref}}$
$\quad\quad\quad\quad |\ \textbf{\textit{mkstruct}}\ i_{\text{tag}}\ t^*$
$\quad\quad\quad\quad |\ \textbf{\textit{unary}}\ uop\ t$
$\quad\quad\quad\quad |\ \textbf{\textit{binary}}\ bop\ t_1\ t_2$

$t \in TExp ::= x$ trivial expressions
$\quad\quad\quad\quad |\ lit$
$\quad\quad\quad\quad |\ \lambda_{\text{fc}}().e$
$\quad\quad\quad\quad |\ \lambda_{\text{sc}}(x^*).e$

$e \in Exp\quad ::= @_{\text{fc}}\ t_{\text{fc}}$ cps expressions
$\quad\quad\quad\quad |\ @_{\text{sc}}\ t_{\text{sc}}\ t^*$
$\quad\quad\quad\quad |\ @_{\text{p}}\ proc\ t^*\ t_{\text{fc}}\ t_{\text{sc}}$
$\quad\quad\quad\quad |\ @_{\text{lab}}\ lab\ t^*$
$\quad\quad\quad\quad |\ \textbf{\textit{let}}\ lab(x^*) = e_1\ \textbf{\textit{in}}\ e_2$
$\quad\quad\quad\quad |\ \textbf{\textit{let}}\ x = t\ \textbf{\textit{in}}\ e$
$\quad\quad\quad\quad |\ \textbf{\textit{let}}\ x = o\ \textbf{\textit{in}}\ e$
$\quad\quad\quad\quad |\ \textbf{\textit{let}}\ (x_{\text{deref}}, x_{\text{hdr}}) = \textbf{\textit{inspectbox}}\ t\ \textbf{\textit{in}}\ e$
$\quad\quad\quad\quad |\ \textbf{\textit{restore}}\ t\ e$
$\quad\quad\quad\quad |\ \textbf{\textit{switch}}\ t\ (c:e)^*\ e_{\text{def}}$

$Prog\ ::= (proc = \lambda_{\text{p}}(x^*, x_{\text{fc}}, x_{\text{sc}}).e)^+$ programs

Figure 8.2: Summary of CPS representation

reasons, there are different operators for immediate and boxed types. Also for efficiency reasons, there is a special *inspectbox* construct that both dereferences a boxed value and fetches its header.

Choosing representations for user-declared `datatypes` is done as follows:

1. If no constructor takes any arguments, then the datatype is treated as an enumerated type. The constructors become small integers.

   The built-in boolean type, defined as

   ```
   datatype bool = false | true
   ```

   represents `false` as 0 and `true` as 1.

2. A value-carrying constructor will be represented as a boxed object, containing a tag and the argument values.

3. If there is a mix of constant and value-carrying constructors, then *all* constructors are represented as boxed objects. The tags are small integers.

   This is intended to make data inspection more efficient, for two reasons. First, inspecting a data type whose values can be either immediate or boxed requires an *isptr* test, followed by separate tests for the immediate and boxed cases. Second, due to logical variables all values must be dereferenced before inspection. The generic dereference operator is less efficient than the one specialized for boxed values. The representation of a boxed constant constructor becomes a static literal, causing no dynamic allocation overhead.

   The built-in list type, defined as

   ```
   datatype 'a list = nil | cons of 'a * 'a list
   ```

   represents `nil` as a one-element structure with tag 0. A `cons` is a three-element structure with tag 1.

4. If there is just a single constructor, and it takes a single value, then it is not represented at all.

   This means that simple 'type wrappers' such as

   ```
   datatype tag = TAG of int
   ```

   do not cause any allocation or matching overheads.

8.2.2   Local Optimizations on CPS

Figures 8.3 to 8.5 show the transformations currently used by RML's CPS optimizer. The rules assume that all bound variables have unique names, and thus that substitution is trivial. This condition is easily maintained.

The first group, shown in Figure 8.3, attempts to discover when primitive operators can be replaced by constants. The first rule is by far the most important, since it identifies source-level constant data structures.

For trivial expressions, only one optimization is attempted: η-reduction. Often, other optimizations make it possible to turn the last procedure call in a procedure's body into a tailcall (c.f. last-call optimization in Prolog).

Figure 8.5 lists the rules for simplifying CPS expressions. Most of these are essentially compile-time β-reductions: inlining continuations and procedures, propagating constants and variables, deleting unused values. As a basis for inlining and removal decisions, reference counts are needed on all continuations, procedures, labels, and bound variables. This requires a simple, per-module, reference count analysis. A procedure exported from a module is considered to have an infinite number of uses.

In several cases, trivial expressions are removed when their values are unused. As a benefit of CPS, these expressions are known to have no side-effects, so deleting them cannot affect evaluation.

8.3   Translating CPS to Code

The purpose of the translation from CPS to Code is to realize high-level or implicit operations at a level corresponding to machine resources. While keeping the simple structure of CPS, the Code level makes storage allocation and initialization, allocation of literals, parameter passing, and pointer tagging explicit. See Figure 8.6 for the definition of the Code representation.

8.3.1   Control

Every CPS continuation, label, and procedure becomes a *Code label*. Every application expression becomes a *tailcall* to a value that is a Code label.

Before a call, ordinary (non-continuation) arguments are evaluated and placed in the global argument variables (*A0* etc.) using the *bind* operator. A success continuation argument is placed in the *SC* variable, and a failure continuation is placed in *FC*. Then a *tailcall* is performed to branch to the target label. The body of this label will fetch its parameters from the global argument and continuation variables into local variables. The reason for using global variables is that tailcalls must usually be *emulated*, and so ordinary function parameter passing cannot be used.

Continuations in general have free variables; therefore they are represented as *closure records*. A closure contains a code label in its first field,

(1)	$[\![mkstruct\ i_{\text{tag}}\ lit^*]\!]$	$\Rightarrow$	$[\![struct\ i_{\text{tag}}\ lit^*]\!]$
(2)	$[\![unary\ derefimm\ lit]\!]$	$\Rightarrow$	$[\![lit]\!]$
(3)	$[\![unary\ derefbox\ lit]\!]$	$\Rightarrow$	$[\![lit]\!]$
(4)	$[\![unary\ (fetch\ 0)\ (const\ r)]\!]$	$\Rightarrow$	$[\![const\ realhdr]\!]$
(5)	$[\![unary\ (fetch\ 0)\ (const\ s)]\!]$ $[\![const\ (stringhdr\ i_{\text{len}})]\!]$ where i_{len} is the length of s	$\Rightarrow$	
(6)	$[\![unary\ (fetch\ 0)\ (struct\ i_{\text{tag}}\ lit^*)]\!]$ $[\![const\ (structhdr\ i_{\text{len}}\ i_{\text{tag}})]\!]$ where i_{len} is the length of lit^*	$\Rightarrow$	
(7)	$[\![unary\ (fetch\ i)\ (struct\ i_{\text{tag}}\ \cdots\ lit_i\ \cdots)]\!] \Rightarrow [\![lit_i]\!]$		
(8)	$[\![unary\ isptr\ (const\ w)]\!]$	$\Rightarrow$	$[\![const(fixnum\ 0)]\!]$
(9)	$[\![unary\ isptr\ (const\ r)]\!]$	$\Rightarrow$	$[\![const(fixnum\ 1)]\!]$
(10)	$[\![unary\ isptr\ (const\ s)]\!]$	$\Rightarrow$	$[\![const(fixnum\ 1)]\!]$
(11)	$[\![unary\ isptr\ (struct\ i_{\text{tag}}\ lit^*)]\!]$	$\Rightarrow$	$[\![const(fixnum\ 1)]\!]$

Figure 8.3: Simplifying primitive operations

(12)	$[\![\lambda_{\text{fc}}().@_{\text{fc}}\ t_{\text{fc}}]\!]\quad \Rightarrow t_{\text{fc}}$
(13)	$[\![\lambda_{\text{sc}}(x^*).@_{\text{sc}}\ t_{\text{sc}}\ x^*]\!] \Rightarrow t_{\text{sc}}$ if no x in x^* occurs free in t_{sc}

Figure 8.4: Simplifying trivial expressions

(14) $[\![@_{\text{fc}} \ (\lambda_{\text{fc}}().e)]\!]$ $\qquad\qquad\qquad \Rightarrow e$

(15) $[\![@_{\text{sc}} \ (\lambda_{\text{sc}}(\langle x_1, \cdots, x_n \rangle).e) \ \langle t_1, \cdots, t_n \rangle]\!] \Rightarrow$
$[\![\textit{let} \ x_1 = t_1 \ \textit{in} \ \cdots \ \textit{let} \ x_n = t_n \ \textit{in} \ e]\!]$

(16) $[\![@_{\text{p}} \ \textit{proc} \ \langle t_1, \cdots, t_n \rangle \ t_{\text{fc}} \ t_{\text{sc}}]\!]$ $\qquad\qquad \Rightarrow$
$[\![\textit{let} \ x_1 = t_1 \ \textit{in} \ \cdots \ \textit{let} \ x_{\text{fc}} = t_{\text{fc}} \ \textit{in} \ \textit{let} \ x_{\text{sc}} = t_{\text{sc}} \ \textit{in} \ e]\!]$
if $[\![\textit{proc} = \lambda_{\text{p}}(\langle x_1, \cdots, x_n \rangle, x_{\text{fc}}, x_{\text{sc}}).e]\!] \in \textit{Prog}$,
and *proc* is used only once

(17) $[\![@_{\text{lab}} \ \textit{lab} \ \langle t_1, \cdots, t_n \rangle]\!]$ $\qquad\qquad\qquad \Rightarrow$
$[\![\textit{let} \ x_1 = t_1 \ \textit{in} \ \cdots \ \textit{let} \ x_n = t_n \ \textit{in} \ e]\!]$
if this is in the scope of $[\![\textit{let} \ \textit{lab}(\langle x_1, \cdots, x_n \rangle) = e \ \cdots]\!]$
and this was the only use of *lab*

(18) $[\![\textit{let} \ \textit{lab}(x^*) = e_1 \ \textit{in} \ e_2]\!]$ $\qquad\qquad \Rightarrow e_2$
if *lab* is unused

(19) $[\![\textit{let} \ x_1 = x_2 \ \textit{in} \ e]\!]$ $\qquad\qquad \Rightarrow e \ [x_1 \mapsto x_2]$

(20) $[\![\textit{let} \ x = l \ \textit{in} \ e]\!]$ $\qquad\qquad\qquad \Rightarrow e \ [x \mapsto l]$

(21) $[\![\textit{let} \ x = t_\lambda \ \textit{in} \ e]\!]$ $\qquad\qquad\quad \Rightarrow e \ [x \mapsto t_\lambda]$
if x is used at most once in e

(22) $[\![\textit{let} \ x = o \ \textit{in} \ e]\!]$ $\qquad\qquad\qquad \Rightarrow e$
if x is unused and o has no serious side-effect (i.e. not *unify*)

(23) $[\![\textit{let} \ (x_{\text{deref}}, x_{\text{hdr}}) = \textit{inspectbox} \ l \ \textit{in} \ e]\!] \Rightarrow$
$[\![\textit{let} \ x_{\text{deref}} = l \ \textit{in} \ \textit{let} \ x_{\text{hdr}} = \textit{unary} \ (\textit{fetch} \ 0) \ l \ \textit{in} \ e]\!]$

(24) $[\![\textit{restore} \ t \ (@_{\text{fc}} \ t_{\text{fc}})]\!]$ $\qquad\qquad \Rightarrow [\![@_{\text{fc}} \ t_{\text{fc}}]\!]$

(25) $[\![\textit{switch} \ c \ \langle \cdots (c' : e) \cdots \rangle \ e_{\text{def}}]\!]$ $\qquad \Rightarrow e$
if $c = c'$

(26) $[\![\textit{switch} \ c \ \textit{case}^* \ e_{\text{def}}]\!]$ $\qquad\qquad \Rightarrow e_{\text{def}}$
if no *case* has tag c

(27) $[\![\textit{switch} \ x \ \langle \cdots (c : e) \cdots \rangle \ e_{\text{def}}]\!]$ $\qquad \Rightarrow$
$[\![\textit{switch} \ x \ \langle \cdots (c : e \ [x \mapsto c]) \cdots \rangle \ e_{\text{def}}]\!]$

(28) $[\![\langle \cdots, \ \textit{proc} = \lambda_{\text{p}}, \ \cdots \rangle]\!]$ $\qquad \Rightarrow [\![\langle \cdots, \ \cdots \rangle]\!]$
if *proc* is unused

Figure 8.5: Simplifying CPS expressions

Abstract Syntax

$id \in Ident$		identifiers
$x \in Var$	$::= global\ id\ \mid\ local\ id$	variables
$lab \in Label$		labels
$w \in Word$	$::= fixnum\ i\ \mid\ uncoded\ i$	words
	$\mid\ structhdr\ i_{\text{len}}\ i_{\text{tag}}\ \mid\ unboundhdr$	
	$\mid\ realhdr\ \mid\ stringhdr\ i_{\text{len}}$	
$lid \in LitId$		literal 'names'
$lref \in LitRef$	$::= intval\ w\ \mid\ label\ lab$	literal references
	$\mid\ real\ lid\ \mid\ string\ lid\ \mid\ struct\ lid$	
$ldef \in LitDef$	$::= real\ r\ \mid\ string\ s$	literal definitions
	$\mid\ struct\ i_{\text{tag}}\ lref^*$	
$v \in Value$	$::= var\ x$	values
	$\mid\ rawint\ w$	
	$\mid\ literal\ lref$	
	$\mid\ offset\ v\ i$	
	$\mid\ fetch\ v$	
	$\mid\ untagptr\ v$	
	$\mid\ tagptr\ v$	
	$\mid\ call\ lab\ v^*$	
$case \in Case$	$::= w\ \mid\ r\ \mid\ s$	'case' tags
$c \in Code$	$::= tailcall\ v$	code
	$\mid\ store\ v_{\text{dst}}\ v_{\text{src}}\ ;\ c$	
	$\mid\ bind\ x_{\text{opt}}\ v\ ;\ c$	
	$\mid\ inspectbox\ x_{\text{deref}}\ x_{\text{hdr}}\ v\ ;\ c$	
	$\mid\ switch\ v\ (case : c)^*\ c_{\text{def}}$	
$def \in LabDef$	$::= labdef\ lab\ i_{\text{alloc}}\ c$	label definitions
$m \in Module$	$::= module\ (lid, lref)^*\ def^*$	modules

Auxiliaries

$SP, FC, SC, A0, A1, A2, \cdots : Var$	global variables
$deref, isptr, marker, unify, unwind, \cdots : Label$	primops

Figure 8.6: Summary of Code representation

while the remaining fields contain the values of the free variables. Continuation records are stored on a global stack – pointed to by *SP*. Creating a continuation is done by first pushing the values of its free variables onto the stack, and then pushing the code label of the continuation's body. The resulting stack pointer is used as the continuation 'value'.

To invoke a continuation, ordinary parameters are placed in the argument variables, the continuation pointer is placed in the corresponding continuation variable (*SC* or *FC* depending on whether it is a success or failure continuation), the code label is fetched from the first word of the pointed-to record, and a tailcall is made to this label. The invoked label will use the continuation variable as the new stack pointer, fetch its free variables from the record, and pop the record off the stack.

Since a continuation record only contains those variables it will need later, an effect similar to the *Environment Trimming* optimization of the WAM is achieved. The difference is that rml2c would completely pop the record and then create a new one for the next call, while the WAM would try to reuse the old record.

Non-inlined primitive CPS operators are also represented by labels. However, these labels may only be invoked by the *call* operator, as they are called recursively rather than in tailcalls. For instance, the CPS *marker* and *restore* constructs become calls to the *marker* and *unwind* labels.

8.3.2 Copy Propagation

As a result of the need to emulate tailcalls, parameters are passed through global variables. On exit from a label, it is not uncommon to find that one or more of the global variables will be assigned the same values they had on entry to the label. A simple *copy-propagation* optimization [3, Chapter 10] will discover when this happens and remove the unnecessary stores. Sometimes, the initial load can also be removed. A C compiler can in general not do this optimization, since any recursive C-level call, to a runtime primitive say, can potentially modify all global locations.

8.3.3 Memory Allocation

The CPS *mkref* and *mkstruct* operators allocate heap space. Due to the CPS *switch* control-flow construct, it is in general not possible to compute the exact amount of memory needed for a procedure or continuation body. Instead the maximum along any path from the start of the body to its end – always a *tailcall* – is used as an upper approximation.

The very first action of a translated body is to call a runtime primitive to allocate any storage it needs. A pointer to this memory block is stored in a local variable. During translation, the compiler keeps track of its current offset in the memory block. A *mkref* or *mkstruct* will become a sequence of *store* instructions to initialize the structure, before a tagged pointer to the first word is constructed to represent the value itself.

Since at most one request for memory is made in each translated body, the overhead of checking for garbage collection is kept low. Furthermore, this request is made before parameters or free variables have been loaded into local variables. Hence, should a garbage collection be necessary, all live values are reachable from known global locations. This *safe points* policy makes the interface to the memory allocation subsystem very simple [7, Section 13.2].

8.3.4   Data

To distinguish between immediate and boxed values, pointers to boxed objects are *tagged*. Consequently, pointers must be *untagged* before objects can be inspected. As in CPS, the actual encodings used for pointer tags and boxed objects' headers are not known. Symbolic operators are used instead: the *tagptr* and *untagptr* operations manipulate pointer tags, and object headers are constructed using the *Word* operators.

All forms of array indexing are translated into pointer arithmetic using the *offset* operator.

All non-immediate literals occurring in a CPS module are collected into a set. Equivalent literals are merged. A reference to a structured literal becomes a *typed*[2] reference to the *name* bound to the literal.

8.4   Translating Code to C

Translating Code to C is basically straightforward: global (local) variables become global (local) C variables, the stack and trail[3] are implemented as global arrays, values become C expressions, code becomes sequences of C statements, and structured literals become statically allocated C data structures.

The only technical problems are how to represent labels and how to implement tailcalls. Labels are essentially *code addresses* and tailcalls are gotos. Because of tail-recursiveness, the C stack cannot be used for calls or parameter passing. Some languages allow *functions* to be passed around as first-class values; a standard solution is therefore to represent labels as parameterless functions [166, 171]. To control the execution, a *dispatch* function calls the first label (i.e. function). When it exits with a tailcall, the target label (a function) is *returned* back to the dispatcher, which loops to call the new

---

[2]This is a workaround for machines where `double` has stricter alignment than `void*`. The ANSI-C standard [5] defines *alignment* as "a requirement that objects of a particular type be located on storage boundaries with addresses that are particular multiples of a byte address." On modern RISC machines, the "multiple" is usually 2^n for simple values, where n is the size in bytes of the value.

[3]The trail records bindings of logical variables that are to be undone during backtracking; see also Section 3.3.3.

function, and so on. In C, function pointers are used to represent labels. Parameters and results are passed in global variables and/or a simulated stack. (Chapter 9 discusses this and several other schemes for implementing tailcalls.)

8.4.1 Data Representation

The generated C code *still* does not 'know' anything about actual data representation. All representation-level operations and all primitive operators become calls to macros that hide the actual details. However, the runtime system uses essentially the same representation on all machines.

Values are tagged machine words, normally 32 or 64 bits, represented as the C void* type. Boxed data objects are required to be aligned on even addresses. Immediate values are integers shifted up one step, hence their lowest bit is zero. Tagging the address of a boxed object is done by adding 3 to the (even) address, which results in an odd value.[4] (For a good survey of tagging options, see [71].)

Boxed objects are sequences of words. The first word is a header: the high 24 (or 56) bits contain the number of data words in the object, and the low 8 bits are a tag used by the garbage collector, other parts of the runtime system, and the application itself. Since RML is statically typed, the tag is not used to distinguish one type from another, but to convey representation information to the collector or to the application. A single bit in the tag distinguishes string-like objects (strings and floating-point numbers) from structures. The interpretation of the other bits depends on the type of the object. User-defined datatypes use the remaining bits as 'case tags' for pattern-matching.

A string needs to record its length in bytes, but the high bits of the header only record its length in words. Hence, the high bits of the tag (adjacent to the low bit of the word length) are specially encoded. On a 32-bit machine, the high $24 + 2$ bits of a string's header are defined as $n + 4$, where n is the string's length in bytes. (For compatibility with 'foreign' C functions, the last character in a string is always followed by a zero byte.) The string's byte length is thus retrieved by down-shifting the header 6 steps, and then subtracting 4.

8.4.2 Memory Management

Memory is managed by a simple generational copying garbage collector. The younger generation is a fixed *allocation arena* (a.k.a. *nursery*). The older generation is split into two regions, *current* and *reserve*. When the nursery is full, a minor collection is performed to copy live objects from the nursery to the current older region. When that one fills up, all live data is copied to the reserve older region, and the rôles of these regions are interchanged. (More

---

[4] Any small positive odd offset may be used. The value 3 is my personal preference, for obscure historical reasons.

information on garbage collection can be found in Wilson's survey [179]. Logic programming languages have additional problems, see for example [20] or [23].)

8.5 A Code Generation Example

Figures 8.7 to 8.10 show a simple RML relation, and its CPS and C representations. The RML relation, which maps a tuple of integers to their sum as a one-element list, incorporates most important operational features: data inspection, continuation creation and invocation, calling mechanisms, and storage allocation.

```
relation test =
  rule  int_add(x, y) => z
        ----------------
        test((x,y)) => [z]
end
```

Figure 8.7: Code generation example: RML source

The CPS version illustrates the control flow and some details about data layout. The empty list ('#(0)) is a structure with 0 data slots and tag 0, while a cons cell has 2 data slots and tag 1. A plain n-tuple is represented as a structure with n slots and tag 0. (In reality, the call to int_add would be inlined and replaced by a few tests and an int_add operator. We keep this sub-optimal version in order to illustrate continuation manipulations.)

The C code illustrates the use of global variables for parameter passing, how continuation closures are represented as stack-allocated records, explicit heap allocation and structure initialization, and pointer tagging and untagging.

```
(define (test v102 fc100 sc101)
  ;; v102 is a tuple of integers
  ;; fc100 is the failure continuation
  ;; sc101 is the success continuation
  ;; first dereference and fetch header, bind v103 to
  ;; the dereferenced value and v104 to its header
  (let (([v103 v104] (inspectbox v102)))
  ;; inspect header
  (switch v104
    ((STRUCTHDR 2 0)
      ;; argument was a 2-tuple with tag 0
      ;; get its components, x=v105, y=v106
      (let ((v106 (fetch 2 v103)))
      (let ((v105 (fetch 1 v103)))
      ;; call int_add with x and y
      (@p int_add v105 v106 fc100
            ;; success continuation sc114 binds z=v111
            ;; it has free variables [sc101]
            (lambda sc114 (v111)
              ;; construct [z] = z::nil
              (let ((v113 (mkstruct 1 v111 '#(0))))
              ;; return to original caller
              (@sc sc101 v113)))))))
    ;; argument was not a 2-tuple
    ;; no alternatives left, so fail
    (else (@fc fc100)))))
```

Figure 8.8: Code generation example: intermediate CPS code

```
/* cast f to function pointer
 * invoke, get back next f
 * repeat
 */
void motor(void *f)
{
    for(;;)
      f = ((void*(*)(void))f)();
}

void *test(void) /* code for test */
{
    { void *sc101 = rmlSC;
    { void *fc100 = rmlFC;
    { void *sp154 = rmlSP;
    { void *v102 = rmlA0;
    { void *v103, v104;
    INSPECTBOX(v103, v104, v102);
    switch( (int)v104 ) {
      case STRUCTHDR(2,0):
        { void *v106 = FETCH(OFFSET(UNTAGPTR(v103), 2));
        { void *v105 = FETCH(OFFSET(UNTAGPTR(v103), 1));
        /* make closure for lambda sc114:
           push free vars [sc101], then label */
        STORE(OFFSET(sp154, -1), sc101);
        STORE(OFFSET(sp154, -2), LABVAL(lamsc114));
        /* setup arguments for int_add */
        rmlA1 = v106;
        rmlA0 = v105;
        rmlSC = OFFSET(sp154, -2);
        rmlSP = OFFSET(sp154, -2);
        rmlFC = fc100; /*redundant*/
        /* invoke int_add */
        TAILCALLQ(rml_int_add);}}
      default:
        /* fail: invoke fc100 */
        rmlFC = fc100; /*redundant*/
        TAILCALL(FETCH(fc100));}}}}}}
}
```

Figure 8.9: Code generation example: C code for test

```
/* empty list, nil, is empty tuple with tag 0 */
static const DEFSTRUCT0LIT(lit0,0);

static void *lamsc114(void) /* code for sc114 */
{
    /* get 3 words for the [z] cons cell, 1 live arg reg */
    { void *v116;
    ALLOC(v116, 3, 1);
    /* get free vars: [sc101] */
    { void *sc157 = rmlSC;
    { void *sc101 = FETCH(OFFSET(sc157, 1));
    /* new stack pointer */
    { void *sp156 = OFFSET(sc157, 2);
    /* bind formals: v111 = z */
    { void *v111 = rmlA0;
    /* construct v113 = [z] = z::nil */
    STORE(v116, IMMEDIATE(STRUCTHDR(2,1)));
    STORE(OFFSET(v116, 1), v111); /*car=v111=z*/
    STORE(OFFSET(v116, 2), REFSTRUCTLIT(lit0));
    { void *v113 = TAGPTR(v116);
    /* return to original caller */
    rmlA0 = v113;
    rmlSC = sc101;
    rmlSP = sp156;
    TAILCALL(FETCH(sc101));}}}}}}
}
```

Figure 8.10: Code generation example: C code for sc114

Chapter 9

Simulating Tailcalls in C

J mplementations of modern high-level languages sometimes generate C
as their 'machine code'. While this can lead to a reasonable degree
of portability and efficiency of the generated code, some features are
difficult to express correctly, portably, and efficiently in C. One such feature
is the *tailcall*, which is present in most functional and logic programming
languages. This chapter describes and evaluates a number of techniques for
simulating tailcalls in C.

Since RML can only express loops by tailcalls, and our compiler uses a
continuation-passing style intermediate representation, efficient and correct
implementation of tailcalls is of utmost importance to the rml2c compiler.

9.1 The Problem

Compiled implementations of modern high-level languages sometimes generate C code rather than machine code. This has some obvious advantages: C
is (effectively) universally available, C allows most of the necessary low-level
manipulations to be expressed, C compilers often generate excellent code,
and the generated C code can be ported to many different machines.

The are also disadvantages in using C. Efficient implementations of high-
level languages often use peculiar data structure representations, memory
management policies, and calling conventions. C often does not allow such
conventions – for instance, associating activation record descriptors with return addresses – to be expressed as directly, if at all, as in assembly language.
Some machine features, such as carry or overflow flags, are hidden from the
C code, often making arithmetic in Lisp/Scheme/ML-like languages less efficient than had assembly code been used.

Some languages have no primitive iteration constructs, instead they require function calls to be 'tail-recursive'. A *tailcall* is a call that occurs as
the last action in the caller, before the caller itself returns. In a *tail-recursive*

implementation, a function making a tailcall must first release *its own* activation record before branching to the called function. In a stack-based implementation, this means that a series of tailcalls executes in constant stack space.

Other features, such as exceptions, coroutines, or backtracking, require the generated code to be able to manipulate the activation records in ways that are not supported by the C calling mechanisms. Implementations based on a *Continuation-Passing Style* (CPS) transformation represent the continuation(s) using explicit data structures. Invoking a continuation then becomes a tailcall to its code pointer.

Alas, C function calls are not guaranteed to be tail-recursive.

9.1.1 Overview

Several techniques for expressing tailcalls in compiler-generated C code are described in this chapter. Section 9.2 briefly discusses why C compilers in general do not, and probably never will, generate properly tail-recursive code. Section 9.3 then describes a typical intermediate representation and our running-example program expressed in it. Some terminology is also defined there. Section 9.4 describes the standard 'dispatching labels' technique. An often overlooked detail is how to access global state variables; here we describe four variants that can exhibit surprisingly large performance variations. Section 9.5 describes the use of a giant switch/case to reduce the overheads associated with the dispatching technique. This technique is however rather impractical; Section 9.6 describes a combination of the dispatching and switching techniques that appears to be both practical and efficient, according to our experimental data. Section 9.7 describes a completely different idea based on identifying the C stack with the youngest generation of a generational copying garbage collector. Section 9.8 describes a non-portable technique based on pushing the use of GCC's first-class labels to the extreme. Section 9.9 describes another technique, claimed to be portable, using inserted assembly code. Section 9.10 briefly mentions a few approaches to the problem of compiling high-level languages that fail to be properly tail-recursive. Our experimental results are presented in Section 9.11 and Chapter 10. Section 9.12 concludes.

Our contributions are as follows:

- We describe, in reasonable detail, most known techniques for simulating tailcalls in C.

- We show an original way of making the 'dispatching switches' technique efficient. (Section 9.6)

- We report on and evaluate the first known (to us) implementation of the 'pushy labels' technique. (Section 9.7)

9.2 Why is C not Tail-Recursive?

A C compiler is subject to many constraints [93] when implementing function calls. When combined, these constraints typically result in a calling convention that does not support tailcalls. There are two major causes for this: the need to support variadic functions, and the relatively weak type system.

Before the introduction of ANSI-C and function prototypes, there was no mechanism for declaring a function to be variadic (taking a variable number of arguments, e.g. `printf`). Therefore, a compiler had to use the *same* calling convention for both normal and variadic function calls.

During a variadic call, only the caller knows the exact number and types of arguments. The callee can inspect a *prefix* of the arguments, but is not required to inspect any or all of them. Therefore, the callee cannot be responsible for deallocating the arguments when it returns to the caller, that has to be the caller's task. Since there could be no difference between normal and variadic calls, it follows that in *all* calls, it is the caller that deallocates the arguments after the callee has returned.

A possible alternative would be to pass, as an additional hidden argument, the total size of the argument list. While this would allow the callee to deallocate the arguments, it would also be unnecessarily inefficient for normal calls. And since there can be only one calling convention, this is not a viable solution.

The typical calling convention then is the following:

1. The caller evaluates the arguments and places them *in sequence* starting at a known location.

2. The caller saves its return address and branches to the callee.

3. The callee can reference a prefix of the arguments, since it knows the location of the first one.

4. The callee returns to the caller by branching to the return address.

5. The caller deallocates the arguments.

On a stack-based implementation, step 1 typically pushes the arguments in reverse order on the stack, and step 5 adjusts the stack pointer by a constant amount.

On a RISC machine, the first few arguments are often passed in registers, with the remaining ones being placed at a known place in the caller's activation record. Usually, this area is allocated once and for all when the caller is initially invoked. Step 1 places the arguments in reserved registers or fixed locations in the activation record, and step 5 is a no-op.

9.2.1   Why do not Prototypes Help?

With the introduction of prototypes in ANSI-C, compilers *can* use different calling conventions for normal and variadic function calls.

A fixed-arity function could itself deallocate its arguments. In a stack-based implementation, this is easy. On a RISC machine, this would require the callee to be able to adjust the caller's activation record. This could be done, if the overflow argument area is near the bottom of the activation record, but the disadvantage then is that the caller must allocate this area before every call that needs it. Due to the added complexity, and slight performance degradation, this alternative will probably not become standard.

A second reason, and for now equally serious, is that changing calling conventions is not without costs. Most machines and operating systems to-day have been in existence since before the introduction of ANSI-C. Hence, the calling conventions in these environments cannot differentiate between variadic and normal function calls. Since binary compatibility is important on the market, these environments are not likely to suddenly change their calling conventions and invalidate existing binaries, just because prototypes *could* allow different calling conventions.

The sad end result is that C compilers have little if any reason to start supporting tailcalls as a matter of course.

9.2.2   ANDF

ANDF – Architecture Neutral Distribution Format – has been proposed as a common intermediate language for compilers. Research at the Defence Research Agency (DRA) in England and the Open Software Foundation's (OSF) research institute has resulted in a definition of ANDF, a C compiler front end, and a back end based on the Gnu C compiler back end.

The current version of ANDF does not cater for tailcalls in any way. As a result of an effort to implement the Dylan language, tailcalls are scheduled to be added to ANDF in the near future.[1] Should ANDF back-ends become commonplace, it might be a better alternative to use ANDF instead of C in compilers for high-level languages. But for now, ANDF offers little advantage over C.

9.3   Preliminaries

To make the following more concrete, we assume that the compiler for our high-level language uses an intermediate representation akin to that shown in figure 9.1. It is intended for a strict functional language after CPS and *closure-conversion* [7, 164], but could also be used for lazy or logic programming languages.

---

[1]C. Fabre, OSF Research Institute, e-mail, March 17, 1995.

$$
\begin{array}{lll}
x \in \text{Var} & & \text{variables} \\
l \in \text{Label} & & \text{labels} \\
i \in \text{Int} & & \text{integers} \\
c \in \text{Con} & ::= l \mid i \mid \textbf{nil} \mid \textbf{true} \mid \textbf{false} \mid \cdots & \text{constants} \\
v \in \text{Val} & ::= x \mid c \mid \textbf{null? } v & \text{(pure) values} \\
& \mid \textbf{car } v \mid \textbf{cdr } v \mid \textbf{cloref } v\ i & \\
o \in \text{Oper} & ::= \textbf{cons } v_1\ v_2 \mid \textbf{closure } l\ v^* & \text{(primitive) operations} \\
& \mid \textbf{add } v_1\ v_2 \mid \textbf{mul } v_1\ v_2 \mid \cdots & \\
e \in \text{Exp} & ::= \textbf{tailcall } v_{\text{label}}\ v^* & \text{(CPS) expressions} \\
& \mid \textbf{let } x = v \textbf{ in } e & \\
& \mid \textbf{let } x = o \textbf{ in } e & \\
& \mid \textbf{if } v \textbf{ then } e_1 \textbf{ else } e_2 & \\
\text{Prog} & ::= (\textbf{define } l\ x^* = e)^* & \text{programs}
\end{array}
$$

Figure 9.1: Prototypical intermediate language

An intermediate program is a collection of functions. Every function has a name (label), a number of formal parameters, and a body which is an expression. We identify a function with its label. The body of a label describes a control-flow tree: execution flows forward over atomic operations and conditionals/forks, eventually ending in a tailcall to another label. There are no global variables/registers, only formal parameters and local variables. There are no assignments to variables either, but there may be primitive operators to update data structures.

Loops and joins in the control-flow graph can only occur at tailcalls. A useful consequence is that the heap allocation needs (due to the cons and closure primops) for any label's definition can be statically estimated. (This is an upper estimate due to the conditional.) This allows a single allocation test to be performed at the beginning of a label's body, which simplifies the interface to the garbage collector.

Below we will show a simple source-level function, and convert it in steps to the intermediate language. The resulting representation is used in the remainder of this chapter to illustrate different compilation techniques for tailcalls. The map function, which applies a function f to each element of a list xs and constructs a list of the results, might be written as follows in a hypothetical strict functional language:

```
define map f xs =
  if null? xs then nil
  else cons (f (car xs)) (map f (cdr xs))
```

During CPS conversion, we replace recursion by continuations – functions that know how to 'continue'. All functions now take an additional continuation argument, which we prepend to the list of arguments. By convention,

continuations variables are called k. Where an original function would have
returned a value v, the converted function will call the continuation k with v
as an argument. See Section 3.3 and Chapter 8 for more information about
CPS.

After CPS conversion, the example becomes:

```
define map k0 f xs =
  if null? xs then k0 nil
  else
    let fun k1 y = let fun k2 ys = k0 (cons y ys)
                   in map k2 f (cdr xs)
    in f k1 (car xs)
```

Closure conversion replaces closures – functions and their free variables –
with concrete data structures. Several options are available, subject only to
the condition that the creator of, callers of, and code for a closure all agree
on the calling convention. Here we use a traditional and simple convention:
A closure becomes a record, the first field of which contains the code pointer
(i.e. label) of the code to invoke. The remaining fields contain the values of
the free variables. For example, closure mapk1 f xs k0 creates a closure
with the code pointer mapk1 and the values of f, xs, and k0. By convention,
the closure record itself is passed as the first argument to the code, to allow
access to free variables. Since free variables have been removed, all code
labels are placed in the same global scope.

After closure conversion, the example becomes:

```
define map clo k0 f xs =
  if null? xs then tailcall (cloref k0 0) k0 nil
  else
    let k1 = closure mapk1 f xs k0
    in tailcall (cloref f 0) f k1 (car xs)

define mapk1 k1 y =
  let f = cloref k1 1 in
  let xs = cloref k1 2 in
  let k0 = cloref k1 3 in
  let k2 = closure mapk2 k0 y in
  tailcall map nil k2 f (cdr xs)

define mapk2 k2 ys =
  let k0 = cloref k2 1 in
  let y = cloref k2 2 in
  let zs = cons y ys in
  tailcall (cloref k0 0) k0 zs
```

As should be obvious from this example, there are two main implementation constraints that must be satisfied:

1. labels must be first-class values

2. the `tailcall` operator must behave like a `goto`

9.3.1 Tailcall Classification

We will classify tailcalls as follows: *known* calls are those where the called label is known at compile-time, other calls are *unknown*; *intramodule* calls are those where the calling and called labels are defined in the same compilation unit (typically a single file), other calls are *intermodule* calls. These classifications can be combined in the obvious ways.

9.4 Plain Dispatching Labels

While machine code labels are not first-class in C, *function pointers* are. Hence, one can encode a label and its body as a function, the return value of which is the label (function pointer) to call next. A dispatcher loops invoking these labels, for ever. This idea is so old and obvious that it probably has been reinvented many times [62, 110, 136, 143, 166, 171].

The C code for a label's body is straightforward: bindings to variables become assignments to local C variables, values become C expressions, and primops become sequences of statements (when initializing data structures) or expressions (arithmetic).

Since recursive C calls are not used, parameters to labels are passed by assigning to global variables before returning the label to the dispatcher loop. The called label will then have to fetch its arguments from the global to its local variables.

The interface to the garbage collector is fairly simple. As mentioned previously, it suffices to make a single allocation request at the start of a label's body. At this point, the *only live values are those reachable from the global argument variables.* (This is called a *safe points* policy [7, Section 13.2].) Then, should a garbage collection be necessary, it suffices to call the collector with arguments indicating which globals are live and the amount of memory needed. After the collection, the code in the body can load the global variables into locals and proceed as usual. Allocations within the body simply store values at known offsets in the newly allocated chunk of memory.

There are some obvious disadvantages though:

- Tailcalls become a series of (at least) two jumps. First a return from the caller back to the dispatcher, and then a call from the dispatcher to the callee. The return from the caller might actually first jump to some cleanup code at the end of the function, before the actual 'return'. Some improvements might result if self-calls are recognized and turned into gotos.

- Callee-saved registers will have to be saved and restored by the generated functions. This is largely redundant, since the caller of these functions is always the dispatcher, and it uses very few registers compared to the invoked functions. It would be better if most registers were caller-saved.

- Accessing global variables for parameter passing is typically slower than accessing local variables, even if they are allocated in the stack frame rather than in registers. Although GCC allows global variables to be allocated to fixed registers, typically only a few registers are suitable for global variables. Also, interfacing with pre-compiled libraries or object modules can be tricky.

Here is an example showing how the C translation of the body of mapk1 might look. In this and following code examples, issues of data representation, pointer tagging and untagging, and primitive operations are skimmed over, as they are necessarily language- and implementation-specific.

```
extern void *gloKONT, *gloCLO, *gloARG1, ...;
#define ALLOC(VAR,NWORDS,NARGS) ...
#define APPLY(LABVAL) (*(void*(*)(void))(LABVAL))

void dispatcher(void *f)
{
    while( TRUE )
        f = APPLY(f)();
}

void *mapk1(void)
{
  { void **mem;
    /* get 4 words for the closure; 1 live global */
    ALLOC(mem,4,1);
    /* fetch incoming arguments */
  { void *k1 = gloKONT;
  { void *y = gloARG1;
    /* body starts here */
  { void *f = CLOREF(k1,1);
  { void *xs = CLOREF(k1,2);
  { void *k0 = CLOREF(k1,3);
    /* create closure k2 */
    mem[0] = CLOSUREHDR(3);
    mem[1] = IMMEDIATE(mapk2);
    mem[2] = k0;
    mem[3] = y;
  { void *k2 = &mem[0];
```

```
    /* assign outgoing arguments */
    gloARG2 = CDR(xs);
    gloARG1 = f;
    gloKONT = k2;
    gloCLO = NIL;
    return IMMEDIATE(map);
  }}}}}}
}
```

9.4.1 Alternative Access Methods for Globals

A possible problem with the way parameters are passed between labels via global variables is that accessing a global variable often requires a separate address calculation before the actual access. There are several ways of reducing this cost.

A first step might be to join the globals into a single global record (C struct). This way, the C compiler could compute just a single address to this record, and then load (or store) with an immediate offset when accessing fields in it. Another possible gain is that data locality might be improved.

It may be that the C compiler needs more explicit guidance to make this transformation. We can instead arrange to have the dispatcher loop pass *the address* of the record as the only C-parameter to labels. In the body, explicit pointer accesses are made. The code generated by the KLIC and Gambit-C compilers always use this approach [42, 62].

Yet another alternative is to let the body of a label start by binding a local variable to the address of the global record. This can help the register allocator make better spilling decisions.

The following code example shows these variants in more detail. As the evaluation in Chapter 10 indicates, the best choice is both machine- and compiler-dependent, and the best choice may yield up to 10% faster code than the worst.

```
/* SPLIT: separate variables */
int a, b, c, d;

void f1(void)
{
    d = (a + b) * c;
}

/* JOING: JOINed Globals */
struct globals { int a, b, c, d; };
struct globals glo;

void f2(void)
```

```
{
    glo.d = (glo.a + glo.b) * glo.c;
}

/* AGPTR: Argument Globals PoinTeR */
void f3(struct globals *gp)
{
    gp->d = (gp->a + gp->b) * gp->c;
}

/* LGPTR: Locally bound Globals PoinTeR */
void f4(void)
{
    struct globals *gp = &glo;
    gp->d = (gp->a + gp->b) * gp->c;
}
```

The Gnu C compiler allows global variables to be allocated to registers. Since usually only a few global registers are available, it will take a great deal of benchmarking to discover exactly which subset should be so allocated. Here is how to express this for the SPARC:

```
register int a asm("%g2");
register int b asm("%g3");
```

Finally, non-trivial performance improvements can be gained if we apply a *copy-propagation* optimization [3] to the global variables. Suppose that in a tailcall, one of the globals will be assigned the same value it had on entry to the calling label. In this case, the assignment is redundant and can be removed. If there are no other references to this variable, then there is no need to load it in the first place. C compilers will often not discover this opportunity, either because asynchronous events may modify the global variable, or because the body of the label contains C function calls to runtime routines, in which case the C compiler has to assume that any global location can be modified. We have observed (Chapter 10) performance improvements in the 2-17% range from this optimization.

9.5   The Monster Switch

The disadvantages of the 'plain' technique (tailcalls become series of at least two jumps, unnecessary saves/restores of registers, expensive parameter passing) can be alleviated by collecting all labels into a single large switch-statement in a single C function. Every label has a tag, a natural number that is used to represent the label when it is passed around as a value. Unknown calls use the tag to switch to the code for the label. A label can also have an ordinary C label to allow direct gotos for known calls.

Since all code is collected in a single C function, parameters can be passed using local C variables (hoping that they will be allocated to hardware registers), and frequently accessed global state variables (such as the heap pointer) can be cached as local variables.

The disadvantages are severe: separate compilation is no longer possible, and the generated switch can easily be tens of thousands lines long. Disabling optimizations may allow compilation times to be acceptable, but then performance suffers so much that there is little point in using this rather than the 'plain' technique. The Janus compiler jc [72] is one of the implementations using this technique, in spite of its problems.

Here is a portion of our running example, illustrating the 'monster switch'.

```
/* declare the labels */
enum label {
    label_map, label_mapk1, label_mapk2,
    ...
};

void monster(enum label label)
{
    void *argKONT, *argCLO, *arg1, ...;
dispatch:
    switch( label ) {
...
case label_mapk1: /* entry for unknown calls */
entry_mapk1:       /* entry for known calls */
    ...
    /* make known tailcall */
    arg2 = CDR(xs);
    arg1 = f;
    argKONT = k2;
    argCLO = NIL;
    goto entry_map;

case label_mapk2:
entry_mapk2:
    ...
    /* make unknown tailcall */
    arg1 = zs;
    argKONT = k0;
    label = (enum label)CLOREF(k0,0);
    goto dispatch;
...
    } /* end of switch */
}
```

Even this code has some inefficiencies. Unknown calls must go via the `switch`. In C, if the value `switched` upon is not among the `cases`, then control is to flow to the next statement after the `switch`. The range-checking code inserted by the C compiler is redundant for our purposes, but there is no portable standard mechanism for removing it. (As described later in this chapter, the first-class labels implemented by GCC does allow `switch` statements to be replaced by jump tables, thereby eliminating the range-checking overhead.)

9.6   Dispatching Switches

It is probably true of many languages that in most calls, the caller and callee are lexically 'close'. There are two reasons for this: (1) source-level calls are often recursions between a set (perhaps a singleton) of related functions placed in the same source-level 'module', and (2) since recursion is frequently used, source-level 'returns' are also often to lexically 'close' code. Modules, whether just source files or finer-grained language elements, typically consist of such lexically close code.

Our measurements in the `rml2c` compiler indicate a 10-to-1 ratio between intramodular and intermodular calls. Due to source-level tailcalls, the share of the intramodular calls being known is closer to 60% rather than 50%, but this still leaves us with a large number of unknown intramodular calls. Hence, intramodule calls, whether known or unknown, should be made as efficient as possible.

In this section we develop an efficient technique in three steps: first known intramodule calls are dealt with, then problems associated with unknown intramodule calls are discussed, and then our solution to these problems is presented. A final section mentions some spin-off benefits from our technique.

9.6.1   Step 1: Fast Known Intramodule Calls

Our first step is to collect the code for all labels within a module into a single C 'module function'. Every label is headed by a C label of the same name. Known intramodule calls use local C variables for argument passing, and simple `goto`s for branching, as in the 'monster switch'. Unknown and known intermodule calls use the global argument variables and relay control using the dispatcher, as in the 'plain' technique.

Since labels may be passed around as values, a proper representation of them must be introduced. A simple choice is to use function pointers, just as in the 'plain' scheme. Every label that *escapes*[2] from a module is given an *entry function*: a C function that simply calls the module function with an integer tag indicating which label to invoke. The module function then uses

---

[2]A label escapes if it is globally known, or if it is given away as part of a data structure, for instance a continuation closure.

a switch to branch to the actual code. (A similar technique was used by the
Interlisp-10 Block Compiler [172].) The initial call into a module also loads
the local argument variables from the globals. The locals must be flushed
before garbage collections and reloaded afterwards. The code for this would
look roughly as follows:

```
enum label { label_map, ... }; /* tags for 'switch' */

/* declare entry functions */
void *entry_map(void) { return modfun(label_map); }

void *modfun(enum label entry) /* the module function */
{
    switch( entry ) {
    case label_map: /* for incoming calls */
    direct_map:     /* intramodule known calls */
      /* code for map here */
...
    }
}
```

While this results in code that can make very fast known intramodule
calls, our measurements indicated an overall performance *decrease*. The reasons for this were:

1. Entering a module became more expensive than in the 'plain' scheme.

2. Leaving a module had the same cost as before.

3. The runtime calling sequences typically consisted of very short bursts
   of known intramodule calls (rarely longer than 3-4 calls), separated by
   unknown intramodule or intermodule, calls. The performance improvements for these bursts were often outweighed by the increased costs for
   leaving and entering modules.

9.6.2   Step 2: Recognizing Unknown Intramodule Calls

It is clear that something has to be done to allow an unknown intramodule
call without leaving and reentering the module. Some kind of runtime test has
to be able to inspect a label (in its first-class value representation), determine
whether or not it denotes a C label in the current module and, if so, which
one.

There is certainly a multitude of design choices here! We list a few, before
describing the one we developed in the next section.

- The stub entry functions can be replaced by records, each containing
  two fields: the address of the module function and the integer tag used

to switch to the corresponding code. (This requires a trivial change
to the dispatcher.) At an unknown call, the record's module function
pointer is compared with the address of the current module function,
and then an intramodule or intermodule code sequence is selected. The
code for an unknown call would look as follows:

```
targetLab = <expr>;
if( targetLab->modfun == my_modfun ) {
    /* eval args for intramodule call */
    goto the_switch; /* branch via 'switch' */
} else {
    /* eval args for intermodule call */
    return targetLab; /* back to dispatcher */
}
```

(From inspection of the generated code, it appears that ICOT's KL1-to-
C compiler klic does something along these lines [42].) There are two
disadvantages: having each unknown call expand into a test followed by
two separate code sequences causes code bloat, and comparing function
pointers is not always terribly efficient (HP-PA/HP-UX uses a runtime
library routine for this).

• Different modules can use different switch tags. The high-level compiler can maintain a database of all labels used in the application program and the runtime system. The labels within a module are given
the consecutive non-negative tags $[i, \cdots, k]$. The runtime test to see if
label l is in this sequence can then be expressed as (l-i) <= (k-i).
This works thanks to C's unsigned arithmetic, because if l < i, then
l-i will wrap around to become a large positive number, larger than
k-i. (This is a standard trick for range testing in C.) Although the
range test is very cheap, there is still the problem of code bloat. Another problem is that separate compilation or dynamic loading of code
at runtime becomes more involved.

9.6.3   Step 3: Fast Unknown Intramodule Calls

Our idea is to streamline the execution of unknown intramodule calls by *spec-
ulatively* assuming all unknown calls to be intramodule. A runtime mechanism is introduced to make unknown *intermodule* calls cause a software *trap*
to a handler, while unknown intramodule calls proceed at almost the same
speed as known intramodule calls.

Each module has its own private *bit-mask* variable, which is all-zeros when
the module is inactive, and all-ones when it is active. (A module is active
when the currently executing label in defined within it.) Exactly *one* module
is active at any given time. The bit-mask is set on entry to and cleared

on every exit from the module. We let the module functions do this work, although it could be delegated to the dispatcher.

A label is represented as a record with three elements: the pointer to the module function, the label's integer tag, and *a pointer to* the module's bit-mask variable. The dispatcher fetches the tag and passes it as an argument to the module function.

```
typedef struct label {
    struct label *(*modfun)(unsigned);
    unsigned tag;
    unsigned *mask;
} label_t;

void dispatcher(label_t *f)
{
    while( TRUE )
        f = (*f->modfun)(f->tag);
}
```

An unknown call proceeds almost as a known intramodular call: the arguments are evaluated and placed in the local C argument variables. The target label is evaluated, resulting in a pointer to a label record which is placed in a local variable. Then a bitwise 'and' of the label's tag and its pointed-to bit-mask is computed, and a switch is made to the result. Now, one of two things can happen:

1. The call was intramodular. Since this is the active module, its bit-mask is all-ones; the 'and' of the label's tag and its bit-mask is the tag itself, and the switch jumps directly to the correct label.

2. The call was intermodular. The label's bit-mask must be all-zeros, so the 'and' of the tag and bit-mask is zero. Case zero of the switch is reserved for the trap handler, which simply unloads the local C argument variables to the global ones and leaves the module, returning the label record pointer to the dispatcher which will then invoke the target module and label.

The advantage of this technique is that we *re-use* the tests done by the switch to also perform the inter/intra-module test. Other alternatives, such as inspecting the bit-mask (*is it zero or non-zero?*) before the switch or comparing module function pointers, makes the code executed for unknown intramodular calls longer and less pipeline-friendly.

The code for our map example would be as follows:

```
void *gloKONT, *gloCLO, *gloARG1, ...;

static unsigned my_mask = 0;
```

```
static label_t *my_module(unsigned);
label_t map = {my_module, 1, &my_mask};
label_t mapk1 = {my_module, 2, &my_mask};
label_t mapk2 = {my_module, 3, &my_mask};

static label_t *my_module(unsigned tag)
{
    void *argKONT, *argCLO, *arg1, ...;
    label_t *label;
    /* entry code */
    my_mask = ~0; /* all-ones */
    argKONT = gloKONT;
    ...
    goto dispatch;
mask_dispatch:
    tag = label->tag & *label->mask;
dispatch:
    switch( tag ) {
case 0: /* trap handler for unknown intermodule calls */
    gloKONT = argKONT;
    gloARG1 = arg1;
    ...
    my_mask = 0;
    return label;
case 1:
entry_map:
    ...
case 2:
entry_mapk1:
    ...
    mem[0] = CLOSUREHDR(3);
    mem[1] = &mapk2;
    mem[2] = k0;
    mem[3] = y;
  { void *k2 = &mem[0];
    /* do a known intramodule call */
    arg2 = CDR(xs);
    arg1 = f;
    argKONT = k2;
    argCLO = UNIT;
    goto entry_map;
  }
case 3:
entry_mapk2:
```

```
    . . .
    /* do an unknown call */
    arg1 = zs;
    argKONT = k0;
    label = (label_t)CLOREF(k0,0);
    goto mask_dispatch;
    } /* end of switch */
}
```

Different methods for accessing the global variables can be applied here, just as for the 'plain' technique.

Using GCC's first-class labels, the switch statement can be replaced by a jump table, further reducing the cost of unknown calls. If the tags are assigned numbers that are multiples of the machine's word size, and the jump table is pointed to by a char* local variable, then the scaling normally done for array indexing can be eliminated, resulting in extremely fast dispatch code. The map example would become:

```
label_t map = {my_module, 1*sizeof(void**), &my_mask};
. . .
static label_t *my_module(unsigned tag)
{
    static void ** const entry_tab[] = { /* jump table */
        &&entryTrapHandler, &&entry_map, ...
    };
    const char *entry_ptr = (const char*)labels_tab;
    /* prologue code as before */
dispatch:
    goto **(const void**)(entry_ptr + tag);
entryTrapHandler:
    . . .
entry_map:
    . . .
}
```

There are potential problems with regard to code size, similar to the case for the 'monster switch'. Compiling a high-level language to C often results in code expanding in the order of 5-10 times. Even a moderately-sized source module can result in a C module of several thousand lines. Some C compilers need to be coerced into optimizing such large functions.

Finally, we note that an independent study [53] of some techniques came to the conclusion that the KLIC scheme (of which our 'dispatching switches' is an improvement) is to be preferred over both the 'monster switch' and the 'warped gotos' (described later in Section 9.8).

9.6.4   Additional Benefits

An additional feature of the 'dispatching switches' scheme is that it allows meta-information to be stored in labels.

Consider for instance an implementation of a lazy functional language using the G-machine [142]. To make dispatching instructions efficient, the tag stored in a node is typically *not* a small integer, but a pointer to a table of code addresses, one address for each dispatching instruction. Invoking one of these pieces of code requires two indirections (load the tag, load code pointer) and a jump.

Since the EVAL instruction is very frequent, a common optimization is to let the tag be the address of the code for EVAL, with the rest of the table stored just *before* this code, thus saving one indirection for EVAL. Accessing the other code addresses just requires the second indirection to use a different (negative) offset from the tag pointer.

In C it is not possible to place data and code together like this. But suppose now that the tag in a node is the label for EVAL, represented as in the 'dispatching switches' scheme. The other labels can be stored directly in EVAL's label, as meta-data. This allows a very similar optimization to be expressed.

Garbage collectors can also make use of meta-data in labels. Suppose closures (including perhaps continuations) are represented as heap-allocated records. Heap records often need a header for the GC to be able to inspect them. Since closure records tend to be small, having to allocate and initialize a header word can cause significant overhead.

But for any particular label, all closures for that label will have the same layout and the same header. Hence, one could store the header in the label itself, as meta-data. Pointers to closures must then use a different encoding, so that the GC can differentiate between plain records and closures.

In an informal experiment with our rml2c compiler [136], we converted the code generator to place continuation records in the heap instead of the stack. Initially, this slowed the code down by some 52%, partly because of the increased heap consumption, partly because the records now had to have a header field added and initialized. Using the above-mentioned trick, the slowdown was reduced to 26%. (A better closure conversion and calling convention, à la Shao and Appel [164], might have reduced this overhead further.)

9.7   Pushy Labels

If the C stack is infinite, then tailcalls *can be allowed* to be recursive. A label can be a separate C function, as in the 'plain' technique, but tailcalls become ordinary recursive C calls and parameters are passed as ordinary C function parameters (often in registers on modern machines). As a bonus, since the

C stack never shrinks, most storage allocations can be implemented as local variables in the C functions (Need a cons cell? Just declare a C variable to *be* of the cons type.) Allocations of statically-unknown sizes can either use alloca() or a separate heap.[3]

In reality, though, the C stack is of limited size. To prevent unbounded stack growth, a check is added to the start of every generated function. When the stack is sufficiently large, a continuation closure is created (on the C stack) containing the address of the function that detected the stack overflow, and all its actual parameters. Then a copying garbage collector is called with this closure as its root. (There may be other roots as well.) Live data in the stack are relocated to the heap. The C stack is then contracted by using longjmp() to back up to the initial activation record. Finally the continuation closure is invoked to resume the interrupted function.

It should be obvious now that the C stack is identified with the youngest generation (often called the *nursery* or *allocation arena*) of a generational copying garbage collector, and that the C stack pointer *is* the heap allocation pointer.

This idea was proposed recently by Henry Baker [16]. Augmenting Fischer's proof that CPS-converted programs only need stack storage [65] with a garbage collector results in the same idea.

Another characterization is to say that we remove the requirement that a caller must deallocate its activation record before a tailcall, as long as we guarantee that it is deallocated *eventually*. A fixed-size C stack is then used to *buffer* many such operations into a single one.

Here we see how mapk1 would be expressed:

```
extern char *stack_limit;
extern void gc(void **cont); /* never returns */

void mapk1(void *k1, void *y)
{
    /* max 4 words needed along any control path */
    void *mem[4];
    /* stack overflow check */
    if( (char*)mem < stack_limit ) {
        /* overflow: create continuation for the gc */
        mem[0] = CLOSUREHDR(3);
        mem[1] = IMMEDIATE(mapk1);
        mem[2] = k1;
        mem[3] = y;
        gc(mem);
    }
```

---

[3]alloca() is a non-portable but widely available procedure that allocates memory in its caller's activation record on the stack. This memory is automatically deallocated when the calling function returns.

```
  /* real body starts here */
{ void *f = CLOREF(k1,1);
{ void *xs = CLOREF(k1,2);
{ void *k0 = CLOREF(k1,3);
  mem[0] = CLOSUREHDR(3);
  mem[1] = IMMEDIATE(mapk2);
  mem[2] = k0;
  mem[3] = y;
{ void *k2 = &mem[0];
  map(NIL, k2, f, CDR(xs));
}}}}
}
```

(Some C compilers have problems compiling functions with many nested scopes containing local arrays or structures. This formulation, with a single large 'chunk' of memory, is safer.)

This *seems* very nice and appears to solve the various problems of the previous techniques, but there are disadvantages:

1. Every label must contain code for the stack overflow check and creation of the GC continuation closure, making the code somewhat bulky. In the previous cases, only those labels that actually allocate storage needed to perform allocation checks.

2. Loops cannot be expressed as C loops if they allocate storage, unless the non-portable `alloca()` is used.

3. Stack frame layout conventions on RISCs tend to make the stack grow much faster than a separate heap containing only explicitly allocated data. This causes frequent minor collections, which in turn means that `longjmp()` is called often. In some UNIX variants, `setjmp()` saves not only the stack pointer, program counter, and general registers, but also the current *signal mask*. Consequently, `longjmp()` restores the signal mask using a system call. Using a system-dependent implementation of these two procedures to eliminate the system calls may be necessary for acceptable performance.

4. Interfacing this code with 'normal' C code becomes very difficult, if unrestricted calls back and forth between the two worlds are needed. In effect, this code *must* be implemented as a coroutine using its own stack, which requires system-dependent programming. In contrast, the dispatching schemes *are* already coroutines, since their entire state is located in a few global state variables.

5. Our performance measurements (Chapter 10) have shown that choosing a suitable size of the stack buffer is *essential* for acceptable performance, presumably due to caching effects.

9.7.1 Pushy Labels and Register Windows

Recursing on machines such as the SPARC uses both *memory* stack space, and another *register window*. When the machine runs out of free windows, a trap is generated, and the operating system is responsible for flushing one or several windows to memory, in order to allow the user-level recursion to continue.

These traps are expensive, which is unfortunate since 'pushy labels' *only* recurse and never 'return', resulting in frequent traps and significantly degraded performance.

Noting that the current function's window is dead at the point of a tailcall, the problem would be solved if the tailcall *popped* the window before branching to the recursively called label. Using GCC, we can express this using another of its extensions: hi-tech inline assembly code. On a SPARC, we can do the following at a tailcall:

1. Evaluate the arguments, placing the results in the *input* registers of the current window. When the window is later popped, these registers become the output registers of the previous window, which is where the arguments to the called function are supposed to be.

2. Branch to the called function.

3. In the delay slot, `restore` the window while leaving the stack pointer unchanged.

A slight problem is that, as the call no longer looks like a C function call but is done using inline assembly code, GCC may well believe this function to be a *leaf* function. Such functions often need no windows at all, but steps 1 and 3 require the window to be present. A fix is to insert a dummy function call after the assembly instructions, just to make sure that GCC does not remove the window.

Here is how we express this in GCC. If the call is unknown, the `ba` instruction is replaced with `jmp`, and the "g" indicator is replaced with "r".

```
/* known tailcall to F with arguments A and B */
{
    register void *_i0 asm("%i0") = (A);
    register void *_i1 asm("%i1") = (B);
    asm volatile("ba %0; restore %%g0,%%sp,%%sp" :
                 : "g" (F), "r" (_i0), "r" (_i1));
    dummy_call();
}
```

There are alternatives: one is to use a post-compilation text processor to edit the generated assembly code before assembling it. (Such techniques have been used in several interpreters.) Another is to modify GCC to do this transformation whenever a so-called noreturn function is called.[4]

9.8   The 'Warped Gotos' Technique

The Gnu C Compiler has an extension whereby C labels can be used as first-class values, and goto can go to the value of an expression. GCC only guarantees this to work when the target label is defined in the same function as the goto. A typical application is to speed up byte-coded interpreters by replacing switch statements with jump tables.

Under suitable circumstances, it might be possible to actually goto from one function to another. That is, to export a label l from a module, its address (&&l) is placed in a pointer variable p. Then to tailcall l from some other module, goto *p is executed. Two languages in the logic programming family, Erlang [82] and Mercury [165], use this to implement tailcalls. The restrictions these implementations have to observe are severe [165]:

1. *No* function may use *any* local variables. This is because all functions must use identical layouts of their activation records.

2. The C stack frame must be large enough to hold any registers spilled during intermediate expression evaluations.

Here is how map could be rendered in this framework:

```
void *map, *mapk1, *mapk2;
extern void **mem,*local[NUM_LOCALS];

void init_module(void)
{
    /* export labels */
    map = &&entry_map;
    mapk1 = &&entry_mapk1;
    mapk2 = &&entry_mapk2;
    return;
    /* code for label bodies */
entry_map: {
    /* symbolic offsets for our locals */
    enum {clo, k0, f, xs, k1};
    ALLOC(mem,5,2);
    local[clo] = gloCLO; /* redundant */
    local[k0] = gloKONT;
    local[f] = gloARG1;
```

---

[4]Both alternatives have been tried with good results (R. Chritchlow, e-mail, Feb. and Sep. 1994).

```
        local[xs] = gloARG2;
        if( NULLP(local[xs]) ) {
            gloARG1 = NIL;
            gloKONT = local[k0]; /* redundant */
            goto *CLOREF(local[k0],0);
        } else {
            mem[0] = CLOSUREHDR(4);
            mem[1] = IMMEDIATE(&&entry_mapk1);
            mem[2] = local[f];
            mem[3] = local[xs];
            mem[4] = local[k0];
            local[k1] = &mem[0];
            gloARG1 = CAR(local[xs]);
            gloKONT = local[k1];
            gloCLO = local[f];
            goto *CLOREF(local[f],0);
        }}
entry_mapk1: {...}
entry_mapk2: {...}
}
```

The advantage of this technique is that tailcalls branch *directly* to the desired code, regardless of whether the call is known or not, and whether it is intra- or intermodular. The disadvantages are:

1. Run-time initialization is required, since a C label is not visible outside the function in which it is defined.

2. Portability suffers since it absolutely requires GCC.

3. Not having local variables makes the C code much less efficient. The Mercury paper reports a speedup of almost a factor of 2 when augmenting the scheme to also use GCC's global register variables. This, however, requires the implementation of a register allocator in the high-level compiler itself, in order to try to fit the intermediate variables into the available global registers. Doing this job properly would require knowing how many of these there are, which then makes both the compiler and the generated C code machine-dependent. Alternatively, one can just try and use as few 'locals' as possible, have a C-compile-time configuration .h-file, and hope that there are enough global registers to cover the most frequently used locals.

4. The 'no locals' condition is not sufficient. Suppose that GCC computes a Very Busy Expression [3] in one module and caches it in a register. During a control exchange from this module to another (a non-local goto), this register can easily be overwritten, causing incorrect execu-

tion if we ever come back to the first module. No syntactic condition can guarantee that this never happens.

5. Several comparisons of this scheme (Chapter 10, [53]) have found this technique to be less efficient than other more portable ones.

9.9   The `wamcc` Approach

The paper on the `wamcc` Prolog-to-C compiler [45] describes a technique based on the observation that calls on some RISC machines are really just jumps that happen to save a return address in a dedicated register. It is the *callee* that causes stack growth when (if) it allocates its activation record. The `wamcc` approach, then, is the following:

1. A label becomes a parameterless C function, and a tailcall becomes a call followed by a dummy `return`.

2. To prevent stack growth, a new assembly label is inserted into the C compiler's output, at the start of the C function body. The intention is that branching to this label will bypass the activation record setup code in the procedure prologue.

3. This fake label is declared globally as a C function. A tailcall calls the fake label, rather than the function in which it occurs.

4. Parameters are passed through global memory cells.

There are two advantages to this technique: fast C compilation since compilation units are kept small (each label becomes an individual C function), and all calls use the same mechanism, making intermodular calls as simple and fast as intramodular calls.

Our running example would be expressed as follows in this scheme:

```
void entry_mapk1(void), entry_mapk2(void), ...;
void *gloKONT, *gloCLO, *gloARG1, ...;

void wrap_mapk1(void)
{
asm("entry_mapk1:"); /* insert fake label */
    ...
    /* tailcall known label */
    gloARG1 = f;
    gloKONT = k2;
    gloCLO = NIL;
    entry_map();
    return;
}
```

```
void wrap_mapk2(void)
{
asm("entry_mapk2:");
    ...
    /* tailcall unknown label */
    gloARG1 = zs;
    gloKONT = k0;
  { void (*f)(void) = CLOREF(k0,0);
    (*f)();
    return; }
}
```

This technique is claimed in the paper [45] to be 'instantly portable'. When we fetched the actual system and inspected the code, however, we found the situation to be quite different:

- The idealized picture presented in the paper is only used for their SPARC, MIPS, and HP-PA targets. Their Alpha, Intel x86, and Motorola m68k targets use inline assembly code.

- On the x86 and m68k targets, even more assembly code is inserted at some points to manipulate the C stack.

Another problem not mentioned is the fact that optimizing compilers may choose not to emit separate prologue and epilogue sections around procedure bodies. Burger et al. [36] noted that although only about one third of procedure invocations are to *syntactic* leaf procedures, more than two thirds are to *effective* leaf procedures. To exploit this, their Scheme compiler's intraprocedural register allocator delayed saving callee-saved registers as long as possible. In their benchmarks, this resulted in a 43% speedup.

C code generated by the wamcc idea would break if compiled by a C compiler that uses this 'lazy prologue' strategy. The wamcc system's performance lies somewhere in between the interpreted and native-code modes of SICStus Prolog.

9.10 Non-Solutions

Although this chapter only considers *correct* implementations of tailcalls, we should mention that some do accept the loss of tailcall 'completeness'.

One school strives for 'natural' translations from the high-level language to C and in doing so equates source-level functions and function calls with their C level counterparts. This has been used for several Scheme and ML compilers [17, 163, 169]. The reward is simplicity of implementation, and potentially more efficient loops; the price is that some programs 'go wrong' due to stack overflow. Simple cases of tailcalls, typically local loops, can sometimes be recognized and compiled non-recursively.

Some (re-)define their input language to have just those features they can handle efficiently [161].

Some believe that the Gnu C compiler, GCC, handles tailcalls properly. This is not true: while GCC recognizes *some* cases of self-tailcalls, there are still many cases it does not recognize. Therefore, one cannot rely on this feature.

De Bosschere and Tarau [52, section 4] describe a technique for compiling Prolog that appears to be a strange hybrid. Their general mapping is based on the 'single success continuation', using C-level returns for backtracking. They compile all code in a module into a single large C function, much like in the 'monster' or 'dispatching switches' techniques. They use GCC's first-class labels to reduce dispatching overhead. Intermodule calls are *recursive* C function calls and intermodule parameters are C function parameters. On entry to a module, they augment the current return continuation with a new record referring to a local label; this label performs the C-level return when invoked.

They lose tail-recursion twice: first during the recursive C call between modules, then in the virtual machine's data structures because the continuation is extended on entry to a module.

9.11   Experimental Results

Our `rml2c` compiler can generate code according to any of the following schemes: dispatching labels ('plain'), dispatching switches ('switch'), pushy labels ('pushy'), warped gotos ('warped'). In the dispatching schemes, one can also choose between the four different ways for accessing global state.

We have evaluated all of these, for our standard benchmarks. The results are described in Chapter 10.

9.12   Conclusions

Our conclusion is that the 'dispatching switches' scheme is to be preferred. Although 'warped gotos' can have similar performance, this is offset by reduced portability and increased implementation effort.

Any compiler generating C code probably arranges to have the code include a configuration `.h`-file to provide the final details of the translation. Schemes based on dispatching should also delegate the global state access method to the configuration file.

The 'pushy' scheme is elegant, but system effects makes it lose much performance. Extreme non-portable techniques ('warped', 'wamcc') do not appear to have any significant performance advantages.

Chapter 10

Performance Evaluation

$\mathcal{B}$ enchmarking is a key ingredient in performance evaluations. In this chapter, several benchmarks for different code generation methods and variations of runtime structures are described. Then the effects of different optimization levels in the rml2c compiler are evaluated, followed by some comparisons between RML, Typol, two commercial Prolog compilers, and one commercial Pascal compiler.

10.1 Target Systems

The rml2c compiler should run on any machine supported by recent versions of Standard ML of New Jersey (SML/NJ), as explained in Section 5.3. The generated code and the runtime system is known to work on several combinations of architectures, operating systems, and compilers. The following targets were used for the benchmarks:

DECstation 3000/300 with a 150MHz Alpha processor and 48MB memory, OSF/1 V1.3A operating system, DEC C compiler version 3.11 (flags -std1 -O2 -Olimit 1500) and Gnu C compiler 2.7.0 (flags -O2). The nicknames for these targets are *alpha-cc* and *alpha-gcc*.

HP 9000/715/75, 75MHz PA-RISC, 64MB, HP-UX A.09.05, HP C (flags -Aa -D_HPUX_SOURCE +O2 +Onolimit +ESlit) and GCC 2.7.0 (flags -O2). Nicknames *hp-cc* and *hp-gcc*.

HP PC, 66MHz Pentium, 32MB, Solaris 2.4, Sun ProCompiler C 2.0.1 (flags -xO2) and GCC 2.7.0 (flags -O2). Nicknames *i386-cc* and *i386-gcc*.

DECstation 5000/200, 25MHz MIPS R3000, 56MB, Ultrix V4.3, Mips C 2.10 (flags -O2 -Olimit 1600) and GCC 2.7.0 (flags -O2). Nicknames *mips-cc* and *mips-gcc*.

Parsytec GigaCube PowerPlus with 128 80MHz PowerPC 601 and 2GB memory (organized as a network of 64 nodes, each with 2 PowerPCs and 32MB memory), PARIX 1.3.1, Motorola C 1.5 (flags -O3 -w -Ac=mixed) and GCC 2.7.0 (flags `-O2 -mno-stack-check`). Nicknames *ppc-cc* and *ppc-gcc*. For the benchmarks, only a single processor on a single node was used.

Sun SPARCstation 10/40, 40MHz SuperSPARC, 64MB, Solaris 2.4, Sun C 3.0.1 (flags `-xO2`) and GCC 2.6.3 (flags `-O2`). Nicknames *sparc-cc* and *sparc-gcc*. (The code is also known to work under SunOS 4.1.3 with GCC 2.6.3.)

C compiler bugs made some targets less than fully operational:

GCC (both 2.6.3 and 2.7.0) generates incorrect code for the 'plain' and 'switch' runtime systems on the Intel x86 architecture.

The HP C compiler sometimes generates incorrect code for the 'pushy' runtime system, which caused the 'miniml' and 'petrol' examples to fail.

10.2   Overview

The three RML example specifications, `mf`, `miniml`, and `petrol`, were used for the benchmarks. The inputs were fixed as follows:

- The `mf` interpreter was applied to a small functional program computing the first 60 primes using the sieve method. The representation of the test case was built into the interpreter itself, thus obviating any overhead from scanning or parsing.

- The `miniml` type-checker was applied to a 154 line SML program containing 38 definitions of various more-or-less polymorphic functions (combinators, Peano arithmetic, lists, linear algebra, sorting), followed by one extremely polymorphic expression adapted from [113, Example 1.1]. (The expression has more than 4000 schematic type variables.) The reported timings do not include time spent in the scanner or parser.

- The `petrol` compiler was applied to a 2293 line Diesel[1] program, consisting of 128 procedures and functions. (These were collected from the original Diesel compiler's test suite.)

Due to the enormous number of combinations of different code generation options, and runtime system parameters, it is assumed that both the memory allocation arena size, and the state access method, can be measured independently.

First the effects of varying the size of the memory allocation arena for every combination of target system and code generation method will be evaluated. The best choice will then be used during the second test, which is to vary the state access methods for the 'plain' and 'switch' runtime systems.

All of the RML code tested has been compiled with all optimizations enabled. In the next test, the three optimization groups in the `rml2c` compiler are evaluated by disabling each one separately, measuring the effect on code

---

[1] Recall that Petrol is a proper extension of Diesel.

size and runtime performance, and comparing this to the fully optimized code.

In the last round of tests, comparisons are made between code generated by rml2c, two commercial native-code Prolog compilers (Quintus and SICStus Prolog), and Sun's commercial Pascal compiler.

For each test point, i.e. choice of code generation options, runtime system, runtime configuration options, machine, and C compiler, each of the three example specifications is executed 10 times; then the fastest run for the example is chosen as its result. The results for the individual examples are then added together to form the result of the given test point.

The reasons for adding the three examples together rather than presenting their results separately are twofold. First, we are interested in finding those options that give best *overall* results for a range of applications. Hence, we would have had to combine the individual results anyway. Second, presenting individual results as well would take four times as much space as just presenting the combined results, making the number of figures and tables in this chapter grow impractically large.

Having said this, we feel compelled to at least indicate the rough relationships between the three benchmark examples. mf and miniml were roughly comparable, each with typically about 45-48% of the accumulated time. In contrast, petrol typically took about 4-5% of the accumulated time.

10.3 Allocation Arena Size

The first test concerns the size of the memory allocation arena. All runtime systems use the same heap organization, with a fixed allocation arena (sometimes called the nursery or simply the youngest generation), and two equal-sized semi-spaces for the older generation. Data surviving a minor collection of the nursery are copied to the current older generation semi-space; when it in turn fills up, a standard stop-and-copy step is done to perform a major collection.

During these tests, the size of the nursery was varied in steps of 1K words from 1K to 16K words, and then in steps of 4K words from 16K to 128K words. Each of the older generation semi-spaces was 256K words. (A *word* is the size of a pointer, which is 64 bits on the Alpha, and 32 bits on all other targets.)

Figures 10.1 to 10.12 display these results for all targets. In each figure, the x-axis is the allocation arena size in kilowords, and the y-axis is the added time (in seconds) of the three examples. In the plotted curves, ◇ is the 'plain' runtime, + the 'pushy' runtime, □ the 'switch' runtime, and × the 'warped' runtime. (The details of these runtime systems are described in Chapter 9.)

We can make the following observations from these figures.

1. The 'switch' runtime (marked □) is always the fastest, for every target and every choice of nursery size.

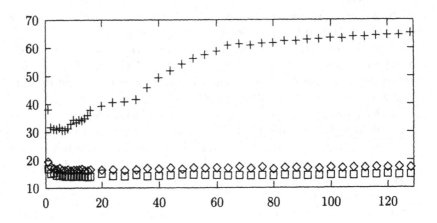

Figure 10.1: alpha-cc

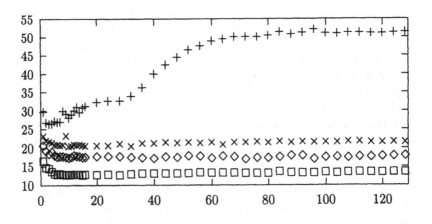

Figure 10.2: alpha-gcc

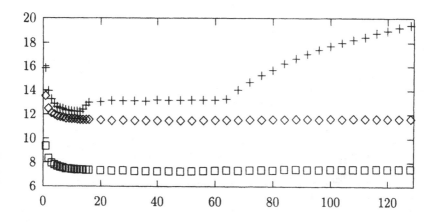

Figure 10.3: hp-cc, only mf example

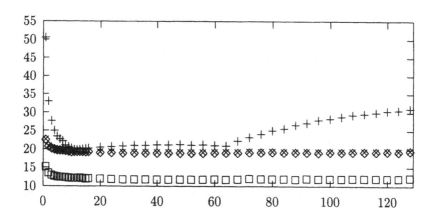

Figure 10.4: hp-gcc

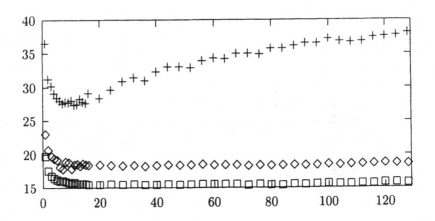

Figure 10.5: i386-cc

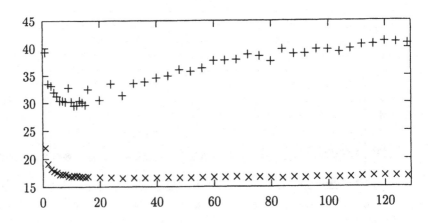

Figure 10.6: i386-gcc, only **pushy** and **warped** runtime systems

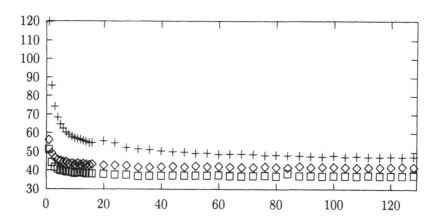

Figure 10.7: mips-cc

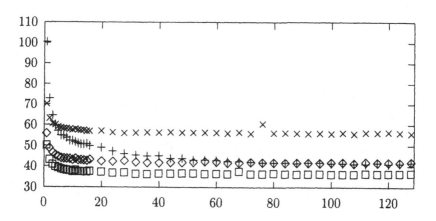

Figure 10.8: mips-gcc

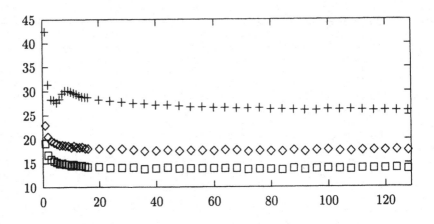

Figure 10.9: ppc-cc

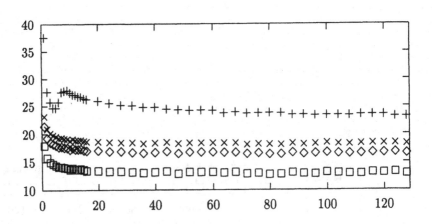

Figure 10.10: ppc-gcc

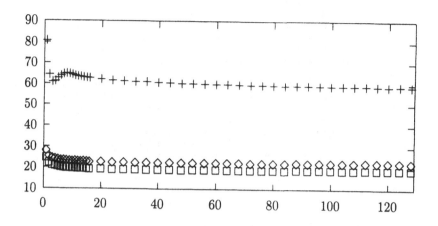

Figure 10.11: sparc-cc

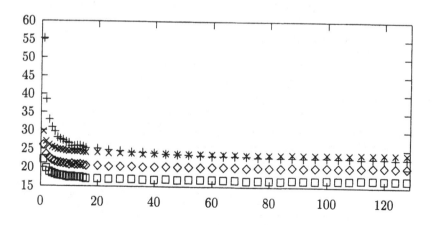

Figure 10.12: sparc-gcc

	switch	plain	pushy	warped
alpha-cc	1.00	1.17	3.40	n/a
alpha-gcc	1.00	1.34	3.00	1.62
hp-cc	1.00	1.56	1.95	n/a
hp-gcc	1.00	1.59	2.03	1.62
i386-cc	1.00	1.18	2.07	n/a
mips-cc	1.00	1.13	1.45	n/a
mips-gcc	1.00	1.15	1.30	1.54
ppc-cc	1.00	1.27	1.97	n/a
ppc-gcc	1.00	1.27	1.88	1.40
sparc-cc	1.00	1.17	3.20	n/a
sparc-gcc	1.00	1.20	1.50	1.41
average	1.00	1.28	2.16	1.52

Table 10.1: Time as a function of tailcall strategy

2. The 'pushy' runtime (marked +) is very sensitive to the nursery size, which in this case is the size of its stack buffer. It is interesting to note that on the *alpha*, *hp*, and *i386* targets, the optimum is reached at a fairly small stack buffer size, and that increasing the size beyond this point can *significantly* reduce performance. In contrast, the other runtime systems are must less sensitive.

3. The 'pushy' runtime almost always had the worst performance, except on the *mips-gcc* where 'warped' (marked ×) performed even worse, and 'pushy' performed almost as good as 'plain' (marked ◇). On the other targets, 'warped' performed like, or only slightly worse than, 'plain'.

To further summarize this data we computed, for each target and runtime system, the sum of its timings at each choice of allocation arena size. For each target, these timings were then normalized with respect to the time taken for the 'switch' runtime system on that target. The data is listed in Table 10.1. Again, the tendency is clear: 'switch' is faster than 'plain', which is faster than both 'pushy' and 'warped'.

The Mercury paper [165] claims a factor of two in speedup when the 'warped' technique is combined with a register allocator and GCC's global register variables. If we assume this to hold also for RML, then the 'warped' runtime would appear to beat the 'switch' runtime, assuming that it still does not use global register variables.

In another paper [53], Demoen and Maris get almost a factor of two in speedup when they used global registers for some important state variables in the KLIC [42] scheme (which is similar in spirit to 'switch'). If we assume this to hold also for RML's 'switch' runtime, then 'switch' will clearly still beat 'warped'.

10.4   State Access Methods

The 'plain' and 'switch' runtime systems implement tailcalls by returning to the dispatcher loop. As a consequence, parameters cannot be passed as C function parameters, but have to be communicated through global memory cells. The caller has to assign these cells, and the callee has to refer to them.

Here we evaluate the state access methods described in Section 9.4.1, for the 'plain' and 'switch' runtime systems. They are:

- SPLIT: the state consists of separate global variables

- JOING: the state is a single global record

- AGPTR: the address of the record is passed to generated functions

- LGPTR: the functions compute the address of the record locally

The results are listed in Table 10.2. There are several observations to be made here:

- The preferred method is always highly machine and compiler dependent. Luckily, it is quite easy for a compiler to generate portable macros, and have a configuration file control the expansion of these into the appropriate version for that system.

- Making a poor choice can cost anywhere from 3% to 10% in the 'plain' runtime. While not catastrophic, this is still overhead one would rather not pay.

- The 'switch' runtime reduces the cost of poor choices, since it reduces the number of times control has to pass through the dispatcher loop.

10.5   Compiler Optimizations

The `rml2c` compiler includes three optional optimization levels: the FOL representation can be simplified using the term-rewriting system described in Chapter 6 (optimization level Ofol), the CPS representation can be optimized using various simple transformations as described in Chapter 8 (Ocps), and (in the non-'pushy' runtime systems) copy propagation can be applied to the Code representation as described in Section 8.3.2 (Ocode).

By default, all of these optimizations are enabled. To measure the efficiency improvements in them, we recompiled the examples for the 'plain' runtime three times, each time disabling one of the optimizations. The effects of this are listed in Tables 10.3, 10.4, 10.5, and 10.6. (In each table, the 'O' column is the default code with all optimizations. The 'abs' columns contain absolute values. The 'rel' columns are relative to the 'O' column.)

	RUNTIME PLAIN				
	SPLIT	JOING	AGPTR	LGPTR	max/min
alpha-cc	16.03	14.61	15.33	15.28	1.10
alpha-gcc	16.36	15.01	16.32	16.47	1.10
hp-cc	22.66	21.93	21.93	22.00	1.03
hp-gcc	19.90	18.82	18.91	19.01	1.06
i386-cc	17.73	17.70	18.91	18.22	1.07
mips-cc	44.95	44.92	41.39	44.48	1.09
mips-gcc	41.67	44.28	41.29	43.71	1.07
ppc-cc	18.65	17.11	17.07	17.20	1.09
ppc-gcc	17.03	16.26	16.36	16.31	1.05
sparc-cc	22.66	21.83	21.42	21.84	1.06
sparc-gcc	20.60	20.34	19.88	20.14	1.04

	RUNTIME SWITCH				
	SPLIT	JOING	AGPTR	LGPTR	max/min
alpha-cc	14.44	14.09	13.90	13.89	1.04
alpha-gcc	13.58	13.09	12.69	13.08	1.07
hp-cc	16.16	16.01	16.30	16.31	1.02
hp-gcc	11.84	11.87	11.61	11.87	1.02
i386-cc	15.07	15.04	15.33	15.42	1.03
mips-cc	38.17	38.33	36.98	38.55	1.04
mips-gcc	35.06	36.39	35.79	36.30	1.04
ppc-cc	13.56	13.40	13.35	13.47	1.02
ppc-gcc	12.61	12.59	12.36	12.58	1.02
sparc-cc	18.84	18.59	18.58	18.52	1.02
sparc-gcc	16.44	16.41	16.42	16.40	1.00

Table 10.2: Timings for different state access methods

	O	no-Ofol		no-Ocps		no-Ocode	
	abs	abs	rel	abs	rel	abs	rel
mf	2141	3115	1.45	3782	1.77	2270	1.06
miniml	4351	5995	1.38	5977	1.37	4647	1.07
petrol	13510	20158	1.49	17544	1.30	14541	1.08
average			1.44		1.48		1.07

Table 10.3: Lines of generated C code for 'plain'

	O	no-Ofol		no-Ocps	
	abs	abs	rel	abs	rel
mf	3390	8595	2.54	4481	1.32
miniml	8868	9005	1.02	8857	1.00
petrol	248	608	2.44	548	2.21
average			2.00		1.51

Table 10.4: Max stack usage in words

	O	no-Ofol		no-Ocps	
	abs	abs	rel	abs	rel
mf	9230676	14954406	1.62	15022709	1.63
miniml	2783084	10190976	3.66	7775259	2.79
petrol	334613	495098	1.48	607076	1.81
average			2.25		2.08

Table 10.5: Number of tailcalls

	O	no-Ofol		no-Ocps		no-Ocode	
	abs	abs	rel	abs	rel	abs	rel
alpha-cc	14.61	40.90	2.80	19.50	1.33	17.03	1.17
alpha-gcc	15.01	45.14	3.01	20.25	1.35	16.66	1.11
hp-cc	21.93	62.43	2.85	30.01	1.37	22.75	1.04
hp-gcc	18.82	55.49	2.95	28.28	1.50	19.98	1.06
i386-cc	17.70	53.35	3.01	23.30	1.32	18.65	1.05
mips-cc	41.39	123.56	2.99	53.49	1.29	43.52	1.05
mips-gcc	41.29	128.77	3.12	55.34	1.34	43.79	1.06
ppc-cc	17.07	50.19	2.94	22.83	1.34	18.09	1.06
ppc-gcc	16.26	48.72	3.00	21.73	1.34	17.00	1.05
sparc-cc	21.42	60.35	2.82	28.28	1.32	21.88	1.02
sparc-gcc	19.88	53.68	2.70	26.04	1.31	20.29	1.02
average			2.93		1.35		1.06

Table 10.6: Accumulated execution times

First, in Table 10.3, we see how much additional C code is generated when the optimizations are disabled. Both the FOL and CPS optimizations are quite effective at reducing the size of the generated code.

Next Table 10.4 shows how stack usage is related to the two high-level optimizations. The FOL optimizations were initially introduced to deal with the extreme stack usage of the original compiler, as discussed in Chapter 6. Now that the language has been modified to be determinate, maximum stack usage is less severe, but the FOL optimizations still reduce it further by a significant amount – about a factor of 2.5 for two of the examples. The CPS optimizations recognize many opportunities for tailcall optimizations, which also helps reduce stack usage.

Using less stack translates directly into faster code, since fewer memory cells need to be written and read. Using less of the address range also helps the cache.

Table 10.5 shows how the two high-level optimizations reduce the number of tailcalls. Again, fewer tailcalls translates directly into faster code. This is partly since there are fewer control transfers via the dispatcher loop, and partly because larger intermediate computations (C function bodies) are being optimized by the C compiler.

Finally, in Table 10.6 the accumulated timings for the examples are listed. We see here that the FOL optimizations cut execution times by almost a factor of three, while the CPS optimizations save about 30%-35%. The trivial little copy-propagation optimization saves a stunning 17% on *alpha-cc*; not counting the Alpha, it saves about 5% on average. The effectiveness of this optimization is probably in part due to our low-level calling conventions, which were designed with this in mind.

10.6   Facing the Opposition

10.6.1   Mini-Freja

The Mini-Freja specification was used during an early stage of the development of the rml2c compiler, to allow comparisons between RML and Typol, and RML and Prolog.

The original specification was written in Typol (the version in Centaur 1.2 [91]), and converted to RML. The standard test program – computing primes – was used as the input to the generated interpreters. Table 10.7 shows the results from executing the interpreters on a Sun 10/40.

As is apparent from these figures, Typol's execution time quickly grows to impractical levels: 1130 seconds is almost 19 minutes. From this we conjecture that Typol has been implemented for other purposes than efficient execution of natural semantics specifications. Debugging, teaching, theorem proving, an attractive user interface, were probably considered more impor-

primes	RML	Typol	T/R
3	0.0026	13	5000
4	0.0037	72	19459
5	0.0063	1130	179365

Table 10.7: MF, RML vs. Typol, time in seconds

primes	RML	SICStus	S/R	Quintus	Q/R	machine
18	0.45	5.0	11.1	4.5	10.0	Sun 4/470
18	0.22	2.20	10.0			Sun 10/40
30	0.87	11.20	12.9			Sun 10/40

Table 10.8: MF, RML vs. Prolog, time in seconds

tant goals. (It has been claimed[2] that the Typol version's use of Typol's **recovery** feature contributed to its poor performance. We have not yet investigated this.)

The Mini-Freja specification was also rewritten in Prolog to allow comparisons to be made with commercial native-code Prolog compilers: SICStus Prolog version 2.1 #9, and Quintus Prolog version 3.1.1. When converting the specification to Prolog, we strove to keep the original high-level structure intact: every inference rule became a Prolog clause. We did *not* change the structure to make use of Prolog's disjunctions, conditionals, or cuts, nor did we change the order of arguments in procedures.

The results of this benchmark are shown in Table 10.8.[3] At least for this specification, rml2c generates code that is an order of magnitude faster than that generated by these commercial compilers.

10.6.2   Petrol

We also compared the generated Petrol compiler with the original Diesel compiler, which was hand-written in Pascal. The original Diesel compiler was compiled with optimizations, no debugging, and no array indexing or pointer checks. This test was performed on the *sparc* target, with Sun's Pascal compiler version SC3.0.1, flags -O -notrace; GCC was used as the back-end for rml2c. Timings for both systems now include time spent in the front-ends and time spent emitting the symbolic code to /dev/null. The test input was the same 2293 line Diesel program used before. (The Pascal code, written in true imperative/procedural style, had several fixed-size tables

---

[2]T. Despeyroux, INRIA Sophia-Antipolis, e-mail, May 20, 1994.
[3]The first line contains figures for an old version of rml2c. Due to Quintus licensing and recent machine upgrades, we are unable to re-evaluate Quintus on our current machines.

RML	Pascal	P/R
1.06	1.47	1.39

Table 10.9: Petrol, RML vs. Pascal, time in seconds

that had to be made much larger before it could compile the benchmarking program.)

As witnessed by the results listed in Table 10.9, the optimized Pascal code is actually 39% slower than the code generated by rml2c. While this is a comparison of apples and oranges, it does suggest that the quality of the code generated by rml2c is on or near a 'production quality' level.

10.7 Conclusions

The literature is full of examples of code generation techniques for mapping high-level languages to C [10, 16, 17, 42, 45, 52, 53, 72, 82, 110, 143, 161, 163, 165, 169, 171]. Some of these suggest using non-portable hacks to work around the perceived inefficiencies of portable schemes – such as our 'plain' and 'switch' runtime systems. We believe, following our benchmarks, that well-engineered portable schemes can be competitive. In particular, our 'switch' scheme seems to have an edge.

Baker's elegant 'pushy' scheme has three major flaws: (1) it makes it more difficult to have calls between normal C code and generated code, (2) unless carefully tuned to the particular machine, performance can be significantly reduced, and (3) it appears to always be slower than the 'switch' and 'plain' schemes. Because of these flaws, we feel that the 'pushy' scheme is a non-contender.

We have shown the effectiveness of rml2c's strategy of applying optimizations at all representation levels. We have also shown that relatively simple transformations, unaided by global program analysis, have sufficed to achieve performance levels on par with, or even surpassing, those of commercial systems.

We have shown that optimizing state accesses in dispatching schemes (copy propagation in the compiler, state access macros in the runtime system) can produce small but useful improvements.

Chapter 11

Concluding Remarks

$\mathcal{T}$his chapter marks the end of this book. Here I summarize our contributions and indicate some possibilities for future work.

11.1 Summary

We see the following as our main contributions:

- We have designed and defined the Relational Meta-Language. The important features of this language are: strong static typing via an ML-like polymorphic type system, modules, and determinate proof search. (Chapters 3 and 4, and Appendix A.)

- We have developed an effective compilation strategy resulting in efficient code. The most significant phase in the compiler is the translation to a First-Order Logic representation, followed by transformations to improve determinacy. (Chapters 5, 6, and 10.)

- We have shown that a functional continuation-passing style intermediate representation is useful also for compiling logic-programming languages. (Chapters 8 and 10.)

- We have described most known techniques for mapping tailcalls to properly tail-recursive C code, and also developed a new method for 'block' (module) compilation. We have implemented four techniques in our rml2c compiler, measured the performance of these techniques on several machines, and shown our new method to be superior for our compiler. (Chapters 9 and 10.)

11.2   Future Work

11.2.1   Default Rules

From the discussion in Section 3.4, we saw that limiting the scope of specifications to determinate ones is considered acceptable.[1] This creates an opportunity for introducing *default* rules. Consider:

```
datatype t = C1 of int
           | C2 of string
             ...
relation normalize =
    axiom normalize(C1 _) => C1 0
    axiom normalize(C2 _) => C2 ""
default
    axiom normalize other => other
end
```

This, admittedly contorted, example describes a fairly common situation: there are a large number of possible cases, but only a few need special treatment, all the others are treated similarly. If the `default` keyword is removed, then this example can be executed in RML, and indeed produces the desired result (due to determinacy and the top-down search among rules). However, the example becomes *logically* incorrect, since the default rule also matches the two previous rules.

There are really two different kinds of defaults. The first handles the case when all previous rules *fail*, and is easy to describe. The second kind deals with the case when no previous rule matched the actual parameters. To handle this properly in current RML, it is necessary to describe *explicitly* that the default rule is not applicable for the non-default cases:

```
relation is_c1_or_c2 =
    axiom is_c1_or_c2(C1 _)
    axiom is_c1_or_c2(C2 _)
end

relation normalize =
    axiom normalize(C1 _) => C1 0
    axiom normalize(C2 _) => C2 ""

    rule  not is_c1_or_c2 other
          ----------------
          normalize other => other
end
```

---

[1]This is not so surprising. Consider context-free grammars. Most language designers and compiler writers seem to be quite happy with limiting themselves to the LR(1), LALR(1), or even LL(1) subclasses.

The proposed solution with the `default` keyword is much simpler than this explicit formulation, while retaining the correct operational and logical interpretations. (The Typol 'recovery' feature appears to have a similar operational interpretation, but seems to be intended for error handling rather than defaults.)

11.2.2 Programming Sub-Language

As witnessed by the code emitting phases in the Diesel and Petrol compilers, we prefer to manipulate RML data objects in RML rather than in C. However, these 'programming' tasks become quite verbose when expressed in RML, especially since RML provides no low-level control operators. An SML-like sub-language would allow them to be coded using a more economical and natural form of expression.

11.2.3 Taming Side-Effects

The dynamic semantics is currently inconsistent with the FOL optimizations, since eliminating calls with side-effects may be observed. Note, however, that deterministic calls are never removed. Our current workaround is to warn users: *nondeterministic side-effects are used at one's peril*. It would clearly be desirable to find a formulation of the dynamic semantics that is both sufficiently abstract to admit the FOL optimizations, and sufficiently predictable to allow controlled use of side-effects.

11.2.4 Moded Types

Unknowns, or logical variables, are rare creatures in many specifications. Mini-Freja used them for its illogical realization of recursive objects, but there they could be eliminated by using finite unfolding instead. Only the Mini-ML polymorphic type checker actually *computes* with unknowns. This leads us to believe that unknowns can be replaced by a primitive polymorphic type, whose objects require explicit tests and projections when accessed. This would only affect Mini-ML, and then only in a small part of the specification.

The advantages of introducing this change are twofold. First, it would greatly simplify C code that needs to access RML data, since data representation and accesses would be more straightforward. Second, it would reduce the size of the compiled code and improve its efficiency, since almost all (currently unnecessary) dereferencing operations can be removed.

11.2.5 Linear Types

State-like objects have the property that there is only one handle to them when they are updated. This allows the updates to be destructive. However, this property cannot be expressed in most side-effect free languages, causing state accesses to be asymptotically slower than in imperative languages.

This problem is not new, having been studied in denotational semantics and functional languages under the name of *single-threading*. Recently *linear types* have been proposed as a means for expressing the necessary conditions for allowing destructive updates [83, 177].

An RML user *can* implement state-like objects efficiently in C code linked with the RML specification, but the compiler cannot verify that those objects are handled in a single-threaded manner. (It *is* possible to perform fairly cheap checks at runtime in the C code.) If linear type declarations were possible, the compiler could instead check statically that accesses indeed are linear.

11.2.6 Compile to SML

Since the change of the dynamic semantics to be determinate, choice points and backtracking are really equivalent to SML *exceptions*. If the type system is changed to encode *modes* as types, then compiling RML to SML would become a clear alternative. (The reasons for not doing so now are accounted for in Chapter 5.)

11.2.7 Tuning the Runtime Systems

According to the discussion in Section 10.3, using GCC's global register variables might improve performance by a factor of two for some runtime systems. This possibility is clearly worth investigating.

11.2.8 User-Friendliness

The current compiler is not easy to use. The error messages for incorrect RML code are overly terse, but more seriously, there is no support for runtime debugging or tracing. It is planned to rectify these problems in the near future.

Appendix A

The Definition of RML

A.1 Introduction

This document formally defines RML – the Relational Meta-Language – using Natural Semantics as the specification formalism.

RML is intended as an executable specification language for experimenting with and implementing Natural Semantics. The rationale for the design of the language, and hints on how it may be implemented, are not included here, but may be found in earlier chapters of this thesis.

The style of this document was greatly influenced by the formal definition of the Standard ML language and notation used in denotational semantics. See [120] and [119] for further examples on the kind of Natural Semantics used here.

A.1.1 Differences to SML

RML is heavily influenced by Standard ML, both in the language itself and in its definition. Below we summarize some of the technical differences between these languages.

RML's relations are n-to-m, not 1-to-1 as functions in SML are. Also, RML's datatype constructors are n-ary rather than just unary. The kinds of objects used to represent relation types are therefore slightly more general than those used for SML.

Like SML, RML's datatype declarations can simultaneously introduce a number of type aliases using the withtype construct. SML requires those aliases to be expanded *simultaneously*, while RML (like the SML/NJ implementation) expands them *sequentially*. This allows aliases to depend on other aliases.

The RML module system is very much simpler than that in SML. A module is an environment of type and value bindings. Within a module, no type identifier, constructor, or variable may be multiply bound, and in a program, no module identifier may be multiply bound. For stand-alone applications, RML defines the entry point to be module Main's relation main, which must be of type string list => ().

SML and RML introduce a unique tag to represent a user-level datatype in the type system. Such a tag is known as a *type name*, but is *not* the type identifier used in the datatype declaration. In RML, type names are pairs (*module id*, *type id*). Due to its simpler module system, these pairs are guaranteed to be unique.

Similarly to SML, RML needs to distinguish between different kinds of value identifiers, viz. constructors, relations, and variables. The definition of SML pretends that the lexical analysis phase correctly classifies identifiers, even though such a classification requires static elaboration. In RML the rules for identifier classification are merged into the static semantics.

A.2 Notation for Natural Semantics

A.2.1 Lexical Definitions

Lexical definitions are made primarily using regular expressions. These are written using the following notation[1], in which alternatives are listed in decreasing order of precedence:

c	denotes the character c, if c is not one of `. *+?|(){}\"[]^`
`\t`	denotes a tab character (ASCII 9)
`\n`	denotes a newline character (ASCII 10)
`\`*ddd*	denotes the single character with number *ddd*, where *ddd* is a 3-digit decimal integer in the interval $[0, 255]$
`\`c	denotes the character c
`[...]`	denotes the set of characters listed in `...`
`[^...]`	denotes the complement of `[...]`
c_1-c_2	(within `[...]`) denotes the range of characters from c_1 to c_2
`.`	denotes any character except newline
`"`x`"`	denotes the string of characters x
`{`x`}`	equals the expression bound to the identifier x
`(`x`)`	equals x
x`*`	denotes the Kleene closure of x
x`+`	denotes the positive closure of x
x`?`	denotes an optional occurrence of x
x{n}	denotes n repetitions of x, where n is a small integer
x{n_1,n_2}	denotes between n_1 and n_2 repetitions of x
xy	denotes the concatenation of x and y
x|y	denotes the disjunction of x and y

A.2.2 Syntax Definitions

Syntax definitions are made using extended context-free grammars. The following conventions apply:

- The brackets ⟨ ⟩ enclose optional phrases.

- Alternative forms for each phrase class are listed in *decreasing* order of precedence.

- ε denotes an empty phrase.

- $\cdots$ denotes repetition. It is never a literal token.

- Constraints on the applicability of a production may be added.

- A production may be indicated as being left (right) (non) associative by adding the letter L (R) (N) to its right.

---

[1]This notation coincides with the one used by the `ml-lex` scanner generator.

- References to literal tokens are printed in this style.

- References to syntactic phrases or non-literal lexical items are printed in *this* style.

A.2.3 Sets

If A is a set, then Fin A denotes the set of finite subsets of A.

A.2.4 Tuples

Tuples are ordered heterogeneous collections of fixed finite length.

$(x_1, \cdots, x_n)$ a tuple t formed of x_1 to x_n, in that order
k of t projection; equals x_k if $t = (x_1, \cdots, x_k, \cdots, x_n)$
$T_1 \times \cdots \times T_n$ the type $\{(x_1, \cdots, x_n) \; ; \; x_i \in T_i \; (1 \le i \le n)\}$

The notation k of t is sometimes extended to x of t, where x is a meta-variable ranging over T_k, and t is of type $T_1 \times \cdots T_k \cdots \times T_n$. There must be only one occurrence of the type T_k in $T_1, \cdots, T_n$.

A.2.5 Finite Sequences

Sequences are ordered homogeneous collections of varying, but always finite, length.

$[]$	the empty sequence
$x :: s$	the sequence formed by prepending x to sequence s
$s @ s'$	the concatenation of sequences s and s'
$x^{(n)}$ or $[x_1, \cdots, x_n]$	the sequence $x_1 :: \cdots :: x_n :: []$
x^*	a sequence of 0 or more x's
x^+	a sequence of 1 or more x's
$s \downarrow k$	the k'th element of sequence s (1-based)
$s \setminus k$	the sequence s with its k'th element removed
$\#s$	the length of sequence s
$\rightleftharpoons s$	the reversal of sequence s
$x \in s$	membership test, $\exists k \in [1, \#s] : s \downarrow k = x$
$s \subseteq s'$	$\forall k \in [1, \#s] : s \downarrow k \in s'$
T^k	the type of all T-sequences of length k
T^* or $\cup_{k \ge 0} T^k$	the type of all finite T-sequences
T^+ or $\cup_{k \ge 1} T^k$	the type of all non-empty finite T-sequences

A.2.6 Finite Maps

If A and B are sets, then $A \xrightarrow{\text{fin}} B$ denotes the set of *finite maps* (partial functions with finite domain) from A to B. The domain and range of a finite map, f, are denoted by Dom f and Ran f. A finite map can be written explicitly in the form $\{a_1 \mapsto b_1, \cdots, a_k \mapsto b_k\}, k \ge 0$. The form $\{a \mapsto b \; ; \; \phi\}$

stands for a finite map f whose domain is the set of values a which satisfy the condition ϕ, and whose value on this domain is given by $f(a) = b$. If f and g are finite maps, then $f + g$ (*f modified by g*) is the finite map with domain Dom $f \cup$ Dom g and values

$$(f + g)(a) = \text{if } a \in \text{Dom } g \text{ then } g(a) \text{ else } f(a).$$

A.2.7   Substitutions

If t is a term with variables V of type T, and f is a finite map of type $V \xrightarrow{\text{fin}} T$, then f can be used as a *substitution* on t. The expression tf denotes the effect of substituting free variables v_i in t by $f(v_i)$, when $v_i \in$ Dom f. The definition of 'free' variables depends on the type of the term t. Substitutions are extended element-wise to finite sequences.

A.2.8   Disjoint Unions

The type $T_1 \cup \cdots \cup T_n$ denotes the *disjoint* union of the types $T_1, \ldots, T_n$. Let x be a meta-variable ranging over a disjoint union type T, and x_i range over its summands T_i.

An x_i is injected into T by the expression x_i in T.

Membership test and projection are normally expressed using pattern-matching syntax. Using a meta-variable x_i in a binding position in a function or relation, where the binding position is of type T, constrains an argument to be in the summand T_i; moreover, the formal parameter x_i is bound to the projected value in T_i.

A.2.9   Relations

A relation is a (in general infinite) set of tuples, i.e. a subset of some product $T_1 \times \cdots \times T_n$. It is characterized by a *signature* and is defined by a finite set of *inference rules*.

Signatures

A signature is used to declare the form and type of a relation. It is written as a non-empty sequence of meta-variables, with some auxiliary symbols inserted between some of them. Let $x_1, \ldots, x_n$ be meta-variables for the types $T_1, \cdots, T_n$. Then a signature whose sequence of meta-variables is $x^{(n)}$, declares a relation over $T_1 \times \cdots \times T_n$.

When a relation is seen as defining logical propositions, as is typical for natural semantics, signatures are usually called *judgements*.

Occasionally, the place of a meta-variable will be replaced by a 'prototype' pattern of the form e/e', which denotes an anonymous type $T \cup T'$, where T (T') is the type of e (e').

The auxiliary symbols inserted in a signature have no semantic effect, other than to make the signature easier to read, and to disambiguate different relations having the same type.

Example: Let *ME*, *VE*, *exp*, and τ be the meta-variables for the types ModEnv, ValEnv, Exp, and Type respectively. Then $ME, VE \vdash exp \Rightarrow \tau$ is a signature for a relation over ModEnv $\times$ ValEnv $\times$ Exp $\times$ Type.

Instances

An instance of a signature is formed by instantiating the meta-variables with expressions (or patterns) of appropriate types.

Groups of relations are often viewed as defining a special-purpose logic. In this case, instances are referred to as *propositions* or *sequents*.

Inference Rules

The contents (set of tuples) of a relation is specified using a finite set of inference rules of the form:

$$\frac{premises}{conclusion} \qquad (label)$$

The conclusion is written as an instance of the signature of the relation. The premises impose additional conditions, typically by checking that certain values occur in other relations, that certain values are equal (or not equal), or that certain values occur (or do not occur) in some set or sequence. When the premises are true, the conclusion (the existence of an element in the relation) can be inferred.

We additionally require relations to be *determinate*: for every element in the relation, *exactly one* of the relation's inference rules must hold.[2]

We sometimes use _ in the place of a meta-variable. This syntax is used to make it clear that a particular value is ignored.

Inference rules are often labelled, as indicated by the label written to the right.

In the rules, phrases bracketed by $\langle \rangle$ are *optional*. In an instance of a rule, either all or none of the options must be present. This convention, motivated by optional phrases in syntax definitions, allows a reduction in the number of rules.

A.2.10 Example

These declarations are given for natural and binary numbers:

Here is the specification for a relation expressing a mapping from binary to natural numbers. By convention, we write the relation's signature in a box

---

[2]This ensures some consistency between RML itself and the natural semantics used to define it. However, the current RML compiler does not check that specifications obey this condition. See also the discussion about default rules in Section 4.3.3.

$n \in$ Nat   natural numbers (primitive)

$b \in$ Bin $::= 0 \mid 1 \mid b0 \mid b1$ binary numbers

above and to the right of the rules. We also indicate the type of the main object inspected by writing its name above and to the left of the rules.

Binary Numbers

$$\boxed{b \Rightarrow n}$$

$$\frac{}{0 \Rightarrow 0} \tag{1}$$

$$\frac{}{1 \Rightarrow 1} \tag{2}$$

$$\frac{b \Rightarrow n}{b0 \Rightarrow 2n} \tag{3}$$

$$\frac{b \Rightarrow n}{b1 \Rightarrow 2n + 1} \tag{4}$$

Relations are often used in a directed manner. For example, a query $b \Rightarrow n$ is typically used when b is known to *compute* n. (This distinction of arguments and results is made explicit in the syntax and semantics of RML.)

A.3 Lexical Structure

This section defines the lexical structure of RML.

A.3.1 Reserved Words

The following are the reserved words, including special symbols. The word
-- represents all words generated by the regular expression -(-)+.

```
abstype  and  as  axiom  datatype  end  exists  module
not  of  relation  rule  type  val  with  withtype
&  (  )  *  ,  --  .  :  ::  =  =>  [  ]  _  |
```

A.3.2 Integer Constants

Integer constants are denoted by the token class *icon*, which is defined by
the regular expression (-)?{*natnum*}, where *natnum* is defined as [0-9]+.
Examples: 5   -123 . Non-example: +7 .

A.3.3 Real Constants

Real constants are denoted by the token class *rcon*. A real constant is written
as an integer constant, followed by a fraction and an exponent. Either the
fraction or the exponent, but not both, may be omitted. Examples: 0.7
3.25E5   3E-7 . Non-examples: 23   .3   4.E5 .

$$
\begin{array}{rcl}
fraction & = & \text{"."}\{natnum\} \\
exponent & = & \text{"E"}\{icon\} \\
rcon & = & \{icon\}(\{fraction\}\{exponent\}?\,|\,\{exponent\})
\end{array}
$$

A.3.4 Character Constants

The regular expression [^"\\\n]|\\(\\|n|t|\"), bound to *char*, describes
characters. An underlying alphabet of at least 256 distinct characters numbered 0 to 255 is assumed, such that the characters numbered 0 to 127 coin-
cide with the ASCII character set. \n denotes the newline character (ASCII
10), \t denotes the tab character (ASCII 9), \\ denotes the backslash character (ASCII 92), \" denotes the double quote character, and *c* denotes the
character *c* provided *c* is not a backslash, quote, or newline.

Character constants are denoted by the token class *ccon*, which is defined
by the regular expression #\"{*char*}\". Examples: #"A"   #" "   #"\\" .
Non-examples: #""   #"\e" .

A.3.5 String Constants

String constants are denoted by the token class *scon*, which is defined by the
regular expression \"{*char*}*\". Each item in the sequence is subject to the

same interpretation as described above for character constants. Examples:
`"foo"` `"Backslash is \\"` . Non-examples: `"bar`   `"fum\$"` .

A.3.6   Identifiers

Identifiers are denoted by the token class *id*, which is defined by the regular expression {*alpha*}{*alnum*}*. The *alpha* character class is defined as `[A-Za-z_]`, and *alnum* is defined as `[0-9A-Za-z_']`. An instance of the regular expression for *id* that coincides with a reserved word is interpreted as that reserved word, not as an identifier. Examples: `cons`   `g4711'` .
Non-examples: `5plus`   `axiom`   `$:/%#|!*~+-` .

A.3.7   Type Variables

Types variables are denoted by the token class *tyvar*, which is defined by the regular expression `'`{*alpha*}{*alnum*}*. Examples: `'a` .

A.3.8   Whitespace and Comments

The blank, tab, linefeed, carriage return, and formfeed characters are treated as whitespace characters. Any non-empty sequence of whitespace characters between tokens is ignored, except that it serves to delimit tokens.

   A comment is any character sequence starting with `(*` and ending with `*)` such that any occurrence of `(*` properly within that sequence is balanced by a subsequent occurrence of `*)`. A comment is equivalent to a single blank character. Formally, comments are described by the following grammar:

$$
\begin{aligned}
comment &::= (*\ skipto_{*)} \\
skipto_{*)} &::= *\ after_* \\
&\quad |\ (\ after_(\\
&\quad |\ [\char94*(]\ skipto_{*)} \\
after_* &::=) \\
&\quad |\ *\ after_* \\
&\quad |\ (\ after_(\\
&\quad |\ [\char94)*(]\ skipto_{*)} \\
after_(&::= *\ skipto_{*)}\ skipto_{*)} \\
&\quad |\ (\ after_(\\
&\quad |\ [\char94*(]\ skipto_{*)}
\end{aligned}
$$

A.3.9   Lexical Analysis

Lexical analysis maps a program to a sequence of items, in left to right order. Each item is either a reserved word, an integer, real, character, or string constant, an identifier, or a type variable. Whitespace and comments separate items but are otherwise ignored – except within character and string constants. At each stage, the longest recognizable item is taken.

A.4 Syntactic Structure

This section defines the syntax of RML.

A.4.1 Derived Forms, Full and Core Grammar

First the *full* (concrete) syntax is defined in Figures A.1 to A.6. In these rules, standard *derived* forms are marked with (*). Such forms are subject to term–rewriting transformations specified in Figures A.7 to A.11. The resulting *core* syntax is defined in Figures A.12 to A.16. Figure A.17 defines the implicit syntax of programs, i.e. sequences of modules.

The derived forms for `with` specifications and declarations use string literals to indicate the names of the files in which the intended external modules are located. In the core syntax, the interface of such an external module is made explicit (Figure A.11).

A.4.2 Ambiguity

The full grammar as given is highly ambiguous: the reasons are that an identifier may stand either for a (short) constructor or a variable binding in a pattern, and in an expression it may stand for a constructor or a variable reference. Type information is in general necessary to determine the meaning of an identifier in these contexts.

A parser could produce an ambiguous syntax tree where these possibilities have been joined to a single 'unknown identifier' case. The type checker can then construct an unambiguous syntax tree using the type information it has access to.

The static semantics rules given later assume an unambiguous core syntax tree, but also verify that the identifier classification was correct.

$$
\begin{array}{llll}
tycon & \in \text{TyCon} & ::= id & \text{type constructor} \\
con & \in \text{Con} & ::= id & \text{value constructor} \\
var & \in \text{Var} & ::= id & \text{value variable} \\
modid & \in \text{ModId} & ::= id & \text{module name} \\
longtycon & \in \text{longTyCon} & ::= \langle modid . \rangle tycon & \text{long type constructor} \\
longcon & \in \text{longCon} & ::= \langle modid . \rangle con & \text{long value constructor} \\
longvar & \in \text{longVar} & ::= \langle modid . \rangle var & \text{long value variable} \\
lit & \in \text{Lit} & ::= ccon & \text{character constant} \\
& & \mid icon & \text{integer constant} \\
& & \mid rcon & \text{real constant} \\
& & \mid scon & \text{string constant}
\end{array}
$$

Figure A.1: Full grammar: auxiliaries

```
tyvarseq ∈ TyVarSeq ::= ε                              empty (*)
                   | tyvar                          singleton (*)
                   | (tyvar₁, ···, tyvarₙ)               n ≥ 1
      ty ∈ Ty      ::= tyvar                             variable
                   | ⟨tyseq⟩ longtycon              construction (*)
                   | ty₁ * ··· * tyₙ                 tuple, n ≥ 2
                   | tyseq₁ => tyseq₂                    relation
                   | (ty)                                  (*)
    tyseq ∈ TySeq   ::= ()                               empty
                   | ty                             singleton (*)
                   | (ty₁, ···, tyₙ)             sequence, n ≥ 1
```

Figure A.2: Full grammar: types

```
   pat ∈ Pat      ::= _                                 wildcard
                   | lit                                 literal
                   | [pat₁, ···, patₙ]             list, n ≥ 0 (*)
                   | longcon                            constant
                   | var                             variable (*)
                   | longcon patseq                    structure
                   | (pat₁, ···, patₙ)           tuple, n ≠ 1
                   | pat₁ :: pat₂                    cons, R (*)
                   | var as pat                          binding
                   | (pat)                                 (*)
patseq ∈ PatSeq ::= ()                                  empty
                   | pat                            singleton (*)
                   | (pat₁, ···, patₙ)          sequence, n ≥ 1
```

Figure A.3: Full grammar: patterns

```
   exp ∈ Exp     ::= lit                                  literal
                   | [exp₁, ···, expₙ]             list, n ≥ 0 (*)
                   | longcon                            constant
                   | longvar                            variable
                   | longcon expseq                    structure
                   | (exp₁, ···, expₙ)           tuple, n ≠ 1
                   | exp₁ :: exp₂                    cons, R (*)
                   | (exp)                                 (*)
expseq ∈ ExpSeq ::= ()                                  empty
                   | exp                            singleton (*)
                   | (exp₁, ···, expₙ)          sequence, n ≥ 1
```

Figure A.4: Full grammar: expressions

$$
\begin{array}{llll}
goal \in \text{Goal} & ::= & longvar \; \langle expseq \rangle \; \langle \texttt{=>} \; \langle patseq \rangle \rangle & \text{call (*)} \\
& | & var = exp & \text{unification} \\
& | & \texttt{exists} \; var & \text{existential} \\
& | & \texttt{not} \; goal & \text{negation} \\
& | & goal_1 \; \texttt{\&} \; goal_2 & \text{sequence} \\
& | & \langle goal \rangle & \text{(*)} \\
clause \in \text{Clause} & ::= & \texttt{rule} \; \langle goal \rangle \; \texttt{--} \; var \; \langle patseq \rangle \; \langle \texttt{=>} \; \langle expseq \rangle \rangle & \text{rule (*)} \\
& | & \texttt{axiom} \; var \; \langle patseq \rangle \; \langle \texttt{=>} \; \langle expseq \rangle \rangle & \text{axiom (*)} \\
& | & clause_1 \; clause_2 & \text{sequence}
\end{array}
$$

Figure A.5: Full grammar: goals and clauses

$$
\begin{array}{llll}
conbind \in \text{ConBind} & ::= & con \; \langle \texttt{of} \; ty_1 \; \texttt{*} \; \cdots \; \texttt{*} \; ty_n \rangle & \langle n \geq 1 \rangle \\
& | & conbind_1 \; | \; conbind_2 & \\
datbind \in \text{DatBind} & ::= & tyvarseq \; tycon = conbind & \\
& | & datbind_1 \; \texttt{and} \; datbind_2 & \\
typbind \in \text{TypBind} & ::= & tyvarseq \; tycon = ty & \\
& | & typbind_1 \; \texttt{and} \; typbind_2 & \\
withbind \in \text{WithBind} & ::= & \langle \texttt{withtype} \; typbind \rangle & \\
relbind \in \text{RelBind} & ::= & var \; \langle \texttt{:} \; tyseq_1 \; \texttt{=>} \; tyseq_2 \rangle = clause & \\
& | & relbind_1 \; \texttt{and} \; relbind_2 & \\
spec \in \text{Spec} & ::= & \texttt{with} \; scon & \text{(*)} \\
& | & \texttt{abstype} \; tyvarseq \; tycon & \\
& | & \texttt{type} \; typbind & \\
& | & \texttt{datatype} \; datbind \; withbind & \\
& | & \texttt{relation} \; var \; \texttt{:} \; tyseq_1 \; \texttt{=>} \; tyseq_2 & \\
& | & \texttt{val} \; var \; \texttt{:} \; ty & \\
& | & spec_1 \; spec_2 & \\
dec \in \text{Dec} & ::= & \texttt{with} \; scon & \text{(*)} \\
& | & \texttt{type} \; typbind & \\
& | & \texttt{datatype} \; datbind \; withbind & \\
& | & \texttt{relation} \; relbind & \\
& | & \texttt{val} \; var = exp & \\
& | & dec_1 \; dec_2 & \\
interface \in \text{Interface} & ::= & \texttt{module} \; modid \; \texttt{:} \; spec \; \texttt{end} & \\
module \in \text{Module} & ::= & interface \; dec &
\end{array}
$$

Figure A.6: Full grammar: declarations

Derived Form   Equivalent Form

Type Variable Sequences *tyvarseq*

ε	()
tyvar	(*tyvar*)

Types *ty*

longtycon	() *longtycon*

Type Sequences *tyseq*

ty	(*ty*)

Figure A.7: Derived forms of type variable sequences, types, and type sequences

Derived Form   Equivalent Form

Patterns *pat*

var	*var* **as** _	
$pat_1 :: pat_2$	`rml.cons`(pat_1, pat_2)	
[]	`rml.nil`	
$[pat_1, \cdots, pat_n]$	$pat_1 :: \cdots :: pat_n ::$ []	$(n \geq 1)$
(*pat*)	*pat*	

Pattern Sequences *patseq*

pat	(*pat*)

Pattern Sequences ⟨*patseq*⟩

ε	()

Figure A.8: Derived forms of patterns and pattern sequences

Derived Form   Equivalent Form

Expressions *exp*

$exp_1 :: exp_2$	`rml.cons(`exp_1`,` exp_2`)`
`[]`	`rml.nil`
$[exp_1, \cdots, exp_n]$	$exp_1 :: \cdots :: exp_n :: $ `[]` $(n \geq 1)$
(exp)	exp

Expression Sequences *expseq*

exp	(exp)

Expression Sequences ⟨*expseq*⟩

ε	`()`

Figure A.9: Derived forms of expressions and expression sequences

Derived Form   Equivalent Form

Goals *goal*

longvar ⟨*expseq*⟩	*longvar* ⟨*expseq*⟩ `=>` `()`
⟨*goal*⟩	*goal*

Clauses *clause*

`rule` ⟨*goal*⟩ `--` *var* ⟨*patseq*⟩	`rule` ⟨*goal*⟩ `--` *var* ⟨*patseq*⟩ `=>`
`axiom` *var* ⟨*patseq*⟩ ⟨`=>` ⟨*expseq*⟩⟩	`rule` `--` *var* ⟨*patseq*⟩ ⟨`=>` ⟨*expseq*⟩⟩

Figure A.10: Derived forms of goals and clauses

Derived Form Equivalent Form

Specifications *spec*

`with` *scon*	`with` *interface*

Declarations *dec*

`with` *scon*	`with` *interface*

Figure A.11: Derived forms of specifications and declarations

$tyvarseq \in$ TyVarSeq	$::= (tyvar_1, \cdots, tyvar_n)$	$n \geq 0$
$ty \in$ Ty	$::= tyvar$	variable
	$\mid tyseq\ longtycon$	construction
	$\mid ty_1 * \cdots * ty_n$	tuple, $n \geq 2$
	$\mid tyseq_1 \Rightarrow tyseq_2$	relation
$tyseq \in$ TySeq	$::= (ty_1, \cdots, ty_n)$	sequence, $n \geq 0$

Figure A.12: Core grammar: types

$pat \in$ Pat	$::= \_$	wildcard
	$\mid lit$	literal
	$\mid longcon$	constant
	$\mid longcon\ patseq$	structure
	$\mid (pat_1, \cdots, pat_n)$	tuple, $n \neq 1$
	$\mid var$ **as** pat	binding
$patseq \in$ PatSeq	$::= (pat_1, \cdots, pat_n)$	sequence, $n \geq 0$

Figure A.13: Core grammar: patterns

$exp \in$ Exp	$::= lit$	literal
	$\mid longcon$	constant
	$\mid longvar$	variable
	$\mid longcon\ expseq$	structure
	$\mid (exp_1, \cdots, exp_n)$	tuple, $n \neq 1$
$expseq \in$ ExpSeq	$::= (exp_1, \cdots, exp_n)$	sequence, $n \geq 0$

Figure A.14: Core grammar: expressions

$goal \in$ Goal	$::= longvar\ expseq \Rightarrow patseq$	call
	$\mid var = exp$	unification
	$\mid$ **exists** var	existential
	$\mid$ **not** $goal$	negation
	$\mid goal_1$ & $goal_2$	sequence
$clause \in$ Clause	$::=$ **rule** $\langle goal \rangle$ -- $var\ patseq \Rightarrow expseq$	rule
	$\mid clause_1\ clause_2$	sequence

Figure A.15: Core grammar: goals and clauses

$$
\begin{array}{lll}
conbind \in \text{ConBind} & ::= con \ \langle\text{of}\ ty_1 * \cdots * ty_n\rangle & \langle n \geq 1 \rangle \\
& \mid\ conbind_1 \mid conbind_2 & \\
datbind \in \text{DatBind} & ::= tyvarseq\ tycon = conbind & \\
& \mid\ datbind_1\ \textbf{and}\ datbind_2 & \\
typbind \in \text{TypBind} & ::= tyvarseq\ tycon = ty & \\
& \mid\ typbind_1\ \textbf{and}\ typbind_2 & \\
withbind \in \text{WithBind} & ::= \langle\text{withtype}\ typbind\rangle & \\
relbind \in \text{RelBind} & ::= var\ \langle:\ tyseq_1\ \text{=>}\ tyseq_2\rangle = clause & \\
& \mid\ relbind_1\ \textbf{and}\ relbind_2 & \\
spec \in \text{Spec} & ::= \textbf{with}\ interface & \\
& \mid\ \textbf{abstype}\ tyvarseq\ tycon & \\
& \mid\ \textbf{type}\ typbind & \\
& \mid\ \textbf{datatype}\ datbind\ withbind & \\
& \mid\ \textbf{relation}\ var\ :\ tyseq_1\ \text{=>}\ tyseq_2 & \\
& \mid\ \textbf{val}\ var\ :\ ty & \\
& \mid\ spec_1\ spec_2 & \\
dec \in \text{Dec} & ::= \textbf{with}\ interface & \\
& \mid\ \textbf{type}\ typbind & \\
& \mid\ \textbf{datatype}\ datbind\ withbind & \\
& \mid\ \textbf{relation}\ relbind & \\
& \mid\ \textbf{val}\ var = exp & \\
& \mid\ dec_1\ dec_2 & \\
interface \in \text{Interface} & ::= \textbf{module}\ modid\ :\ spec\ \textbf{end} & \\
module \in \text{Module} & ::= interface\ dec & \\
\end{array}
$$

Figure A.16: Core grammar: declarations

$$
\begin{array}{ll}
modseq \in \text{ModSeq} & ::= module \\
& \mid\ modseq_1\ modseq_2 \\
\end{array}
$$

Figure A.17: Auxiliary grammar: programs

A.5 Static Semantics

This section presents the rules for the static semantics of RML. First the semantic objects involved are defined. Then inference rules (written in the style of Natural Semantics) are given.

A.5.1 Simple Objects

All semantic objects in the static semantics are built from the atomic objects found in the syntax, Figure A.1. In the static semantics, we let α range over TyVar.

A.5.2 Compound Objects

The compound objects for the static semantics are shown in Figure A.18.

For notational convenience, we identify TyVarSeq with TyVar*, TySeq with Ty*, PatSeq with Pat*, and ExpSeq with Exp*.

$$
\begin{aligned}
t \text{ or } (modid, tycon) &\in \text{TyStamp} = \text{ModId} \times \text{TyCon} \\
\tau &\in \text{Type} = \text{TyVar} \cup \text{TupleType} \cup \text{RelType} \cup \text{ConsType} \\
&\quad \text{TypeSeq} = \cup_{k \geq 0} \text{Type}^k \\
&\quad \text{TupleType} = \text{TypeSeq} \\
\tau^{(k)} \lceil \Rightarrow \rceil \tau'^{(k')} &\in \text{RelType} = \text{TypeSeq} \times \text{TypeSeq} \\
\tau^{(k)} t &\in \text{ConsType} = \cup_{k \geq 0} (\text{Type}^k \times \text{TyStamp}) \\
\theta \text{ or } \Lambda \alpha^{(k)}.\tau &\in \text{TypeFcn} = \cup_{k \geq 0} (\text{TyVar}^k \times \text{Type}) \\
\sigma \text{ or } \forall \alpha^{(k)}.\tau &\in \text{TypeScheme} = \cup_{k \geq 0} (\text{TyVar}^k \times \text{Type}) \\
valkind &\in \text{ValKind} = \{\text{con, rel, var}\} \\
VE &\in \text{ValEnv} = (\text{Var} \cup \text{Con}) \overset{\text{fin}}{\to} (\text{ValKind} \times \text{TypeScheme}) \\
tykind &\in \text{TyKind} = \{\text{abs, nonabs}\} \\
TE &\in \text{TyEnv} = \text{TyCon} \overset{\text{fin}}{\to} (\text{TyKind} \times \text{TypeFcn}) \\
ME &\in \text{ModEnv} = \text{ModId} \overset{\text{fin}}{\to} (\text{TyEnv} \times \text{ValEnv})
\end{aligned}
$$

Figure A.18: Compound semantic objects

Type stamps are pairs of module names and type constructor names. This device is used to uniquely identify all constructed types. Neither module names nor type constructor names may be redefined. The only exception to this rule concerns `abstype` specifications. However, their implementation types are guaranteed to have the same type stamps and equal type functions as those inferred from their specifications.

The structure of types, constructed types, type schemes and type functions is almost identical to that in Standard ML.

Value environments map variables (relations or local variables) and constructors to tagged type schemes. The tags distinguish constructors from non-constructors, since these classes behave differently in patterns. They also distinguish variables arising from relation bindings from other variables. (This turns out to be important for separate compilation.) Since the only polymorphic objects in RML are globally declared (relations and datatype constructors), type schemes bind either all or none of their type variables.

Type environments map type constructors to tagged type functions. Abstract types (arising from `abstype` specifications) must be rebound in the module's body, whereas other types may not be rebound.

A.5.3 Initial Static Environments

The initial static environments ME_0, TE_0, and VE_0 are defined in Section A.7.1.

A.5.4 Inference Rules

Type Functions
$$\boxed{appTyFcn(\theta, \tau^{(k)}) \Rightarrow \tau'}$$

$$\frac{k = k' \quad \tau\{\alpha_i \mapsto \tau_i \; ; \; 1 \leq i \leq k\} = \tau'}{appTyFcn(\Lambda\alpha^{(k)}.\tau, \tau^{(k')}) \Rightarrow \tau'} \tag{1}$$

Types
$$\boxed{tyvars \; \tau \Rightarrow \alpha^*}$$

$$\frac{}{tyvars \; \alpha \Rightarrow [\alpha]} \tag{2}$$

$$\frac{tyvars' \; \tau^* \Rightarrow \alpha^*}{tyvars \; \tau^* \Rightarrow \alpha^*} \tag{3}$$

$$\frac{tyvars' \; \tau_1^* \Rightarrow \alpha_1^* \quad tyvars' \; \tau_2^* \Rightarrow \alpha_2^*}{tyvars \; \tau_1^* \lceil \Rightarrow \rceil \tau_2^* \Rightarrow \alpha_1^* \cup \alpha_2^*} \tag{4}$$

$$\frac{tyvars' \; \tau^* \Rightarrow \alpha^*}{tyvars \; \tau^* t \Rightarrow \alpha^*} \tag{5}$$

$$\boxed{tyvars' \; \tau^* \Rightarrow \alpha^*}$$

$$\frac{tyvars \; \tau_i \Rightarrow \alpha_i^* \; (1 \leq i \leq k) \quad \bigcup_{1 \leq i \leq k} \alpha_i^* = \alpha'^*}{tyvars' \; \tau^{(k)} \Rightarrow \alpha'^*} \tag{6}$$

Comment: For conciseness, we identify finite sets and non-repeating sequences.

$$\boxed{Close \; \tau \Rightarrow \sigma}$$

$$\frac{tyvars \; \tau \Rightarrow \alpha^*}{Close \; \tau \Rightarrow \forall \alpha^*.\tau} \tag{7}$$

Comment: This operation closes τ by abstracting all of its type variables.

Type Schemes

$$\boxed{\sigma \succ \tau}$$

$$\frac{\tau\{\alpha_i \mapsto \tau_i' \; ; \; 1 \leq i \leq k\} = \tau''}{\forall \alpha^{(k)}.\tau \succ \tau''} \tag{8}$$

Comment: This operation instantiates a type scheme by substituting types for the abstracted type variables.

Long Type Constructors

$$\boxed{ME, TE \vdash longtycon \Rightarrow \theta}$$

$$\frac{TE(tycon) = (\_, \theta)}{ME, TE \vdash tycon \Rightarrow \theta} \tag{9}$$

$$\frac{ME(modid) = (TE', \_) \quad TE'(tycon) = (\_, \theta)}{ME, TE \vdash modid . tycon \Rightarrow \theta} \tag{10}$$

Type Expressions

$$\boxed{ME, TE\langle, \alpha^*\rangle \vdash ty \Rightarrow \tau}$$

$$\frac{\langle \alpha \in \alpha^* \rangle}{ME, TE\langle, \alpha^*\rangle \vdash \alpha \Rightarrow \alpha} \tag{11}$$

$$\frac{ME, TE\langle, \alpha^*\rangle \vdash tyseq \Rightarrow \tau^* \quad ME, TE \vdash longtycon \Rightarrow \theta}{appTyFcn(\theta, \tau^*) \Rightarrow \tau} \tag{12}$$
$$\overline{ME, TE\langle, \alpha^*\rangle \vdash tyseq \; longtycon \Rightarrow \tau}$$

$$\frac{ME, TE\langle, \alpha^*\rangle \vdash ty^{(k)} \Rightarrow \tau^{(k)}}{ME, TE\langle, \alpha^*\rangle \vdash ty_1 * \cdots * ty_k \Rightarrow \tau^{(k)} \; in \; Type} \tag{13}$$

$$\frac{ME, TE\langle, \alpha^*\rangle \vdash tyseq_1 \Rightarrow \tau_1^* \quad ME, TE\langle, \alpha^*\rangle \vdash tyseq_2 \Rightarrow \tau_2^*}{ME, TE\langle, \alpha^*\rangle \vdash tyseq_1 \; \texttt{=>} \; tyseq_2 \Rightarrow \tau_1^* \lceil \Rightarrow \rceil \tau_2^*} \tag{14}$$

Comments:

(11) When present, α^* serves to constrain type expressions to only have type variables in α^*. This is used when elaborating *typbinds* and *datbinds*. It does *not* suffice to elaborate a type expression to a type τ, and then check that *tyvars* $\tau \Rightarrow \alpha'^*$ and $\alpha'^* \subseteq \alpha^*$, since type functions θ may 'forget' some of their type variables. The following example does not elaborate: `type 'a t = int type tt = 'b t`.

Type Expression Sequences $\boxed{ME,\, TE\langle,\alpha^*\rangle \vdash ty^{(k)} \Rightarrow \tau^{(k)}}$

$$\frac{ME,\, TE\langle,\alpha^*\rangle \vdash ty_i \Rightarrow \tau_i \;(1 \le i \le k)}{ME,\, TE\langle,\alpha^*\rangle \vdash ty^{(k)} \Rightarrow \tau^{(k)}} \tag{15}$$

Type Variable Sequences $\boxed{nodups\ \alpha^*}$

$$\frac{}{nodups\ []} \tag{16}$$

$$\frac{\alpha \notin \alpha^* \quad nodups\ \alpha^*}{nodups\ \alpha :: \alpha^*} \tag{17}$$

Comment: *nodups* α^* verifies that α^* contains no duplicates, as required when elaborating type, datatype and abstype.

Type Bindings $\boxed{ME,\, TE \vdash typbind \Rightarrow TE}$

$$\frac{tycon \notin \mathrm{Dom}\ TE \quad nodups\ \alpha^* \quad ME,\, TE_0 + TE, \alpha^* \vdash ty \Rightarrow \tau}{ME,\, TE \vdash \alpha^*\ tycon = ty \Rightarrow TE + \{tycon \mapsto (\mathrm{nonabs}, \Lambda\alpha^*.\tau)\}} \tag{18}$$

$$\frac{ME,\, TE \vdash typbind_1 \Rightarrow TE_1 \quad ME,\, TE_1 \vdash typbind_2 \Rightarrow TE_2}{ME,\, TE \vdash typbind_1 \text{ and } typbind_2 \Rightarrow TE_2} \tag{19}$$

$$\boxed{ME,\, TE \vdash withbind \Rightarrow TE}$$

$$\frac{ME,\, TE \vdash typbind \Rightarrow TE'}{ME,\, TE \vdash \text{withtype } typbind \Rightarrow TE'} \tag{20}$$

$$\frac{}{ME,\, TE \vdash \varepsilon \Rightarrow TE} \tag{21}$$

Comment: As implied by the sequential elaboration of a *typbind*, the type aliases after withtype are expanded sequentially. This is a deliberate change from SML.

Constructor Bindings $\boxed{ME,\, TE,\, VE, \alpha^*, \tau \vdash conbind \Rightarrow VE}$

$$\frac{con \notin \mathrm{Dom}\ VE \quad Close\ \tau \Rightarrow \sigma}{ME,\, TE,\, VE, \alpha^*, \tau \vdash con \Rightarrow VE + \{con \mapsto (\mathrm{con}, \sigma)\}} \tag{22}$$

$$\frac{\begin{array}{c} con \notin \mathrm{Dom}\ VE \quad ME, TE, \alpha^* \vdash ty^{(k)} \Rightarrow \tau'^{(k)} \\ Close\ \tau'^{(k)} \lceil \Rightarrow \rceil [\tau] \Rightarrow \sigma \quad VE' = VE + \{con \mapsto (con, \sigma)\} \end{array}}{ME, TE, VE, \alpha^*, \tau \vdash con\ of\ ty_1 * \cdots * ty_k \Rightarrow VE'} \quad (23)$$

$$\frac{\begin{array}{c} ME, TE, VE, \alpha^*, \tau \vdash conbind_1 \Rightarrow VE_1 \\ ME, TE, VE_1, \alpha^*, \tau \vdash conbind_2 \Rightarrow VE_2 \end{array}}{ME, TE, VE, \alpha^*, \tau \vdash conbind_1 \mid conbind_2 \Rightarrow VE_2} \quad (24)$$

Datatype Bindings $\boxed{ME, TE, VE \vdash datbind \Rightarrow VE}$

$$\frac{TE(tycon) = (\_, \Lambda\alpha^*.\tau) \quad ME, TE, VE, \alpha^*, \tau \vdash conbind \Rightarrow VE'}{ME, TE, VE \vdash \_\ tycon = conbind \Rightarrow VE'} \quad (25)$$

$$\frac{\begin{array}{c} ME, TE, VE \vdash datbind_1 \Rightarrow VE_1 \\ ME, TE, VE_1 \vdash datbind_2 \Rightarrow VE_2 \end{array}}{ME, TE, VE \vdash datbind_1\ \mathbf{and}\ datbind_2 \Rightarrow VE_2} \quad (26)$$

$$\boxed{TE, modid \vdash datbind \Rightarrow TE}$$

$$\frac{\begin{array}{c} tycon \notin \mathrm{Dom}\ TE \ \vee\ TE(tycon) = (\mathrm{abs}, \_) \\ nodups\ \alpha^* \quad \theta = \Lambda\alpha^*.\alpha^*(modid, tycon) \end{array}}{TE, modid \vdash \alpha^*\ tycon = \_ \Rightarrow TE + \{tycon \mapsto (\mathrm{nonabs}, \theta)\}} \quad (27)$$

$$\frac{TE, modid \vdash datbind_1 \Rightarrow TE_1 \quad TE_1, modid \vdash datbind_2 \Rightarrow TE_2}{TE, modid \vdash datbind_1\ \mathbf{and}\ datbind_2 \Rightarrow TE_2} \quad (28)$$

Comment: Normally, once an identifier has been bound in an environment, it may not be rebound. Rule (27) is the only place where this does not hold: an abstract type declared in an interface can (indeed must) be rebound in the module's body by a *datbind*. This relies crucially on the fact that both the abstype specification and the *datbind* will produce equal type functions (up to renaming of type variables). See also rule (31).

$$\boxed{ME, TE, VE, modid \vdash datbind, withbind \Rightarrow TE, VE}$$

$$\frac{\begin{array}{c} TE, modid \vdash datbind \Rightarrow TE' \quad ME, TE' \vdash withbind \Rightarrow TE'' \\ ME, TE_0 + TE'', VE \vdash datbind \Rightarrow VE' \end{array}}{ME, TE, VE, modid \vdash datbind, withbind \Rightarrow TE'', VE'} \quad (29)$$

Specifications $\boxed{ME, TE, VE, modid \vdash spec \Rightarrow ME, TE, VE}$

$$\frac{\begin{array}{c} ME \vdash interface \Rightarrow ME', TE', VE', modid' \\ ME'' = ME + \{modid' \mapsto (TE', VE')\} \end{array}}{ME, TE, VE, modid \vdash \texttt{with}\ interface \Rightarrow ME'', TE, VE} \quad (30)$$

$$\frac{\begin{array}{c} tycon \notin \mathrm{Dom}\ TE \quad nodups\ \alpha^* \\ TE' = TE + \{tycon \mapsto (\mathrm{abs}, \Lambda\alpha^*.\alpha^*(modid, tycon))\} \end{array}}{ME, TE, VE, modid \vdash \texttt{abstype}\ \alpha^*\ tycon \Rightarrow ME, TE', VE} \quad (31)$$

$$\frac{ME, TE \vdash typbind \Rightarrow TE'}{ME, TE, VE, modid \vdash \texttt{type}\ typbind \Rightarrow ME, TE', VE} \quad (32)$$

$$\frac{ME, TE, VE, modid \vdash datbind, withbind \Rightarrow TE', VE'}{ME, TE, VE, modid \vdash \texttt{datatype}\ datbind\ withbind \Rightarrow ME, TE', VE'} \quad (33)$$

$$\frac{\begin{array}{c} var \notin \mathrm{Dom}\ VE \quad ME, TE_0 + TE \vdash tyseq_1 \texttt{=>} tyseq_2 \Rightarrow \tau \\ Close\ \tau \Rightarrow \sigma \quad VE' = VE + \{var \mapsto (\mathrm{rel}, \sigma)\} \end{array}}{ME, TE, VE, modid \vdash \texttt{relation}\ var : tyseq_1 \texttt{=>} tyseq_2 \Rightarrow ME, TE, VE'} \quad (34)$$

$$\frac{\begin{array}{c} var \notin \mathrm{Dom}\ VE \quad ME, TE_0 + TE \vdash ty \Rightarrow \tau \\ Close\ \tau \Rightarrow \sigma \quad VE' = VE + \{var \mapsto (\mathrm{var}, \sigma)\} \end{array}}{ME, TE, VE, modid \vdash \texttt{val}\ var : ty \Rightarrow ME, TE, VE'} \quad (35)$$

$$\frac{\begin{array}{c} ME, TE, VE, modid \vdash spec_1 \Rightarrow ME_1, TE_1, VE_1 \\ ME_1, TE_1, VE_1, modid \vdash spec_2 \Rightarrow ME_2, TE_2, VE_2 \end{array}}{ME, TE, VE, modid \vdash spec_1\ spec_2 \Rightarrow ME_2, TE_2, VE_2} \quad (36)$$

Interfaces $\boxed{ME \vdash interface \Rightarrow ME, TE, VE, modid}$

$$\frac{modid \notin \mathrm{Dom}\ ME \quad ME_0, \{\}, \{\}, modid \vdash spec \Rightarrow ME', TE, VE}{ME \vdash \texttt{module}\ modid : spec\ \texttt{end} \Rightarrow ME', TE, VE, modid} \quad (37)$$

Literals $\boxed{\vdash lit \Rightarrow \tau}$

$$\frac{}{\vdash ccon \Rightarrow [](\texttt{rml}, \texttt{char})} \quad (38)$$

$$\frac{}{\vdash icon \Rightarrow [](\texttt{rml}, \texttt{int})} \quad (39)$$

$$\overline{\vdash rcon \Rightarrow [](\texttt{rml},\texttt{real})} \tag{40}$$

$$\overline{\vdash scon \Rightarrow [](\texttt{rml},\texttt{string})} \tag{41}$$

Comment: The type expressions are equal to the parameterless constructed types used in TE_0 for char, int, real, and string respectively.

Long Value Constructors $\qquad\boxed{ME,\ VE \vdash longcon \Rightarrow \sigma}$

$$\frac{VE(con) = (con,\sigma)}{ME,\ VE \vdash con \Rightarrow \sigma} \tag{42}$$

$$\frac{ME(modid) = (\_,\ VE')\quad VE'(con) = (con,\sigma)}{ME,\ VE \vdash modid\,.\,con \Rightarrow \sigma} \tag{43}$$

Patterns $\qquad\boxed{ME,\ VE \vdash pat \Rightarrow VE, \tau}$

$$\frac{}{ME,\ VE \vdash \_ \Rightarrow VE, \tau} \tag{44}$$

$$\frac{\vdash lit \Rightarrow \tau}{ME,\ VE \vdash lit \Rightarrow VE, \tau} \tag{45}$$

$$\frac{ME,\ VE \vdash longcon \Rightarrow \sigma \quad \sigma \succ \tau^*t}{ME,\ VE \vdash longcon \Rightarrow VE, \tau^*t} \tag{46}$$

$$\frac{ME,\ VE \vdash longcon \Rightarrow \sigma \quad ME,\ VE \vdash patseq \Rightarrow VE', \tau^* \quad \sigma \succ \tau^*[\Rightarrow][\tau]}{ME,\ VE \vdash longcon\ patseq \Rightarrow VE', \tau} \tag{47}$$

$$\frac{ME,\ VE \vdash pat^{(k)} \Rightarrow VE', \tau^{(k)}}{ME,\ VE \vdash (pat_1, \cdots, pat_k) \Rightarrow VE', \tau^{(k)}\ \text{in Type}} \tag{48}$$

$$\frac{ME,\ VE \vdash pat \Rightarrow VE', \tau \quad var \notin \text{Dom } VE'}{ME,\ VE \vdash var \text{ as } pat \Rightarrow VE' + \{var \mapsto (var, \forall[].\tau)\}, \tau} \tag{49}$$

Pattern Sequences $\qquad\boxed{ME,\ VE \vdash pat^{(k)} \Rightarrow VE, \tau^{(k)}}$

$$\frac{ME,\ VE_i \vdash pat_i \Rightarrow VE_{i+1}, \tau_i\ (1 \le i \le k)}{ME,\ VE_1 \vdash pat^{(k)} \Rightarrow VE_{k+1}, \tau^{(k)}} \tag{50}$$

Long Variables

$$\boxed{ME, VE \vdash longvar \Rightarrow \sigma}$$

$$\frac{VE(var) = (valkind, \sigma) \quad valkind \neq \mathrm{con}}{ME, VE \vdash var \Rightarrow \sigma} \tag{51}$$

$$\frac{ME(modid) = (\_, VE') \quad VE'(var) = (valkind, \sigma) \quad valkind \neq \mathrm{con}}{ME, VE \vdash modid . var \Rightarrow \sigma} \tag{52}$$

Expressions

$$\boxed{ME, VE \vdash exp \Rightarrow \tau}$$

$$\frac{\vdash lit \Rightarrow \tau}{ME, VE \vdash lit \Rightarrow \tau} \tag{53}$$

$$\frac{ME, VE \vdash longcon \Rightarrow \sigma \quad \sigma \succ \tau^* t}{ME, VE \vdash longcon \Rightarrow \tau^* t} \tag{54}$$

$$\frac{ME, VE \vdash longvar \Rightarrow \sigma \quad \sigma \succ \tau}{ME, VE \vdash longvar \Rightarrow \tau} \tag{55}$$

$$\frac{ME, VE \vdash longcon \Rightarrow \sigma \quad ME, VE \vdash expseq \Rightarrow \tau^* \quad \sigma \succ \tau^* \lceil \Rightarrow \rceil [\tau]}{ME, VE \vdash longcon \; expseq \Rightarrow \tau} \tag{56}$$

$$\frac{ME, VE \vdash exp^{(k)} \Rightarrow \tau^{(k)}}{ME, VE \vdash (exp_1, \cdots, exp_k) \Rightarrow \tau^{(k)} \text{ in Type}} \tag{57}$$

Expression Sequences

$$\boxed{ME, VE \vdash exp^{(k)} \Rightarrow \tau^{(k)}}$$

$$\frac{ME, VE \vdash exp_i \Rightarrow \tau_i \; (1 \leq i \leq k)}{ME, VE \vdash exp^{(k)} \Rightarrow \tau^{(k)}} \tag{58}$$

Goals

$$\boxed{ME, VE \vdash goal \Rightarrow VE}$$

$$\frac{\begin{array}{c} ME, VE \vdash longvar \Rightarrow \sigma \quad ME, VE \vdash expseq \Rightarrow \tau_1^* \\ ME, VE \vdash patseq \Rightarrow VE', \tau_2^* \quad \sigma \succ \tau_1^* \lceil \Rightarrow \rceil \tau_2^* \end{array}}{ME, VE \vdash longvar \; expseq \Rightarrow patseq \Rightarrow VE'} \tag{59}$$

$$\frac{ME, VE \vdash exp \Rightarrow \tau \quad var \notin \mathrm{Dom} \; VE}{ME, VE \vdash var = exp \Rightarrow VE + \{var \mapsto (var, \forall[].\tau)\}} \tag{60}$$

$$\frac{ME, VE \vdash exp \Rightarrow \tau \quad var \in \mathrm{Dom} \; VE \quad VE(var) = (\_, \sigma) \quad \sigma \succ \tau}{ME, VE \vdash var = exp \Rightarrow VE} \tag{61}$$

$$\frac{var \notin \mathrm{Dom}\ VE}{ME, VE \vdash \texttt{exists}\ var \Rightarrow VE + \{var \mapsto (var, \forall[].\tau)\}} \tag{62}$$

$$\frac{ME, VE \vdash goal \Rightarrow VE'}{ME, VE \vdash \texttt{not}\ goal \Rightarrow VE} \tag{63}$$

$$\frac{ME, VE \vdash goal_1 \Rightarrow VE_1 \quad ME, VE_1 \vdash goal_2 \Rightarrow VE_2}{ME, VE \vdash goal_1\ \texttt{\&}\ goal_2 \Rightarrow VE_2} \tag{64}$$

Comments: (63) A negative goal produces no visible bindings.

$$\boxed{ME, VE \overset{\shortmid}{\vdash} \langle goal \rangle \Rightarrow VE}$$

$$\frac{ME, VE \vdash goal \Rightarrow VE'}{ME, VE \overset{\shortmid}{\vdash} goal \Rightarrow VE'} \tag{65}$$

$$\frac{}{ME, VE \overset{\shortmid}{\vdash} \varepsilon \Rightarrow VE} \tag{66}$$

Clauses
$$\boxed{ME, VE, \tau \vdash clause}$$

$$\frac{\begin{array}{c} ME, VE \vdash patseq \Rightarrow VE_1, \tau_1^* \quad ME, VE_1 \overset{\shortmid}{\vdash} \langle goal \rangle \Rightarrow VE_2 \\ ME, VE_2 \vdash expseq \Rightarrow \tau_2^* \quad \tau = \tau_1^* \lceil \Rightarrow \rceil \tau_2^* \end{array}}{ME, VE, \tau \vdash \texttt{rule}\ \langle goal \rangle\ \texttt{--}\ \_\ patseq\ \texttt{=>}\ expseq} \tag{67}$$

$$\frac{ME, VE, \tau \vdash clause_1 \quad ME, VE, \tau \vdash clause_2}{ME, VE, \tau \vdash clause_1\ clause_2} \tag{68}$$

Relation Bindings
$$\boxed{ME, VE \vdash relbind}$$

$$\frac{VE(var) = (\mathrm{rel}, \forall\_.\tau) \quad ME, VE, \tau \vdash clause}{ME, VE \vdash var\ \langle : \_ \texttt{=>} \_ \rangle\ \texttt{=}\ clause} \tag{69}$$

$$\frac{ME, VE \vdash relbind_1 \quad ME, VE \vdash relbind_2}{ME, VE \vdash relbind_1\ \texttt{and}\ relbind_2} \tag{70}$$

$$\boxed{ME, TE, VE, VE' \vdash relbind \Rightarrow VE''}$$

$$\frac{var \notin \mathrm{Dom}\ VE \quad var \notin \mathrm{Dom}\ VE' \\ ME, TE \vdash tyseq_1\ \texttt{=>}\ tyseq_2 \Rightarrow \tau \quad Close\ \tau \Rightarrow \sigma}{ME, TE, VE, VE' \vdash var\ :\ tyseq_1\ \texttt{=>}\ tyseq_2\ \texttt{=}\ \_ \Rightarrow VE' + \{var \mapsto (\mathrm{rel}, \sigma)\}} \tag{71}$$

$$\frac{var \notin \mathrm{Dom}\ VE \quad var \notin \mathrm{Dom}\ VE' \quad \sigma = \forall[].\tau}{ME, TE, VE, VE' \vdash var = \_ \Rightarrow VE' + \{var \mapsto (\mathrm{rel}, \sigma)\}} \quad (72)$$

$$\frac{\begin{array}{c} ME, TE, VE_1, VE_2 \vdash relbind_1 \Rightarrow VE_2' \\ ME, TE, VE_1, VE_2' \vdash relbind_2 \Rightarrow VE_2'' \end{array}}{ME, TE, VE_1, VE_2 \vdash relbind_1 \ \text{and}\ relbind_2 \Rightarrow VE_2''} \quad (73)$$

Variable Environments $\boxed{Close\ VE \Rightarrow VE'}$

$$\frac{Close\ \tau_i \Rightarrow \sigma_i \ \ (1 \leq i \leq k)}{Close\ \{var_i \mapsto (\mathrm{rel}, \forall\_.\tau_i)\ ;\ 1 \leq i \leq k\} \Rightarrow \{var_i \mapsto (\mathrm{rel}, \sigma_i)\ ;\ 1 \leq i \leq k\}}$$
$$(74)$$

Declarations $\boxed{ME, TE, VE, modid \vdash dec \Rightarrow ME, TE, VE}$

$$\frac{\begin{array}{c} ME \vdash interface \Rightarrow ME', TE', VE', modid' \\ ME'' = ME + \{modid' \mapsto (TE', VE')\} \end{array}}{ME, TE, VE, modid \vdash \text{with}\ interface \Rightarrow ME'', TE, VE} \quad (75)$$

$$\frac{ME, TE \vdash typbind \Rightarrow TE'}{ME, TE, VE, modid \vdash \text{type}\ typbind \Rightarrow ME, TE', VE} \quad (76)$$

$$\frac{ME, TE, VE, modid \vdash datbind, withbind \Rightarrow TE', VE'}{ME, TE, VE, modid \vdash \text{datatype}\ datbind\ withbind \Rightarrow ME, TE', VE'} \quad (77)$$

$$\frac{\begin{array}{c} ME, TE_0 + TE, VE, \{\} \vdash relbind \Rightarrow VE' \\ ME, VE_0 + VE + VE' \vdash relbind \quad Close\ VE' \Rightarrow VE'' \end{array}}{ME, TE, VE, modid \vdash \text{relation}\ relbind \Rightarrow ME, TE, VE + VE''} \quad (78)$$

$$\frac{\begin{array}{c} var \notin \mathrm{Dom}\ VE \quad ME, VE_0 + VE \vdash exp \Rightarrow \tau \\ Close\ \tau \Rightarrow \sigma \quad VE' = VE + \{var \mapsto (\mathrm{var}, \sigma)\} \end{array}}{ME, TE, VE, modid \vdash \text{val}\ var = exp \Rightarrow ME, TE, VE'} \quad (79)$$

$$\frac{\begin{array}{c} ME, TE, VE, modid \vdash dec_1 \Rightarrow ME_1, TE_1, VE_1 \\ ME_1, TE_1, VE_1, modid \vdash dec_2 \Rightarrow ME_2, TE_2, VE_2 \end{array}}{ME, TE, VE, modid \vdash dec_1\ dec_2 \Rightarrow ME_2, TE_2, VE_2} \quad (80)$$

Specifications $\boxed{TE_{\mathrm{dec}}, VE_{\mathrm{spec}}, VE_{\mathrm{dec}} \vdash spec}$

$$\frac{VE_{\mathrm{spec}}(var) = (\mathrm{rel}, \forall\alpha^*.\tau_{\mathrm{spec}}) \quad VE_{\mathrm{dec}}(var) = (\mathrm{rel}, \sigma_{\mathrm{dec}}) \quad \sigma_{\mathrm{dec}} \succ \tau_{\mathrm{spec}}}{TE_{\mathrm{dec}}, VE_{\mathrm{spec}}, VE_{\mathrm{dec}} \vdash \text{relation}\ var : \_ \Rightarrow \_}$$
$$(81)$$

$$\frac{VE_{\text{spec}}(var) = (\text{var}, \forall \alpha^*.\tau_{\text{spec}}) \quad VE_{\text{dec}}(var) = (\_, \sigma_{\text{dec}}) \quad \sigma_{\text{dec}} \succ \tau_{\text{spec}}}{TE_{\text{dec}}, VE_{\text{spec}}, VE_{\text{dec}} \vdash \text{val } var : \_} \tag{82}$$

$$\frac{TE_{\text{dec}}(tycon) = (\text{nonabs}, \Lambda\alpha^*.\tau) \quad \#\alpha^* = \#\alpha'^*}{TE_{\text{dec}}, VE_{\text{spec}}, VE_{\text{dec}} \vdash \text{abstype } \alpha'^* \; tycon} \tag{83}$$

$$\frac{TE_{\text{dec}}, VE_{\text{spec}}, VE_{\text{dec}} \vdash spec_1 \quad TE_{\text{dec}}, VE_{\text{spec}}, VE_{\text{dec}} \vdash spec_2}{TE_{\text{dec}}, VE_{\text{spec}}, VE_{\text{dec}} \vdash spec_1 \; spec_2} \tag{84}$$

$$\frac{spec = \text{with } \_ \lor spec = \text{type } \_ \lor spec = \text{datatype } \_}{TE_{\text{dec}}, VE_{\text{spec}}, VE_{\text{dec}} \vdash spec} \tag{85}$$

Comments: (81) (82) Note that σ_{dec} cannot be more specific than τ_{spec}.
(81) A relation specification requires a corresponding relation declaration.

Modules $\boxed{\vdash module \Rightarrow modid, VE}$

$$ME_0 \vdash \text{module } modid : spec \text{ end} \Rightarrow ME, TE, VE, modid$$
$$VE' = \{con \mapsto VE(con) \; ; \; VE(con) = (\text{con}, \_)\}$$
$$\frac{ME, TE, VE', modid \vdash dec \Rightarrow ME', TE', VE'' \quad TE', VE, VE'' \vdash spec}{\vdash \text{module } modid : spec \text{ end } dec \Rightarrow modid, VE}$$

$$\tag{86}$$

Comment: The VE arising from the elaboration of the interface contains bindings for both constructors and non-constructors. Only the constructor bindings are retained (in VE') when the module body is elaborated.

Module Sequences $\boxed{ME \vdash modseq \Rightarrow ME'}$

$$\frac{\vdash module \Rightarrow modid, VE \quad modid \notin \text{Dom } ME}{ME \vdash module \Rightarrow ME + \{modid \mapsto (\{\}, VE)\}} \tag{87}$$

$$\frac{ME \vdash modseq_1 \Rightarrow ME_1 \quad ME_1 \vdash modseq_2 \Rightarrow ME_2}{ME \vdash modseq_1 \; modseq_2 \Rightarrow ME_2} \tag{88}$$

Programs $\boxed{\vdash modseq}$

$$\frac{ME_0 \vdash modseq \Rightarrow ME \quad ME(\text{Main}) = (\_, VE) \quad VE(\text{main}) = (\text{rel}, \sigma)}{\vdash modseq}$$
$$\tau = [[](\text{rml}, \text{string})](\text{rml}, \text{list}) \quad \sigma \succ [\tau][\Rightarrow][]$$

$$\tag{89}$$

Comment: A program is a collection of modules. The program's entry point is module Main's relation main, which must have type string list => ().

A.6 Dynamic Semantics

A.6.1 Simple Objects

All objects in the dynamic semantics are built from syntactic objects and the object classes shown in Figure A.19.

$$
\begin{array}{ll}
a \in \text{Answer} = \{\text{Yes}, \text{No}\} \text{ final answers} & \\
l \in \text{Loc} & \text{denumerable set of locations} \\
prim \in \text{PrimOp} & \text{primitive procedures} \\
\{\text{FAIL}\} & \text{failure token} \\
\{\text{unbound}\} & \text{unbound token}
\end{array}
$$

Figure A.19: Simple semantic objects

A.6.2 Compound Objects

The compound objects for the dynamic semantics are shown in Figures A.20 and A.21.

$$
\begin{array}{l}
\text{Closure} = \text{Clause} \times \text{MEnv} \times \text{VEnv} \times \text{VEnv} \\
ev \in \text{EVal} = \text{Loc} \cup \text{Closure} \cup \text{PrimOp} \cup \text{Lit} \cup (\text{Con} \times \text{EVal}^*) \cup \text{EVal}^* \\
VE \in \text{VEnv} = \text{Var} \xrightarrow{\text{fin}} \text{EVal} \\
ME \in \text{MEnv} = \text{ModId} \xrightarrow{\text{fin}} \text{VEnv} \\
sv \in \text{SVal} = \text{EVal} \cup \{\text{unbound}\} \\
\sigma \in \text{Store} = \text{Loc} \xrightarrow{\text{fin}} \text{SVal} \\
s \in \text{State} = \text{Store} \times \cdots \\
m \in \text{Marker} = \text{Store}
\end{array}
$$

Figure A.20: Compound semantic objects

$$
\begin{array}{lll}
fc \in \text{FCont} ::= & \texttt{orhalt} & \text{failure continuations} \\
& | \ \texttt{orelse}(m, clause, ev^*, ME, VE, fc, pc) & \\
& | \ \texttt{ornot}(m, gc, VE, fc) & \\
gc \in \text{GCont} ::= & \texttt{andhalt} & \text{goal continuations} \\
& | \ \texttt{andthen}(goal, ME, gc) & \\
& | \ \texttt{andnot}(fc) & \\
& | \ \texttt{andreturn}(ME, exp^*, pc) & \\
pc \in \text{PCont} ::= & \texttt{retmatch}(pat^*, VE, gc, fc) & \text{procedure continuations}
\end{array}
$$

Figure A.21: Grammar of continuation terms

Expressible values are literals, primops, tuples, constructor applications, closures, or logical variables.

Closures are clauses closed with the module and variable environments in effect when the closure (resulting from evaluating a *relbind*) was created. The last component of a closure describes the recursive part of the closure's environment. This component will be successively unfolded during recursions, giving each level of the recursion access to a 'virtually recursive' environment without actually creating a recursive object.

Logical variables behave like write-once references. A logical variable is represented by a location, and the store maps this location either to an expressible value (when the variable has been instantiated) or to the token 'unbound' (before it has been instantiated).

Markers are used to record whatever information is necessary to restore a store to an earlier configuration, viz. the configuration at the time the marker was created. (The *formal* specification of this is trivial, but it can easily be extended to more intelligent schemes.)

The state is a tuple of a store σ and some unspecified external component (simply called X in the inference rules). The external component is not recorded in markers, and thus not restored during backtracking.

The backtracking control flow is modelled using continuations. In contrast to denotational semantics, these continuations are encoded as first-order data structures that are interpreted by special-purpose relations.

A.6.3   Initial Dynamic Objects

The initial dynamic objects ME_0, VE_0, and s_0, and the contents of the set PrimOp are defined in Section A.7.2.

The function $APPLY(prim, ev^*, s) \Rightarrow (ev'^*, s')/(\text{FAIL}, s')$ describes the effect of calling a primitive procedure. It is also defined in Section A.7.2.

A.6.4   Inference Rules

States and Markers $\boxed{marker\ s \Rightarrow m}$

$$\frac{s = (\sigma, \_)}{marker\ s \Rightarrow \sigma} \tag{90}$$

$\boxed{restore(m, s) \Rightarrow s'}$

$$\frac{s' = (\sigma, X)}{restore(\sigma, (\_, X)) \Rightarrow s'} \tag{91}$$

$$\boxed{new\ s \Rightarrow l, s'}$$

$$\frac{s = (\sigma, X) \quad l \notin \mathrm{Dom}\ \sigma}{new\ s \Rightarrow l, (\sigma + \{l \mapsto \mathrm{unbound}\}, X)} \tag{92}$$

$$\boxed{bind(s, l, ev) \Rightarrow s'}$$

$$\frac{\sigma(l) = \mathrm{unbound} \quad s' = (\sigma + \{l \mapsto ev\}, X)}{bind((\sigma, X), l, ev) \Rightarrow s'} \tag{93}$$

$$\boxed{lookup(s, l) \Rightarrow sv}$$

$$\frac{}{lookup((\sigma, \_), l) \Rightarrow \sigma(l)} \tag{94}$$

Dereferencing Values $\boxed{deref(ev, s) \Rightarrow ev'}$

$$\frac{lookup(s, l) \Rightarrow ev \quad deref(ev, s) \Rightarrow ev'}{deref(l, s) \Rightarrow ev'} \tag{95}$$

$$\frac{lookup(s, l) \Rightarrow \mathrm{unbound}}{deref(l, s) \Rightarrow l} \tag{96}$$

$$\frac{ev \notin \mathrm{Loc}}{deref(ev, s) \Rightarrow ev} \tag{97}$$

Unifying Values $\boxed{unify(ev_1, ev_2, s) \Rightarrow s'/(\mathrm{FAIL}, s')}$

$$\frac{deref(ev_1, s) \Rightarrow ev'_1 \quad deref(ev_2, s) \Rightarrow ev'_2}{\quad unify'(ev'_1, ev'_2, s) \Rightarrow s'/(\mathrm{FAIL}, s') \quad}{unify(ev_1, ev_2, s) \Rightarrow s'/(\mathrm{FAIL}, s')} \tag{98}$$

$$\boxed{unify'(ev_1, ev_2, s) \Rightarrow s'/(\mathrm{FAIL}, s')}$$

$$\frac{l_1 = l_2}{unify'(l_1, l_2, s) \Rightarrow s} \tag{99}$$

$$\frac{l_1 \neq ev_2 \quad bind(s, l_1, ev_2) \Rightarrow s'}{unify'(l_1, ev_2, s) \Rightarrow s'} \tag{100}$$

$$\frac{l_2 \neq ev_1 \quad bind(s, l_2, ev_1) \Rightarrow s'}{unify'(ev_1, l_2, s) \Rightarrow s'} \qquad (101)$$

$$\frac{lit_1 = lit_2}{unify'(lit_1, lit_2, s) \Rightarrow s} \qquad (102)$$

$$\frac{lit_1 \neq lit_2}{unify'(lit_1, lit_2, s) \Rightarrow (\text{FAIL}, s)} \qquad (103)$$

$$\frac{con_1 = con_2 \quad unify^*(ev_1^*, ev_2^*, s) \Rightarrow s'/(\text{FAIL}, s')}{unify'((con_1, ev_1^*), (con_2, ev_2^*), s) \Rightarrow s'/(\text{FAIL}, s')} \qquad (104)$$

$$\frac{con_1 \neq con_2}{unify'((con_1, ev_1^*), (con_2, ev_2^*), s) \Rightarrow (\text{FAIL}, s)} \qquad (105)$$

$$\frac{unify^*(ev_1^*, ev_2^*, s) \Rightarrow s'/(\text{FAIL}, s')}{unify'(ev_1^*, ev_2^*, s) \Rightarrow s'/(\text{FAIL}, s')} \qquad (106)$$

Comments: The case of unifying closures or primops is intentionally undefined. The so-called 'occur check' is deliberately omitted.

$$\boxed{unify^*(ev_1^*, ev_2^*, s) \Rightarrow s'/(\text{FAIL}, s')}$$

$$\frac{}{unify^*([], [], s) \Rightarrow s} \qquad (107)$$

$$\frac{unify(ev_1, ev_2, s) \Rightarrow s' \quad unify^*(ev_1^*, ev_2^*, s') \Rightarrow s''/(\text{FAIL}, s'')}{unify^*(ev_1 :: ev_1^*, ev_2 :: ev_2^*, s) \Rightarrow s''/(\text{FAIL}, s'')} \qquad (108)$$

$$\frac{unify(ev_1, ev_2, s) \Rightarrow (\text{FAIL}, s')}{unify^*(ev_1 :: ev_1^*, ev_2 :: ev_2^*, s) \Rightarrow (\text{FAIL}, s')} \qquad (109)$$

Pattern Matching $\boxed{match(pat, VE, ev, s) \Rightarrow VE'/\text{FAIL}}$

$$\frac{deref(ev, s) \Rightarrow ev' \quad match'(pat, VE, ev', s) \Rightarrow VE'/\text{FAIL}}{match(pat, VE, ev, s) \Rightarrow VE'/\text{FAIL}} \qquad (110)$$

$$\boxed{match'(pat, VE, ev, s) \Rightarrow VE'/\text{FAIL}}$$

$$\frac{}{match'(\_, VE, ev, s) \Rightarrow VE} \qquad (111)$$

$$\frac{lit_1 = lit_2}{match'(lit_1, VE, lit_2, s) \Rightarrow VE} \tag{112}$$

$$\frac{lit_1 \neq lit_2}{match'(lit_1, VE, lit_2, s) \Rightarrow \text{FAIL}} \tag{113}$$

$$\frac{con_1 = con_2}{match'(\langle\_\rangle con_1, VE, (con_2, \_), s) \Rightarrow VE} \tag{114}$$

$$\frac{con_1 \neq con_2}{match'(\langle\_\rangle con_1, VE, (con_2, \_), s) \Rightarrow \text{FAIL}} \tag{115}$$

$$\frac{con_1 = con_2 \quad match^*(pat^{(k)}, VE, ev^*, s) \Rightarrow VE'/\text{FAIL}}{match'(\langle\_\rangle con_1 (pat_1, \cdots, pat_k), VE, (con_2, ev^*), s) \Rightarrow VE'/\text{FAIL}} \tag{116}$$

$$\frac{con_1 \neq con_2}{match'(\langle\_\rangle con_1 (pat_1, \cdots, pat_k), VE, (con_2, ev^*), s) \Rightarrow \text{FAIL}} \tag{117}$$

$$\frac{match^*(pat^{(k)}, VE, ev^*, s) \Rightarrow VE'/\text{FAIL}}{match'((pat_1, \cdots, pat_k), VE, ev^*, s) \Rightarrow VE'/\text{FAIL}} \tag{118}$$

$$\frac{match'(pat, VE + \{var \mapsto ev\}, ev, s) \Rightarrow VE'/\text{FAIL}}{match'(var \text{ as } pat, VE, ev, s) \Rightarrow VE'/\text{FAIL}} \tag{119}$$

$$\boxed{match^*(pat^*, VE, ev^*, s) \Rightarrow VE''/\text{FAIL}}$$

$$\frac{}{match^*([], VE, [], s) \Rightarrow VE} \tag{120}$$

$$\frac{match(pat, VE, ev, s) \Rightarrow VE' \quad match^*(pat^*, VE', ev^*, s) \Rightarrow VE''/\text{FAIL}}{match^*(pat :: pat^*, VE, ev :: ev^*, s) \Rightarrow VE''/\text{FAIL}} \tag{121}$$

$$\frac{match(pat, VE, ev, s) \Rightarrow \text{FAIL}}{match^*(pat :: pat^*, VE, ev :: ev^*, s) \Rightarrow \text{FAIL}} \tag{122}$$

Long Variables $\boxed{lookupLongVar(longvar, ME, VE) \Rightarrow ev}$

$$\frac{VE(var) = ev}{lookupLongVar(var, \_, VE) \Rightarrow ev} \tag{123}$$

$$\frac{ME(modid) = VE' \quad VE'(var) = ev}{lookupLongVar(modid \, . \, var, ME, \_) \Rightarrow ev} \tag{124}$$

Expressions $\boxed{eval(exp, ME, VE) \Rightarrow ev}$

$$\frac{}{eval(lit, ME, VE) \Rightarrow lit \text{ in EVal}} \qquad (125)$$

$$\frac{}{eval(\langle modid.\rangle con, ME, VE) \Rightarrow (con, [])} \qquad (126)$$

$$\frac{lookupLongVar(longvar, ME, VE) \Rightarrow ev}{eval(longvar, ME, VE) \Rightarrow ev} \qquad (127)$$

$$\frac{eval'(exp^{(k)}, ME, VE) \Rightarrow ev^{(k)}}{eval(\langle modid.\rangle con(exp_1, \cdots, exp_k), ME, VE) \Rightarrow (con, ev^{(k)})} \qquad (128)$$

$$\frac{eval'(exp^{(k)}, ME, VE) \Rightarrow ev^{(k)}}{eval((exp_1, \cdots, exp_k), ME, VE) \Rightarrow ev^{(k)} \text{ in EVal}} \qquad (129)$$

$\boxed{eval'(exp^{(k)}, ME, VE) \Rightarrow ev^{(k)}}$

$$\frac{eval(exp_i, ME, VE) \Rightarrow ev_i \ (1 \leq i \leq k)}{eval'(exp^{(k)}, ME, VE) \Rightarrow ev^{(k)}} \qquad (130)$$

Recursive Values $\boxed{unfold_{ev}(VE, ev) \Rightarrow ev'}$

$$\frac{}{unfold_{ev}(VE, (clause, ME, VE', \_)) \Rightarrow (clause, ME, VE', VE)} \qquad (131)$$

$$\frac{ev \notin \text{Closure}}{unfold_{ev}(VE, ev) \Rightarrow ev} \qquad (132)$$

Comment: (131) The first *VE* parameter is the environment in which this closure was bound. The effect of this step is to create a new closure in which an additional level of recursion is available.

Recursive Value Environments $\boxed{unfold_{VE} \ VE \Rightarrow VE'}$

$$\frac{VE = \{var_1 \mapsto ev_1, \cdots, var_k \mapsto ev_k\} \quad unfold_{ev}(VE, ev_i) \Rightarrow ev'_i \ (1 \leq i \leq k)}{unfold_{VE} \ VE \Rightarrow \{var_1 \mapsto ev'_1, \cdots, var_k \mapsto ev'_k\}} \qquad (133)$$

Comment: This rule unfolds every closure bound in the environment, thus enabling each of them to recurse one step.

Failure Continuations $\boxed{fail(fc, s) \Rightarrow a}$

$$\frac{restore(m, s') \Rightarrow s \quad invoke(clause, ev^*, ME, VE, fc, pc, s) \Rightarrow a}{fail(\texttt{orelse}(m, clause, ev^*, ME, VE, fc, pc), s') \Rightarrow a} \quad (134)$$

$$\frac{restore(m, s') \Rightarrow s \quad proceed(gc, VE, fc, s) \Rightarrow a}{fail(\texttt{ornot}(m, gc, VE, fc), s') \Rightarrow a} \quad (135)$$

$$\frac{}{fail(\texttt{orhalt}, s') \Rightarrow \text{No}} \quad (136)$$

Goal Continuations $\boxed{proceed(gc, VE, fc, s) \Rightarrow a}$

$$\frac{exec(goal, ME, VE, fc, gc, s) \Rightarrow a}{proceed(\texttt{andthen}(goal, ME, gc), VE, fc, s) \Rightarrow a} \quad (137)$$

$$\frac{fail(fc', s) \Rightarrow a}{proceed(\texttt{andnot}(fc'), VE, fc, s) \Rightarrow a} \quad (138)$$

$$\frac{eval'(exp^*, ME, VE) \Rightarrow ev^* \quad return(pc, ev^*, s) \Rightarrow a}{proceed(\texttt{andreturn}(ME, exp^*, pc), VE, \_, s) \Rightarrow a} \quad (139)$$

$$\frac{}{proceed(\texttt{andhalt}, VE, fc, s) \Rightarrow \text{Yes}} \quad (140)$$

Comment: (139) The failure continuation in effect at the time of the return is abandoned in favour of the one recorded in the procedure continuation *pc* itself. This restricts relations to be determinate.

Procedure Continuations $\boxed{return(pc, ev^*, s) \Rightarrow a}$

$$\frac{match^*(pat^*, VE, ev^*, s) \Rightarrow VE' \quad proceed(gc, VE', fc, s) \Rightarrow a}{return(\texttt{retmatch}(pat^*, VE, gc, fc), ev^*, s) \Rightarrow a} \quad (141)$$

$$\frac{match^*(pat^*, VE, ev^*, s) \Rightarrow \text{FAIL} \quad fail(fc, s) \Rightarrow a}{return(\texttt{retmatch}(pat^*, VE, gc, fc), ev^*, s) \Rightarrow a} \quad (142)$$

Procedure Calls

$$\boxed{call(ev, ev^*, fc, pc, s) \Rightarrow a}$$

$$\frac{unfold_{VE} \; VE' \Rightarrow VE'' \quad invoke(clause, ev^*, ME, VE + VE'', fc, pc, s) \Rightarrow a}{call((clause, ME, VE, VE'), ev^*, fc, pc, s) \Rightarrow a}$$

$$(143)$$

$$\frac{APPLY(prim, ev^*, s) \Rightarrow (ev'^*, s') \quad return(pc, ev'^*, s') \Rightarrow a}{call(prim, ev^*, \_, pc, s) \Rightarrow a} \quad (144)$$

$$\frac{APPLY(prim, ev^*, s) \Rightarrow (FAIL, s') \quad fail(fc, s') \Rightarrow a}{call(prim, ev^*, fc, pc, s) \Rightarrow a} \quad (145)$$

$$\frac{fail(fc, s) \Rightarrow a}{call(l, ev^*, fc, pc, s) \Rightarrow a} \quad (146)$$

Goals

$$\boxed{exec(goal, ME, VE, fc, gc, s) \Rightarrow a}$$

$$\frac{\begin{array}{c} lookupLongVar(longvar, ME, VE) \Rightarrow ev \quad deref(ev, s) \Rightarrow ev'' \\ eval'(exp^*, ME, VE) \Rightarrow ev'^* \\ pc = \mathbf{retmatch}(pat^*, VE, gc, fc) \quad call(ev'', ev'^*, fc, pc, s) \Rightarrow a \end{array}}{exec(longvar \; exp^* \; \texttt{=>} \; pat^*, ME, VE, fc, gc, s) \Rightarrow a} \quad (147)$$

$$\frac{\begin{array}{c} eval(exp, ME, VE) \Rightarrow ev \quad var \notin \mathrm{Dom} \; VE \\ proceed(gc, VE + \{var \mapsto ev\}, fc, s) \Rightarrow a \end{array}}{exec(var = exp, ME, VE, fc, gc, s) \Rightarrow a} \quad (148)$$

$$\frac{\begin{array}{c} eval(exp, ME, VE) \Rightarrow ev \quad var \in \mathrm{Dom} \; VE \quad VE(var) = ev' \\ unify(ev, ev', s) \Rightarrow s' \quad proceed(gc, VE, fc, s') \Rightarrow a \end{array}}{exec(var = exp, ME, VE, fc, gc, s) \Rightarrow a} \quad (149)$$

$$\frac{\begin{array}{c} eval(exp, ME, VE) \Rightarrow ev \quad var \in \mathrm{Dom} \; VE \quad VE(var) = ev' \\ unify(ev, ev', s) \Rightarrow (FAIL, s') \quad fail(fc, s') \Rightarrow a \end{array}}{exec(var = exp, ME, VE, fc, gc, s) \Rightarrow a} \quad (150)$$

$$\frac{new \; s \Rightarrow l, s' \quad proceed(gc, VE + \{var \mapsto l \; in \; \mathrm{EVal}\}, fc, s') \Rightarrow a}{exec(\mathbf{exists} \; var, ME, VE, fc, gc, s) \Rightarrow a} \quad (151)$$

$$\frac{\begin{array}{c} marker \; s \Rightarrow m \quad fc' = \mathbf{ornot}(m, gc, VE, fc) \quad gc' = \mathbf{andnot}(fc) \\ exec(goal, ME, VE, fc', gc', s) \Rightarrow a \end{array}}{exec(\mathbf{not} \; goal, ME, VE, fc, gc, s) \Rightarrow a} \quad (152)$$

$$\frac{gc' = \mathbf{andthen}(goal_2, ME, gc) \quad exec(goal_1, ME, VE, fc, gc', s) \Rightarrow a}{exec(goal_1 \; \& \; goal_2, ME, VE, fc, gc, s) \Rightarrow a} \quad (153)$$

$$\boxed{exec'(\langle goal \rangle, ME, VE, fc, gc, s) \Rightarrow a}$$

$$\frac{exec(goal, ME, VE, fc, gc, s) \Rightarrow a}{exec'(goal, ME, VE, fc, gc, s) \Rightarrow a} \tag{154}$$

$$\frac{proceed(gc, VE, fc, s) \Rightarrow a}{exec'(\varepsilon, ME, VE, fc, gc, s) \Rightarrow a} \tag{155}$$

Clauses $\qquad \boxed{invoke(clause, ev^*, ME, VE, fc, pc, s) \Rightarrow a}$

$$\frac{\begin{array}{c} match^*(pat^*, VE, ev^*, s) \Rightarrow VE' \\ gc = \mathtt{andreturn}(ME, exp^*, pc) \quad exec'(\langle goal \rangle, ME, VE', fc, gc, s) \Rightarrow a \end{array}}{invoke(\mathtt{rule}\ \langle goal \rangle\ \mathtt{--}\ \_\ pat^*\ \mathtt{=>}\ exp^*, ev^*, ME, VE, fc, pc, s) \Rightarrow a} \tag{156}$$

$$\frac{match^*(pat^*, VE, ev^*, s) \Rightarrow \mathrm{FAIL} \quad fail(fc, s) \Rightarrow a}{invoke(\mathtt{rule}\ \langle goal \rangle\ \mathtt{--}\ \_\ pat^*\ \mathtt{=>}\ exp^*, ev^*, ME, VE, fc, pc, s) \Rightarrow a} \tag{157}$$

$$\frac{\begin{array}{c} marker\ s \Rightarrow m \quad fc' = \mathtt{orelse}(m, clause_2, ev^*, ME, VE, fc, pc) \\ invoke(clause_1, ev^*, ME, VE, fc', pc, s) \Rightarrow a \end{array}}{invoke(clause_1\ clause_2, ev^*, ME, VE, fc, pc, s) \Rightarrow a} \tag{158}$$

Relation Bindings $\qquad \boxed{evalRel(ME, VE, relbind) \Rightarrow VE'}$

$$\frac{VE' = \{var \mapsto (clause, ME, VE, \{\})\}}{evalRel(ME, VE, var\ \langle:\ \_\ \mathtt{=>}\ \_\rangle\ \mathtt{=}\ clause) \Rightarrow VE'} \tag{159}$$

$$\frac{evalRel(ME, VE, relbind_1) \Rightarrow VE_1 \quad evalRel(ME, VE, relbind_2) \Rightarrow VE_2}{evalRel(ME, VE, relbind_1\ \mathtt{and}\ relbind_2) \Rightarrow VE_1 + VE_2} \tag{160}$$

Declarations $\qquad \boxed{evalDec(ME, VE, dec) \Rightarrow VE'}$

$$\frac{evalRel(ME, VE, relbind) \Rightarrow VE' \quad unfold_{\mathrm{VE}}\ VE' \Rightarrow VE''}{evalDec(ME, VE, \mathtt{relation}\ relbind) \Rightarrow VE + VE''} \tag{161}$$

$$\frac{eval(exp, ME, VE) \Rightarrow ev}{evalDec(ME, VE, \mathtt{val}\ var\ \mathtt{=}\ exp) \Rightarrow VE + \{var \mapsto ev\}} \tag{162}$$

$$\frac{evalDec(ME, VE, dec_1) \Rightarrow VE_1 \quad evalDec(ME, VE_1, dec_2) \Rightarrow VE_2}{evalDec(ME, VE, dec_1\ dec_2) \Rightarrow VE_2} \quad (163)$$

$$\frac{dec = \mathtt{with}\ \_\ \lor\ dec = \mathtt{type}\ \_\ \lor\ dec = \mathtt{datatype}\ \_}{evalDec(ME, VE, dec) \Rightarrow VE} \quad (164)$$

Module Sequences $\boxed{load(ME, modseq) \Rightarrow ME'}$

$$\frac{evalDec(ME, VE_0, dec) \Rightarrow VE}{load(ME, \mathtt{module}\ modid:\ \_\ \mathtt{end}\ dec) \Rightarrow ME + \{modid \mapsto VE\}} \quad (165)$$

$$\frac{load(ME, modseq_1) \Rightarrow ME_1 \quad load(ME_1, modseq_2) \Rightarrow ME_2}{load(ME, modseq_1\ modseq_2) \Rightarrow ME_2} \quad (166)$$

Program Arguments $\boxed{cnvargv\ scon^* \Rightarrow ev}$

$$\frac{}{cnvargv\ [] \Rightarrow (\mathtt{nil}, [])} \quad (167)$$

$$\frac{ev = (scon\ \mathtt{in\ Lit})\ \mathtt{in\ EVal} \quad cnvargv\ scon^* \Rightarrow ev'}{cnvargv\ scon :: scon^* \Rightarrow (\mathtt{cons}, [ev, ev'])} \quad (168)$$

Programs $\boxed{run(modseq, scon^*) \Rightarrow a}$

$$\frac{\begin{array}{c} load(ME_0, modseq) \Rightarrow ME \quad ME(\mathtt{Main}) = VE \quad VE(\mathtt{main}) = ev \\ cnvargv\ scon^* \Rightarrow ev' \quad fc = \mathtt{orhalt} \\ pc = \mathtt{retmatch}([], \{\}, \mathtt{andhalt}, fc) \quad call(ev, [ev'], fc, pc, s_0) \Rightarrow a \end{array}}{run(modseq, scon^*) \Rightarrow a} \quad (169)$$

A.7 Initial Objects

This section defines the initial objects for the static and dynamic semantics. Although there is some overlap in naming (ME_0 and VE_0 occur in both parts), the static and dynamic semantics are completely separated.

A.7.1 Initial Static Objects

Figures A.22 to A.24 show the interface to the standard types, constructors, values, and relations.

Temporarily assume that references to ME_0, TE_0, and VE_0 in the inference rules for the static semantics are replaced by empty environments $\{\}$. Let TE and VE be the environments resulting from the elaboration of the rml interface. Then $TE_0 = TE$, $VE_0 = VE$, and $ME_0 = \{\text{rml} \mapsto (TE_0, VE_0)\}$.

A.7.2 Initial Dynamic Objects

The set PrimOp is equal to the set of variable identifiers bound as relations in the standard rml interface. $VE_0 = \{var \mapsto prim \; ; \; prim \in \text{PrimOp} \wedge var = prim\}$. $ME_0 = \{\text{rml} \mapsto VE_0\}$. $s_0 = (\{\}, X)$, for some unspecified external component X of the state.

Primitive Procedures

The function *APPLY* describes the effect of calling a primitive procedure. We let *true* denote the value of the true constructor, i.e. (true, []) (similarly for *false*).

- $APPLY(\text{clock}, [], s) = ([r], s)$ where r is a real number containing the number of seconds since some arbitrary but fixed (for the current process) past time point. The precision of r is unspecified.

- $APPLY(\text{fail}, [], s) = (\text{FAIL}, s)$

- $APPLY(\text{isvar}, [ev], s) = ([true], s)$ if $deref(ev, s) \in \text{Loc}$, $([false], s)$ otherwise.

- $APPLY(\text{print}, [ev], (\sigma, X)) = ([], (\sigma, X'))$ where X has been modified into X' by recording a textual representation of ev, using the state (σ, X) to look up locations.

- $APPLY(\text{tick}, [], (\sigma, X)) = ([i], (\sigma, X'))$ where i is an integer generated from X, and X' is X where this fact has been recorded so that i is not generated again.

```
module rml:
    (* types *)
    abstype char
    abstype int
    abstype real
    abstype string
    abstype 'a vector
    datatype bool       = false
                        | true
    datatype 'a list    = nil
                        | cons of 'a * 'a list
    datatype 'a option  = NONE
                        | SOME of 'a
    (* booleans *)
    relation bool_and: (bool,bool) => bool
    relation bool_or: (bool,bool) => bool
    relation bool_not: bool => bool
    (* integers *)
    relation int_add: (int,int) => int
    relation int_sub: (int,int) => int
    relation int_mul: (int,int) => int
    relation int_div: (int,int) => int
    relation int_mod: (int,int) => int
    relation int_abs: int => int
    relation int_neg: int => int
    relation int_max: (int,int) => int
    relation int_min: (int,int) => int
    relation int_lt: (int,int) => bool
    relation int_le: (int,int) => bool
    relation int_eq: (int,int) => bool
    relation int_ne: (int,int) => bool
    relation int_ge: (int,int) => bool
    relation int_gt: (int,int) => bool
    relation int_real: int => real
    relation int_string: int => string
```

Figure A.22: Interface of the standard rml module

```
(* reals *)
relation real_add: (real,real) => real
relation real_sub: (real,real) => real
relation real_mul: (real,real) => real
relation real_div: (real,real) => real
relation real_mod: (real,real) => real
relation real_abs: real => real
relation real_neg: real => real
relation real_cos: real => real
relation real_sin: real => real
relation real_atan: real => real
relation real_exp: real => real
relation real_ln: real => real
relation real_floor: real => real
relation real_int: real => int
relation real_pow: (real,real) => real
relation real_sqrt: real => real
relation real_max: (real,real) => real
relation real_min: (real,real) => real
relation real_lt: (real,real) => bool
relation real_le: (real,real) => bool
relation real_eq: (real,real) => bool
relation real_ne: (real,real) => bool
relation real_ge: (real,real) => bool
relation real_gt: (real,real) => bool
```

Figure A.23: Interface of the standard rml module (contd.)

```
(* characters *)
relation char_int: char => int
relation int_char: int => char
(* strings *)
relation string_int: string => int
relation string_list: string => char list
relation list_string: char list => string
relation string_length: string => int
relation string_nth: (string,int) => char
relation string_append: (string,string) => string
(* lists *)
relation list_append: ('a list,'a list) => 'a list
relation list_reverse: 'a list => 'a list
relation list_length: 'a list => int
relation list_member: ('a,'a list) => bool
relation list_nth: ('a list, int) => 'a
relation list_delete: ('a list, int) => 'a list
(* vectors *)
relation vector_length: 'a vector => int
relation vector_nth: ('a vector, int) => 'a
relation vector_list: 'a vector => 'a list
relation list_vector: 'a list => 'a vector
(* miscellaneous *)
relation clock: () => real
relation fail: () => ()
relation isvar: 'a => bool
relation print: 'a => ()
relation tick: () => int
end
```

Figure A.24: Interface of the standard rml module (contd.)

The following operations only apply to instantiated values. First, their arguments are dereferenced in the given state s. Then, any value must either be a character c, an integer i, a real r, a string str, a list lst, a vector vec, or an unbound location. If it is a location, then $APPLY$ returns $(FAIL, s)$. If the operation succeeds yielding a value ev, then $APPLY$ returns $([ev], s)$. If the operation fails, then $APPLY$ returns $(FAIL, s)$. We abbreviate $APPLY(prim, [x], s)$ to $prim\ x$ and $APPLY(prim, [x_1, x_2], s)$ to $prim(x_1, x_2)$ below.

- int_add$(i_1, i_2) = i_1 + i_2$ if the result can be represented by the implementation, otherwise the operation fails.

- int_sub$(i_1, i_2) = i_1 - i_2$ if the result can be represented by the implementation, otherwise the operation fails.

- int_mul$(i_1, i_2) = i_1 \times i_2$ if the result can be represented by the implementation, otherwise the operation fails.

- int_div(i_1, i_2) returns the integer quotient of i_1 and i_2 if $i_2 \neq 0$ and the result can be represented by the implementation, otherwise the operation fails.

- int_mod(i_1, i_2) returns the integer remainder of i_1 and i_2 if $i_2 \neq 0$ and the result can be represented by the implementation, otherwise the operation fails.

- int_abs i returns the absolute value of i if the result can be represented by the implementation, otherwise the operation fails.

- int_neg $i = -i$ if the result can be represented by the implementation, otherwise the operation fails.

- int_max$(i_1, i_2) = i_1$ if $i_1 \geq i_2$, i_2 otherwise.

- int_min$(i_1, i_2) = i_1$ if $i_1 \leq i_2$, i_2 otherwise.

- int_lt$(i_1, i_2) = true$ if $i_1 < i_2$, $false$ otherwise.

- int_le$(i_1, i_2) = true$ if $i_1 \leq i_2$, $false$ otherwise.

- int_eq$(i_1, i_2) = true$ if $i_1 = i_2$, $false$ otherwise.

- int_ne$(i_1, i_2) = true$ if $i_1 \neq i_2$, $false$ otherwise.

- int_ge$(i_1, i_2) = true$ if $i_1 \geq i_2$, $false$ otherwise.

- int_gt$(i_1, i_2) = true$ if $i_1 > i_2$, $false$ otherwise.

- int_real $i = r$ where r is the real value equal to i.

- int_string i returns a textual representation of i, as a string.

- $\texttt{real\_add}(r_1, r_2) = r_1 + r_2$.

- $\texttt{real\_sub}(r_1, r_2) = r_1 - r_2$.

- $\texttt{real\_mul}(r_1, r_2) = r_1 \times r_2$.

- $\texttt{real\_div}(r_1, r_2) = r_1/r_2$, if $r_2 \neq 0$, otherwise the operation fails.

- $\texttt{real\_mod}(r_1, r_2)$ returns the remainder of r_1/r_2. This is the value $r_1 - i \times r_2$, for some integer i such that the result has the same sign as r_1 and magnitude less than the magnitude of r_2. If $r_2 = 0$, the operation fails.

- $\texttt{real\_abs}\ r$ returns the absolute value of r.

- $\texttt{real\_neg}\ r = -r$.

- $\texttt{real\_cos}\ r$ returns the cosine of r (measured in radians).

- $\texttt{real\_sin}\ r$ returns the sine of r (measured in radians).

- $\texttt{real\_atan}\ r$ returns the arc tangent of r.

- $\texttt{real\_exp}\ r$ returns e^r.

- $\texttt{real\_ln}\ r$ returns the natural logarithm of r; fails if $r \leq 0$.

- $\texttt{real\_floor}\ r$ returns the largest integer (as a real value) not greater than r.

- $\texttt{real\_int}\ r$ discards the fractional part of r and returns the integral part as an integer; fails if this value cannot be represented by the implementation.

- $\texttt{real\_pow}(r_1, r_2) = r_1^{r_2}$; fails if this cannot be computed.

- $\texttt{real\_sqrt}\ r = \sqrt{r}$; fails if $r < 0$.

- $\texttt{real\_max}(r_1, r_2) = r_1$ if $r_1 \geq r_2$, r_2 otherwise.

- $\texttt{real\_min}(r_1, r_2) = r_1$ if $r_1 \leq r_2$, r_2 otherwise.

- $\texttt{real\_lt}(r_1, r_2) = true$ if $r_1 < r_2$, *false* otherwise.

- $\texttt{real\_le}(r_1, r_2) = true$ if $r_1 \leq r_2$, *false* otherwise.

- $\texttt{real\_eq}(r_1, r_2) = true$ if $r_1 = r_2$, *false* otherwise.

- $\texttt{real\_ne}(r_1, r_2) = true$ if $r_1 \neq r_2$, *false* otherwise.

- $\texttt{real\_ge}(r_1, r_2) = true$ if $r_1 \geq r_2$, *false* otherwise.

- $\texttt{real\_gt}(r_1, r_2) = true$ if $r_1 > r_2$, *false* otherwise.

- `string_int` *str* = *i* if the string has the lexical structure of an integer constant (as defined by the *icon* token class) and *i* is the value associated with that constant. Otherwise the operation fails.

Derived Dynamic Objects

The behaviour of some standard relations can be defined in RML itself; they include the boolean, list, character, and vector operations, and some string operations. Their definitions are shown in Figures A.25 to A.28. An implementation is expected to supply equivalent, but usually more efficient, implementations of some of these relations. In particular, although the vector and string types can be defined in terms of lists, the `vector_length`, `vector_nth`, `string_length` and `string_nth` relations are intended to execute in constant time.

```
relation bool_and =
    axiom    bool_and(true, true) => true
    axiom    bool_and(true, false) => false
    axiom    bool_and(false, true) => false
    axiom    bool_and(false, false) => false
end

relation bool_or =
    axiom    bool_or(false, false) => false
    axiom    bool_or(false, true) => true
    axiom    bool_or(true, false) => true
    axiom    bool_or(true, true) => true
end

relation bool_not =
    axiom    bool_not false => true
    axiom    bool_not true => false
end

relation list_append =
    axiom    list_append([], y) => y

    rule     list_append(y, z) => w
             ----------------
             list_append(x::y, z) => x::w
end

relation list_reverse =
    axiom    list_reverse [] => []

    rule     list_reverse y => revy &
             list_append(revy, [x]) => z
             ----------------
             list_reverse (x::y) => z
end
```

Figure A.25: Derived types and relations

```
relation list_length =
    axiom   list_length [] => 0

    rule    list_length y => leny & int_add(1,leny) => z
            ----------------
            list_length (_::y) => z
end

relation list_member =
    axiom   list_member(_, []) => false

    rule    x = y
            ----------------
            list_member(x, y::ys) => true

    rule    not x = y & list_member(x, ys) => z
            ----------------
            list_member(x, y::ys) => z
end

relation list_nth =
    axiom   list_nth(x::_, 0) => x

    rule    int_gt(n, 0) => true & int_sub(n, 1) => n' &
            list_nth(xs, n') => x
            ----------------
            list_nth(_::xs, n) => x
end

relation list_delete =
    axiom   list_delete(_::xs, 0) => xs

    rule    int_gt(n, 0) => true & int_sub(n, 1) => n' &
            list_delete(xs, n') => xs'
            ----------------
            list_delete(x::xs, n) => x::xs'
end
```

Figure A.26: Derived types and relations (contd.)

```
datatype 'a vector = VEC of 'a list

relation list_vector =
    rule    list_length l => _
            ----------------
            list_vector l => VEC l
end

relation vector_list =
    axiom   vector_list(VEC l) => l
end

relation vector_length =
    rule    vector_list v => l & list_length l => i
            ----------------
            vector_length v => i
end

relation vector_nth =
    rule    vector_list v => l & list_nth(l, i) => x
            ----------------
            vector_nth(v, i) => x
end

(* the char type must have at least 256 elements *)
val char_max = 255
datatype char = CHR of int (* [0,char_max] *)

relation char_int =
    axiom   char_int(CHR i) => i
end

relation int_char =
    rule    int_ge(i,0) => true & int_le(i,char_max) => true
            ----------------
            int_char i => CHR i
end
```

Figure A.27: Derived types and relations (contd.)

```
datatype string = STR of char vector

relation list_string =
    rule    list_vector l => v
            ----------------
            list_string l => STR v
end

relation string_list =
    rule    vector_list v => l
            ----------------
            string_list(STR v) => l
end

relation string_length =
    rule    vector_length v => i
            ----------------
            string_length(STR v) => i
end

relation string_nth =
    rule    vector_nth(v, i) => c
            ----------------
            string_nth(STR v, i) => c
end

relation string_append =
    rule    string_list s1 => l1 &
            string_list s2 => l2 &
            list_append(l1, l2) => l3 &
            list_string l3 => s3
            ----------------
            string_append(s1, s2) => s3
end
```

Figure A.28: Derived types and relations (contd.)

Bibliography

[1] A. V. Aho, M. Ganapathi, and S. W. K. Tjiang. Code generation using tree matching and dynamic programming. *ACM Transactions on Programming Languages and Systems*, 11(4), October 1989.

[2] A. V. Aho, J. E. Hopcroft, and J. D. Ullman. *Data Structures and Algorithms*. Addison-Wesley, 1987. Reprinted with corrections.

[3] A. V. Aho, R. Sethi, and J. D. Ullman. *Compilers Principles, Techniques, and Tools*. Addison-Wesley, 1986.

[4] Hassan Aït-Kaci. *Warren's Abstract Machine: A Tutorial Reconstruction*. The MIT Press, 1991.

[5] ANSI X3.159-1989. *Programming Language – C*. American National Standards Institute, 1989.

[6] Andrew W. Appel. A runtime system. *Lisp and Symbolic Computation*, 3:343–380, 1990.

[7] Andrew W. Appel. *Compiling with Continuations*. Cambridge University Press, 1992.

[8] Andrew W. Appel and Trevor Jim. Continuation-passing, closure-passing style. In POPL'89 [145], pages 293–302.

[9] Joe Armstrong, Robert Virding, Claes Wikström, and Mike Williams. *Concurrent Programming in ERLANG*. Prentice-Hall, second edition, 1996.

[10] Russ Atkinson, Alan Demers, Carl Hauser, Christian Jacobi, Peter Kessler, and Mark Weiser. Experiences creating a portable Cedar. In *Proceedings of the ACM SIGPLAN '89 Conference on Programming Language Design and Implementation, PLDI'89*, pages 322–329. ACM Press, 1989.

[11] Isabelle Attali. Compiling TYPOL with attribute grammars. In P. Deransart, B. Lorho, and J. Małuszyński, editors, *Proceedings of the International Workshop on Programming Languages Implementation and*

       Logic Programming, PLILP'88, volume 348 of *LNCS*, pages 252–272.
       Springer-Verlag, 1988.

[12]   Isabelle Attali and Jacques Chazarain. Functional evaluation of nat-
       ural semantics specifications. In Pierre Deransart and Martin Jour-
       dan, editors, *International Workshop on Attribute Grammars and their
       Applications, WAGA'90*, volume 461 of *LNCS*. Springer-Verlag, 1990.
       Longer version in INRIA Research Report N° 1218, May, 1990.

[13]   Isabelle Attali and Didier Parigot. Integrating natural semantics and
       attribute grammars: the Minotaur system. Research Report N° 2339,
       INRIA, September 1994.

[14]   Lennart Augustsson. Compiling pattern-matching. In Jean-Pierre
       Jouannaud, editor, *Conference on Functional Programming Languages
       and Computer Architecture, FPCA'85*, volume 201 of *LNCS*, pages
       368–381. Springer-Verlag, 1985.

[15]   Sara Baase. *Computer Algorithms, Introduction to Design and Analy-
       sis*. Addison-Wesley, 2nd edition, 1988.

[16]   Henry G. Baker. CONS should not CONS its arguments, part II: Ch-
       eney on the M.T.A. *ACM SIGPLAN Notices*, 30(9):17–20, September
       1995.

[17]   Joel F. Bartlett. SCHEME->C a portable Scheme-to-C compiler. Re-
       search report 89/1, DEC Western Research Laboratory, Palo Alto, Cal-
       ifornia, January 1989.

[18]   Marianne Baudinet and David MacQueen. Tree pattern match-
       ing for ML (extended abstract), December 6, 1985. Available on
       ftp.research.bell-labs.com in /dist/smlnj/papers/.

[19]   Y. Bekkers and J. Cohen, editors. *International Workshop on Memory
       Management (IWMM)*, volume 637 of *LNCS*. Springer-Verlag, 1992.

[20]   Y. Bekkers, O. Ridoux, and L. Ungaro. Dynamic memory management
       for sequential logic programming languages. In Bekkers and Cohen [19],
       pages 82–102.

[21]   Robert L. Bernstein. Producing good code for the case statement.
       Software – Practice and Experience, 15(10):1021–1024, October 1985.

[22]   Dave Berry. Generating program animators from programming lan-
       guage semantics. Technical Report ECS-LFCS-91-163, University of
       Edinburgh, 1991. Ph.D. thesis.

[23]   J. Bevemyr and T. Lindgren. A simple and efficient copying garbage
       collector for Prolog. In Hermenegildo and Penjam [85], pages 88–101.

[24] Michel Billaud. Prolog control structures: a formalization and its applications. In K. Fuchi and M. Nivat, editors, *Programming of Future Generation Computers*, pages 57–73. North-Holland, 1988.

[25] Michel Billaud. Simple operational and denotational semantics for Prolog with cut. *Theoretical Computer Science*, 71:193 208, 1990.

[26] Michel Billaud. Axiomatizations of backtracking (extended abstract). In *Actes JTASPEFL'91, Analyse statique en programmation équationelle, fonctionelle et logique*, Bigre 74, pages 111 116, 1991.

[27] Michel Billaud. Operational and denotational semantics for Prolog with input-output predicates. In *Proceedings of the France-USSR Symposium "INFORMATICA '91"*, pages 265–276, Grenoble, October 1991.

[28] Michel Billaud. Axiomatizations of backtracking. In A. Finkel and M. Jantzen, editors, *Proceedings of the Annual Symposium on Theoretical Aspects of Computer Science, STACS'92*, volume 577 of *LNCS*, pages 71–82. Springer-Verlag, 1992.

[29] E. Börger, editor. *Specification and Validation Methods*. Oxford University Press, 1994.

[30] Egon Börger. Annotated bibliography on evolving algebras. In Börger [29]. ftp://ftp.eecs.umich.edu/groups/Ealgebras/.

[31] Jürgen Börstler, Ulrich Möncke, and Reinhard Wilhelm. Table compression for tree automata. *ACM Transactions on Programming Languages and Systems*, 13(3):295–314, July 1991.

[32] Koen De Bosschere, Bart Demoen, and Paul Tarau, editors. *ILPS'94 Post-Conference Workshop on Implementation Techniques for Logic Programming Language*, 1994.

[33] Pascal Brisset and Olivier Ridoux. Continuations in λProlog. In David S. Warren, editor, *Proceedings of the Tenth International Conference on Logic Programming*, pages 27–43, Budapest, Hungary, 1993. The MIT Press.

[34] de Bruin, A. Continuation semantics for PROLOG with cut. In J. Díaz and F. Orejas, editors, *Theory and Practice of Software Development, TAPSOFT'89. Volume 1: Proceedings CAAP'89*, volume 351 of *LNCS*, pages 178 192. Springer-Verlag, 1989.

[35] Maurice Bruynooghe, editor. *Logic Programming, Proceedings of the 1994 International Symposium*. The MIT Press, 1994.

[36] Robert G. Burger, Oscar Waddell, and R. Kent Dybvig. Register allocation using lazy saves, eager restores, and greedy shuffling. In *Proceedings of the ACM SIGPLAN '95 Conference on Programming Language Design and Implementation, PLDI'95*, pages 130–138. ACM Press, 1995.

[37] Luca Cardelli. Compiling a functional language. In *Proceedings of the 1984 ACM Conference on Lisp and Functional Programming, LFP'84*, pages 208–217. ACM Press, 1984.

[38] Luca Cardelli. Basic polymorphic typechecking. *Science of Computer Programming*, 8:147–172, 1987.

[39] Mats Carlsson. On implementing Prolog in functional programming. *New Generation Computing*, 2:347–359, 1984.

[40] Mats Carlsson. Freeze, indexing, and other implementation issues in the WAM. In Jean-Louis Lassez, editor, *Proceedings of the Fourth International Conference on Logic Programming*, MIT Press Series in Logic Programming, pages 40–58, Melbourne, 1987. The MIT Press.

[41] Eugene Charniak, Christopher K. Riesbeck, Drew V. McDermott, and James R. Meehan. *Artificial Intelligence Programming*. Lawrence Erlbaum Associates, Inc., second edition, 1987.

[42] Takashi Chikayama, Tetsuro Fujise, and Daigo Sekita. A portable and efficient implementation of KL1. In Hermenegildo and Penjam [85], pages 25–39.

[43] Jeff Chu. Optimal algorithm for the nearest common dominator problem. *Journal of Algorithms*, 13(4):693–697, 1992.

[44] D. Clément, J. Despeyroux, T. Despeyroux, and G. Kahn. A simple applicative language: Mini-ML. In *Proceedings of the 1986 ACM Conference on Lisp and Functional Programming, LFP'86*, pages 13–27. ACM Press, 1986.

[45] Philippe Codognet and Daniel Diaz. wamcc: Compiling Prolog to C. In Leon Sterling, editor, *Proceedings of the Twelfth International Conference on Logic Programming*, pages 317–331, Tokyo, Japan, 1995. The MIT Press.

[46] Jacques Cohen. Describing Prolog by its interpretation and compilation. *Communications of the ACM*, 28(12):1311–1324, 1985.

[47] Charles Consel and Olivier Danvy. For a better support of static data flow. In John Hughes, editor, *5th Conference on Functional Programming Languages and Computer Architecture, FPCA'91*, volume 523 of *LNCS*, pages 496–519. Springer-Verlag, 1991.

[48] Fabio Q. B. da Silva. Towards a formal framework for evaluation of operational semantics. Technical Report ECS-LFCS-90-126, University of Edinburgh, 1990.

[49] D. van Dalen. *Logic and Structure (2nd ed.)*. Springer-Verlag, 1985.

[50] Luis Damas and Robin Milner. Principal type-schemes for functional programs. In *Conference Record of the 9th Annual ACM Symposium on Principles of Programming Languages, POPL'82*, pages 207–212. ACM, 1982.

[51] S. Dawson, C. R. Ramakrishnan, and I. V. Ramakrishnan. Design and implementation of jump tables for fast indexing of logic programs. In M. Hermenegildo and S. D. Swierstra, editors, *Proceedings of the 7th International Symposium on Programming Languages: Implementations, Logics, and Programs, PLILP'95*, volume 982 of *LNCS*, pages 133–150. Springer-Verlag, 1995.

[52] K. De Bosschere and P. Tarau. A continuation-based Prolog-to-C mapping. Technical Report TR 93-02, Département d'Informatique, Université de Moncton, Canada, 1993. Shorter version in Proc. ACM SAC'94.

[53] Bart Demoen and Greet Maris. A comparison of some schemes for translating logic to C. In J. Barklund, B. Jayaraman, and J. Tanaka, editors, *Proceedings of the post-ICLP'94 Workshop on Parallel and Data Parallel Extensions of Logic Programs*, pages 79–91, S. Margherita Ligure, Italy, June 17, 1994. UPMAIL Technical Report No. 78, Uppsala University.

[54] Nachum Dershowitz. Termination of rewriting. *Journal of Symbolic Computation*, 3(1&2):69–116, February/April 1987. Corrigendum: 4(3) (Dec 1987), 409–410.

[55] Nachum Dershowitz and Jean-Pierre Jouannaud. Rewrite systems. In Jan van Leeuwen, editor, *Handbook of Theoretical Computer Science*, volume Volume B: Formal Models and Semantics, pages 243–320. Elsevier Science Publishers B.V., 1990.

[56] Joëlle Despeyroux. Proof of translation in natural semantics. In *Proceedings of the 1st Symposium on Logic in Computer Science, LICS'86*, pages 193–205. IEEE, 1986.

[57] Thierry Despeyroux. Executable specification of static semantics. In Gilles Kahn, editor, *Semantics of Data Types*, volume 173 of *LNCS*, pages 215–233. Springer-Verlag, 1984.

[58] Stephan Diehl. Automatic generation of a compiler and an abstract machine for action notation. Technischer Bericht A 03/95, Fachbereich Informatik, Universität des Saarlandes, Saarbrücken, 1995.

[59] J. R. Driscoll, N. Sarnak, D. D. Sleator, and R. E. Tarjan. Making data structures persistent. *Journal of Computer and System Sciences*, 38:86–124, 1989.

[60] Conal Elliot and Frank Pfenning. A semi-functional implementation of a higher-order logic programming language. In Peter Lee, editor, *Topics in Advanced Language Implementations*, pages 289–325. The MIT Press, 1991.

[61] Johan Fagerström, Peter Fritzson, Johan Ringström, and Mikael Pettersson. A data-parallel language and its compilation to a formally defined intermediate language. In W. W. Koczkodaj, P. E. Lauer, and A. A. Toptsis, editors, *4th International Conference on Computing and Information, ICCI'92*, pages 133–134. IEEE, 1992. Full version in Research Report LiTH-IDA-R-92-15, Linköping University, Sweden.

[62] Marc Feeley. Gambit-C version 2.2, May 1995. Available on the Internet via http://www.iro.umontreal.ca/~gambit/.

[63] Marc Feeley, James S. Miller, Guillermo J. Rozas, and Jason A. Wilson. Compiling higher-order languages into fully tail-recursive portable C. Rapport technique 1078, département d'informatique et r.o., Université de Montréal, August 18, 1997.

[64] Alan Finlay and Lloyd Allison. A correction to the denotational semantics for the Prolog of Nicholson and Foo. *ACM Transactions on Programming Languages and Systems*, 15(1):206–208, January 1993.

[65] Michael J. Fischer. Lambda-calculus schemata. *Lisp and Symbolic Computation*, 6(3/4):259–287, 1993.

[66] Cormac Flanagan, Amr Sabry, Bruce F. Duba, and Matthias Felleisen. The essence of compiling with continuations. In *Proceedings of the ACM SIGPLAN '93 Conference on Programming Language Design and Implementation, PLDI'93*, pages 237–247. ACM Press, 1993.

[67] Christopher W. Fraser and Robert R. Henry. Hard-coding bottom-up code generation tables to save time and space. *Software – Practice and Experience*, 21(1):1–12, January 1991.

[68] Jean H. Gallier. *Logic for Computer Science*. John Wiley & Sons, 1987.

[69] Robert Giegerich and Reinhard Wilhelm. Counter-one-pass features in one-pass compilation: a formalization using attribute grammars. *Information Processing Letters*, 7(6):279–284, October 1978.

[70] John Greiner. Standard ML weak polymorphism can be sound. Technical Report CMU–CS–93–160, Carnegie Mellon University, May 1993.

[71] David Gudeman. Representing type information in dynamically typed languages. Technical Report TR 93-27, University of Arizona, Department of Computer Science, October 1993.

[72] David Gudeman, Koenraad De Bosschere, and Saumya K. Debray. jc: An efficient and portable sequential implementation of Janus. In Krzysztof Apt, editor, *Proceedings of the Joint International Conference and Symposium on Logic Programming*, pages 399–413, Washington, USA, 1992. The MIT Press.

[73] Yuri Gurevich. Evolving algebras 1993: Lipari guide. In Börger [29]. ftp://ftp.eecs.umich.edu/groups/Ealgebras/.

[74] D. Hammer, editor. *Compiler Compilers, Third International Workshop, CC'90*, volume 477 of *LNCS*. Springer-Verlag, October 1990.

[75] Chris Hankin and Daniel Le Métayer. A type-based framework for program analysis. In B. Le Charlier, editor, *Proceedings of the 1st International Static Analysis Symposium, SAS'94*, volume 864 of *LNCS*, pages 380–394. Springer-Verlag, 1994.

[76] John Hannan. Investigating a proof-theoretic meta-language for functional programs. Report 91/1, DIKU Copenhagen, 1991. PhD thesis.

[77] John Hannan. Extended natural semantics. *Journal of Functional Programming*, 3(2):123–152, April 1993.

[78] John Hannan. Operational semantics-directed compilers and machine architectures. *ACM Transactions on Programming Languages and Systems*, 16(4):1215–1247, July 1994.

[79] John Hannan and Dale Miller. From operational semantics to abstract machines. *Journal of Mathematical Structures in Computer Science*, 2(4):415–459, 1992.

[80] Robert Harper. Systems of polymorphic type assignment in LF. Technical Report CMU–CS–90–144, Carnegie Mellon University, June 1990.

[81] Robert Harper and Greg Morrisett. Compiling with non-parametric polymorphism (preliminary report). Technical Report CMU–CS–94–122, Carnegie Mellon University, February 1994.

[82] Bogumił Hausman. Turbo Erlang: Approaching the speed of C. In E. Tick and G. Succi, editors, *Implementations of Logic Programming Systems*, pages 119–135. Kluwer Academic Publishers, 1994.

[83] Fergus Henderson. Strong modes can change the world! Masters Thesis 93/25, Department of Computer Science, University of Melbourne, 1993. http://www.cs.mu.oz.au/tr_db/mu_93_25.ps.gz.

[84] Fritz Henglein. Type inference with polymorphic recursion. *ACM Transactions on Programming Languages and Systems*, 15(2):253–289, April 1993.

[85] M. Hermenegildo and J. Penjam, editors. *Proceedings of the 6th International Symposium on Programming Language Implementation and Logic Programming, PLILP'94*, volume 844 of *LNCS*. Springer-Verlag, 1994.

[86] R. Hindley. The principal type-scheme of an object in combinatory logic. *Transactions of the American Mathematical Society*, 146:29–60, 1969.

[87] My Hoang, John C. Mitchell, and Ramesh Viswanathan. Standard ML weak polymorphism and imperative constructs. In *Proceedings, Eighth Annual IEEE Symposium on Logic in Computer Science*, pages 15–25. IEEE Computer Society Press, 19–23 June 1993.

[88] Cristoph M. Hoffman and Michael J. O'Donnell. Pattern matching in trees. *Journal of the ACM*, 29(1), January 1982.

[89] Paul Hudak *et al.* Report on the programming language Haskell, version 1.2. *ACM SIGPLAN Notices*, 27(5), May 1992. Special issue on Haskell.

[90] G. P. Huet. A unification algorithm for typed λ-calculus. *Theoretical Computer Science*, 1:27–57, 1975.

[91] I. Jacobs. *The Centaur 1.2 Manual*, 1992. Available from INRIA – Sophia Antipolis.

[92] Joxan Jaffar and Michael J. Maher. Constraint logic programming: A survey. *The Journal of Logic Programming*, 19/20:503–581, May/July 1994.

[93] S. C. Johnson and D. M. Ritchie. The C language calling sequence. Computing Science Technical Report No. CSTR-102, Bell Laboratories, September 1981.

[94] Martin Jourdan and Didier Parigot. Application development with the FNC-2 attribute grammar system. In Hammer [74], pages 11–25.

[95] David Kågedal and Peter Fritzson. Generating a Modelica compiler from natural semantics specifications. In *Summer Computer Simulation Conference (SCSC '98)*, 1998.

[96] Gilles Kahn. Natural semantics. In F. J. Brandenburg, G. Vidal-Naquet, and M. Wirsing, editors, *Proceedings of the Symposium on Theoretical Aspects of Computer Science, STACS'87*, volume 247 of *LNCS*, pages 22–39. Springer-Verlag, 1987.

[97] Stefan Kahrs. Mistakes and ambiguities in the definition of Standard ML. Technical Report ECS-LFCS-93-257, Laboratory for Foundations of Computer Science, University of Edinburgh, April 1993. Addendum in `ftp://ftp.dcs.ed.ac.uk/pub/smk/SML/errors-new.ps.Z`.

[98] Sampath Kannan and Todd A. Proebsting. Correction to 'Producing good code for the case statement'. *Software – Practice and Experience*, 24(2):233, February 1994.

[99] Richard Kelsey and Paul Hudak. Realistic compilation by program transformation. In POPL'89 [145], pages 281–292.

[100] J. W. Klop. Term rewriting systems. In S. Abramsky, Dov M. Gabbay, and T. S. E. Maibaum, editors, *Handbook of Logic in Computer Science, Volume 2 Background: Computational Structures*, pages 1–116. Oxford University Press, 1992.

[101] Donald E. Knuth. Semantics of context-free languages. *Mathematical Systems Theory*, 2(2):127–145, 1968. Correction in 5(1):95–96, 1971.

[102] Donald E. Knuth. Semantics of context-free languages: Correction. *Mathematical Systems Theory*, 5(1):95–96, 1971.

[103] C. H. A. Koster. A technique for parsing ambiguous languages. In D. Siefkes, editor, *GI-4.Jahrestagung*, volume 26 of *LNCS*, pages 233–246. Springer-Verlag, 1975. The conference took place in Berlin, October 9–12, 1974.

[104] C. H. A. Koster. Affix grammars for programming languages. In H. Albas and B. Melichar, editors, *Attribute Grammars, Applications and Systems. International Summer School Proceedings*, volume 545 of *LNCS*, pages 358–373. Springer-Verlag, 1991.

[105] David Kranz, Richard Kelsey, Jonathan A. Rees, Paul Hudak, James Philbin, and Norman I. Adams. Orbit: an optimizing compiler for Scheme. In *Proceedings of the ACM SIGPLAN '86 Symposium on Compiler Construction*, pages 219–233. ACM Press, 1986.

[106] Peter J. Landin. The mechanical evaluation of expressions. *The Computer Journal*, 6(4):308–320, 1964.

[107] Xavier Leroy. Unboxed objects and polymorphic typing. In *Conference Record of the 19th Annual ACM Symposium on Principles of Programming Languages, POPL'92*, pages 177–188. ACM, 1992.

[108] Xavier Leroy. Polymorphism by name for references and continuations. In *Conference Record of the 20th Annual ACM Symposium on Principles of Programming Languages, POPL'93*, pages 220–231. ACM, 1993.

[109] Xavier Leroy and Pierre Weis. Polymorphic type inference and assignment. In *Conference Record of the 18th Annual ACM Symposium on Principles of Programming Languages, POPL '91*, pages 291–302. ACM, 1991.

[110] M. R. Levy and R. N. Horspool. Translating Prolog to C: a WAM-based approach. In *Proceedings of the 2nd Compulog-Network Area Meeting on Programming Languages*, Pisa, Italy, May 1993.

[111] Thomas Lindgren. A continuation-passing style for Prolog. In Bruynooghe [35], pages 603–617. Also as UPMAIL Technical Report 86, Computing Science Department, Uppsala University, 1994.

[112] J. W. Lloyd. *Foundations of Logic Programming*. Springer-Verlag, 1984.

[113] Harry G. Mairson. Deciding ML typability is complete for deterministic exponential time. In *Conference Record of the 17th Annual ACM Symposium on Principles of Programming Languages, POPL '90*, pages 382–401. ACM, 1990.

[114] William Marsh and Ian O'Neill. Formal semantics of SPARK. Program Validation Ltd., October 1994.

[115] Stephen McKeever. Generating compilers from natural semantics specifications. Available by anonymous ftp from `ftp.comlab.ox.ac.uk` as `pub/Documents/techpapers/Stephen.McKeever/plilp.ps.Z`.

[116] C. Mellish and S. Hardy. Integrating Prolog in the POPLOG environment. In J. A. Campbell, editor, *Implementations of PROLOG*, pages 147–162. Ellis Horwood Ltd., 1984.

[117] Dale A. Miller and Gopalan Nadathur. Higher-order logic programming. In Ehud Shapiro, editor, *Proceedings of the Third International Conference on Logic Programming*, volume 225 of *LNCS*, pages 448–462, London, 1986. Springer-Verlag.

[118] Robin Milner. A theory of type polymorphism in programming. *Journal of Computer and System Sciences*, 17:348–375, 1978.

[119] Robin Milner and Mads Tofte. *Commentary on Standard ML*. The MIT Press, 1991.

[120] Robin Milner, Mads Tofte, and Robert Harper. *The Definition of Standard ML*. The MIT Press, 1990.

[121] Robin Milner, Mads Tofte, Robert Harper, and David MacQueen. *The Definition of Standard ML (Revised)*. The MIT Press, 1997.

[122] Peter D. Mosses. *Action Semantics*. Cambridge University Press, 1992.

[123] J. A. Muylaert-Filho and G. L. Burn. Continuation passing transformation and abstract interpretation. Research Report DoC 92/21, Imperial College, 1992.

[124] Tim Nicholson and Norman Foo. A denotational semantics for Prolog. *ACM Transactions on Programming Languages and Systems*, 11(4):650–665, October 1989. Correction in [64].

[125] Jørgen Fischer Nilsson. On the compilation of a domain-based Prolog. In R. E. A. Mason, editor, *Information Processing 83*, pages 293–298. North–Holland, 1983.

[126] Jacques Noyé. Backtrackable updates. In Bosschere et al. [32], pages 69–89.

[127] Alexander Ollongren. *Definition of Programming Languages by Interpreting Automata*. A.P.I.C. Studies in Data Processing No. 11. Academic Press, 1974.

[128] John Ophel. An improved mixture rule for pattern matching. *ACM SIGPLAN Notices*, 24(6):91–96, June 1989.

[129] John Peterson and Kevin Hammond (eds.). Report on the programming language Haskell, version 1.3. Technical Report YALEU/DCS/RR-1106, Yale University, May 1, 1996.

[130] Mikael Pettersson. Generating interpreters from denotational definitions using C++ as a meta-language. Research Report LiTH-IDA-R-89-52, Department of Computer and Information Science, Linköping University, December 1989.

[131] Mikael Pettersson. Generating efficient code from continuation semantics. In Hammer [74], pages 165–178. Also presented at the Nordic Workshop on Programming Environments Research, NWPER'90, June 1990, Trondheim, Norway.

[132] Mikael Pettersson. DML – a language and system for the generation of efficient compilers from denotational specifications. Licentiate Thesis No. 319, Department of Computer and Information Science, Linköping University, May 1992.

[133] Mikael Pettersson. A term pattern-match compiler inspired by finite automata theory. In U. Kastens and P. Pfahler, editors, *Compiler Construction, 4th International Conference, CC'92*, volume 641 of *LNCS*, pages 258–270. Springer-Verlag, October 1992.

[134] Mikael Pettersson. Main-memory linear hashing – some enhancements of Larson's algorithm. Research Report LiTH-IDA-R-93-04, Department of Computer and Information Science, Linköping University, March 1993. Revised 12/8/93.

[135] Mikael Pettersson. An overview of the RML language and the RML2C compiler. Presentation at INRIA Sophia-Antipolis, June 16, 1994.

[136] Mikael Pettersson. RML – a new language and implementation for natural semantics. In Hermenegildo and Penjam [85], pages 117–131.

[137] Mikael Pettersson. The RML2C compiler – present and future (extended abstract). In Boris Magnusson, Görel Hedin, and Sten Minör, editors, *Proceedings of the Nordic Workshop on Programming Environment Research, NWPER'94*, pages 303–304, Lund University, June 1–3 1994. Published as Technical Report LU-CS-TR:94-127, Lund University.

[138] Mikael Pettersson. A compiler for natural semantics. In Tibor Gyimóthy, editor, *Compiler Construction, 6th International Conference, CC'96*, volume 1060 of *LNCS*, pages 177–191. Springer-Verlag, April 1996. Also published as research report LiTH-IDA-R-96-05, Department of Computer and Information Science, Linköping University, January 1996.

[139] Mikael Pettersson. Portable debugging and profiling. In Kai Koskimies, editor, *Compiler Construction, 7th International Conference, CC'98*, volume 1383 of *LNCS*, pages 279–293. Springer-Verlag, March/April 1998.

[140] Mikael Pettersson and Peter Fritzson. DML – a meta-language and system for the generation of practical and efficient compilers from denotational specifications. In *4th International Conference on Computer Languages, ICCL'92*, pages 127–136. IEEE, April 1992.

[141] Mikael Pettersson and Peter Fritzson. A general and practical approach to concrete syntax objects within ML. In *Proceedings of the 1992 ACM SIGPLAN Workshop on ML and its Applications*, pages 17–27, San Fransicso, June 1992.

[142] Simon L. Peyton Jones. *The Implementation of Functional Programming Languages*. Prentice-Hall, 1987.

[143] Simon L. Peyton Jones. Implementing lazy functional languages on stock hardware: the spineless tagless G-machine. *Journal of Functional Programming*, 2(2):127–202, April 1992.

[144] Gordon D. Plotkin. A structural approach to operational semantics. Report DAIMI FN-19, Computer Science Department, Aarhus University, Denmark, September 1981.

[145] *Conference Record of the 16th Annual ACM Symposium on Principles of Programming Languages, POPL'89*. ACM, 1989.

[146] Kjell Post. *Analysis and Transformation of Logic Programs*. PhD thesis, University of California, Santa Cruz, December 1994.

[147] Kjell Post. Mutually exclusive rules in logic programming. In Bruynooghe [35], pages 472–486.

[148] Dag Prawitz. *Natural Deduction*. Almqvist & Wiksell, Stockholm, 1965.

[149] Todd A. Proebsting. BURS automata generation. *ACM Transactions on Programming Languages and Systems*, 17(3):461 486, May 1995.

[150] L. Puel and A. Suárez. Compiling pattern matching by term decomposition. In *Proceedings of the 1990 ACM Conference on Lisp and Functional Programming, LFP'90*, pages 273 281. ACM Press, 1990.

[151] John D. Ramsdell. An operational semantics for Scheme. *Lisp Pointers*, V(2):6–10, April-June 1992.

[152] Didier Rémy. Extension of ML type system with a sorted equational theory on types. Research Report N° 1766, INRIA, October 1992.

[153] John C. Reynolds. Definitional interpreters for higher-order programming languages. In *Proceedings of the ACM Annual Conference*, pages 717–740, 1972.

[154] Olivier Ridoux. Imagining CLP($\lambda, \equiv_{\alpha\beta}$). Publication Interne N° 876, IRISA, Université de Rennes 1, France, 1994.

[155] J. A. Robinson. A machine-oriented logic based on the resolution principle. *Journal of the ACM*, 12(1):23–41, January 1965.

[156] Amr Sabry. *The Formal Relationship between Direct and Continuation-Passing Style Optimizing Compilers: A Synthesis of Two Paradigms*. PhD thesis, Department of Computer Science, Rice University, August 1994.

[157] Amr Sabry and Matthias Felleisen. Is continuation-passing useful for data flow analysis? In *Proceedings of the ACM SIGPLAN '94 Conference on Programming Language Design and Implementation, PLDI'94*, pages 1–12. ACM Press, 1994.

[158] Erik Sandewall. Conversion of predicate-calculus axioms to corresponding deterministic programs. *IEEE Transactions on Computers*, C-25(4):342–346, April 1976.

[159] David A. Schmidt. Detecting global variables in denotational specifications. *ACM Transactions on Programming Languages and Systems*, 7(2):299–310, April 1985.

[160] David A. Schmidt. *Denotational Semantics, A Methodology for Language Development.* Allyn and Bacon, Inc., 1986.

[161] Wolfgang Schreiner. Compiling a functional language to efficient SACLIB C. Technical Report 93-49, RISC-Linz, Johannes Kepler University, Linz, Austria, September 1993.

[162] Dana Scott and Christopher Strachey. Towards a mathematical semantics for computer languages. Technical monograph PRG-6, Programming Research Group, University of Oxford, 1971.

[163] M. Serrano and P. Weis. $1 + 1 = 1$: an optimizing Caml compiler. In *ACM SIGPLAN ML'94*, pages 101–111. INRIA Research Report N° 2265, June 1994. Longer version published as INRIA Research Report N° 2301, July 1994.

[164] Zhong Shao and Andrew W. Appel. Space-efficient closure representations. In *Proceedings of the 1994 ACM Conference on Lisp and Functional Programming*, pages 150–161. ACM, ACM Press, 1994.

[165] Zoltan Somogyi, Fergus James Henderson, and Thomas Charles Conway. The implementation of Mercury, an efficient purely declarative logic programming language. In Bosschere et al. [32], pages 31–58.

[166] Guy L. Steele Jr. Rabbit: a compiler for Scheme (a study in compiler optimization). MIT AI Memo 474, Massachusetts Institute of Technology, May 1978. Master's Thesis.

[167] Joseph E. Stoy. *Denotational Semantics: The Scott-Strachey Approach to Programming Language Theory.* The MIT Press, 1977.

[168] Gerald Jay Sussman and Guy L. Steele Jr. SCHEME: An interpreter for extended lambda calculus. MIT AI Memo 349, Massachusetts Institute of Technology, December 1975.

[169] Tanel Tammet. Lambda-lifting as an optimization for compiling Scheme to C. Technical report, Department of Computer Science, Chalmers University, April 1995. Unpublished draft, available via `http://www.cs.chalmers.se/~tammet/`.

[170] Paul Tarau and Michel Boyer. Elementary logic programs. In P. Deransart and J. Małuszyński, editors, *Proceedings of the International Workshop on Programming Language Implementation and Logic Programming, PLILP'90*, number 456 in LNCS, pages 159–173. Springer-Verlag, 1990.

[171] David R. Tarditi, Peter Lee, and Anurag Acharya. No assembly required: Compiling Standard ML to C. *ACM Letters on Programming Languages and Systems*, 1(2):161–177, June 1992.

[172] W. Teitelman. *Interlisp Reference Manual*. Xerox Palo Alto Research Center, third edition, October 1978.

[173] Peter J. Thiemann. Unboxed values and polymorphic typing revisited. In *7th Annual SIGPLAN/SIGARCH/WG2.8 Conference on Functional Programming Languages and Computer Architecture, FPCA '95*, 1995.

[174] Mads Tofte. Type inference for polymorphic references. *Information and Computation*, 89:1–34, 1990.

[175] Peter Lodewijk Van Roy. *Can Logic Programming Execute as Fast as Imperative Programming*. PhD thesis, University of California at Berkeley, 1990.

[176] Philip Wadler. Efficient compilation of pattern-matching. In *The Implementation of Functional Programming Languages* [142], chapter 5.

[177] Philip Wadler. Is there a use for linear logic? In *ACM/IFIP Symposium on Partial Evaluation and Semantics Based Program Manipulation, PEPM '91*, pages 255–273, Yale University, June 17–19 1991. Published as ACM SIGPLAN Notices 26(9), September 1991.

[178] David H.D. Warren. An abstract Prolog instruction set. Technical Note 309, SRI International, October 1983.

[179] Paul R. Wilson. Uniprocessor garbage collection techniques. In Bekkers and Cohen [19], pages 1–42. More of Wilson's GC material can be found on `ftp.cs.utexas.edu` in `pub/garbage/`.

[180] Andrew K. Wright. Typing references by effect inference. In B. Krieg-Brückner, editor, *4th European Symposium on Programming, ESOP '92*, volume 582 of *LNCS*, pages 473–491. Springer-Verlag, February 1992.

[181] Andrew K. Wright. Simple imperative polymorphism. *Lisp and Symbolic Computation*, to appear late 1995. Earlier version in Rice Univ. Dept. of CS Technical Report TR93-200.

Index

Lecture Notes in Computer Science

For information about Vols. 1–1513
please contact your bookseller or Springer-Verlag